SPECIAL COUNSEL

SPECIAL COUNSEL

by

Leon H. Charney

Philosophical Library
New York

Library of Congress Cataloging in Publication Data

Charney, Leon H.
  Special counsel.

  Includes index.
  1. Near East—Foreign relations—United States.
2. Charney, Leon H. 3. United States—Foreign relations—
Near East. 4. Egypt—Foreign relations—Israel.
5. Israel—Foreign relations—Egypt. 6. Jewish-Arab
relations—1973- . 7. Lawyers—United States—
Biography. 8. Diplomats—United States—Biography.
I. Title.
DS63.2.U5C44 1984   327.73056   84-14879
ISBN 0-8022-2444-X

I dedicate this book to my late father,
whose memory I cherish,
and to my beloved mother,
may she live to be 120.

CONTENTS

More than once I have been asked: How did it all happen? How did you get involved? I hope this book will provide the answers.

Counseling, in the broad sense of the concept, is what this book is all about—specifically the excitement, drama, and sometimes tedium of being a *Special Counsel*. Just as coincidence is a major factor in human affairs, so I have learned that thoughtful extemporization is the prime element in advising other people. I have come to appreciate that no law school course or textbook can teach one how to become a special counsel. It just happens.

This is not a lawyer's memoir *per se*, nor the story of courtroom battles. In fact, this book focuses on episodes that actually took me *away* from my law practice. I traveled to far-off capitals to advise and counsel the highest officials, always with the hope of helping my distressed brethren and furthering the cause of peace.

Obviously, the perceptions and observations presented in this book are my subjective recollection of the events portrayed. I take upon myself full responsibility for its contents. It must be appreciated that some of the episodes described took place under extremely complex circumstances. If I have unwittingly omitted reference to a person or an event, I hope I shall be forgiven.

L.H.C.

ACKNOWLEDGMENTS

I wish to thank my hard-working collaborator, Mark Segal, without whom this book would never have seen the light of day. And, of course, there are many others to whom I wish to express my gratitude:

— Don Tanselle, the most faithful of friends and counsel to the special counsel, who was always there when needed, the perfect example of a true friend,

— Robert Lipshutz, that most honorable of Southern Jewish gentlemen who, as the other half of The Odd Couple, made making history such fun,

— my good friends and supportive Swiss partners, Michael Florsheim and Ernst Strauss, without whose forbearance and understanding I could never have become a special counsel,

— Wolf Blitzer for his steadfastness and friendship throughout trying times,

— my favorite Generals: Ezer Weizman, Chaim Barlev, Abraham Tamir, Uri Ben-Ari, Micha Paz, and...my favorite Colonels: Ilan Tehila, Milcha Ben-Ari and U.S. Colonel Bruce Williams.

— Senator Vance Hartke and Jacques Leroy and Dolores

Davis for their great assistance in reconstituting my days at the Senate,

— Robert Parker for his friendship and for having provided me with an oasis of tranquillity in which to complete this book,

— Barbara Taufer for her assistance in the Austrian episode,

— the late Alexander Dekel for his initial encouragement to go into print,

— Mrs. Rose Morse Runes for her patience and advice,

— Sharon Sullivan for her editorial guidance,

— Dr. Benjamin Hirsch and Abraham Siegelman, my old college roommates, for their help in recapitulating my days at Y.U., and Herman Malamod for his cantorial inspirations,

— Ambassador Milton Wolf for his friendship and kind cooperation,

— my devoted office staff, Robert Rubenfeld, Sidney Winoker, and Pamela Case,

— and to all the others I may have omitted mentioning who were helpful, my sincere thanks.

IMPORTANT DATES

1948
May   War of Independence.

1956
May   Suez War.

1967
June   Six-Day War.

1970
Sept.   LC becomes special counsel to Senator Vance Hartke.

1972
            LC first meets Ezer Weizman.

1973
Sept.   LC to Russia with Hartke aide Leroy to urge visas for
            Soviet Jews.
Oct.   Yom Kippur War.
            LC to Israel as correspondent; also as aide to Senator
            Hartke to report on infiltration of Russian weaponry to
            Egyptians and Syrians.

1974

LC again meets Ezer Weizman on flight to Israel; they become friendly.

1975

LC meets Don Tanselle and becomes involved in Israel British Bank case.

1977
April
President Anwar Sadat of Egypt meets Carter in person for the first time. They like each other.
Yitzhak Rabin decides not to run as Prime Minister of Israel from the ruling Labor party.

May
LC becomes special counsel to Ezer Weizman.
Menachem Begin elected Israeli Prime Minister; Ezer Weizman appointed Israeli Defense Minister.

July
Prime Minister and Mrs. Begin visit Washington, meet President Carter.
LC first meets Begin as Prime Minister.

Sept.
Dayan visits Carter in Washington.
Dayan meets secretly with Egyptian representative in Morocco; promises return of the Sinai for start of solid peace talks.

Nov.
Sadat's historic visit to Jerusalem.

Dec.
Begin to Washington with new plan for Sinai region; then to London to present plan to Prime Minister Callaghan and to the Egyptians.
Ismalia Conference. The only agreement is to establish two commissions, a political and a military commission, to study the mechanics of peace.

1978
Jan.
Peace talks on the verge of breaking down; Carter invites Sadat to Washington.
Sadat withdraws Egyptian negotiators from Jerusalem after Lebanon bombings by Israelis, and West Bank settlements. But he agrees to permit Israeli military leaders to come to Egypt because he has confidence in Ezer Weizman.

Feb.
Sadat arrives in Washington to meet with Carter.

	Dayan arrives a few days later and voices Israeli fear that U.S. is now somewhat anti-Israel.
Mar.	Ezer Weizman to Washington. Meets Carter and makes a good impression on Carter and the U.S. media.
	LC meets with Carter in N.Y. and has meaningful discussion about the Middle East.
	35 people killed by PLO. Israel retaliates with a raid into Lebanon.
	Begin meets with Carter in Washington. Meeting does not go well.
May	Begin again in Washington, for the celebration of Israel's 30th anniversary.
July	Foreign Ministers of Egypt and Israel meet at Leeds Castle, England. No positions changed.
	Sadat asks Israeli military commission to leave Egypt.
August	LC returns from visit to Israel, where Ezer Weizman tells him to "keep the channels open." LC offers major plan "fig leaf" to Robert Lipshutz for Jimmy Carter.
	Carter invites Sadat and Begin to Camp David for three-way face-to-face summit meeting on the issues.
Sept.	Sadat and Begin arrive for Camp David meetings, and signing of the Accords on Sept. 17. All are enthusiastic.
Oct	Carter invites Egyptian and Israeli Foreign and Defense Ministers to Washington to work out details of peace agreements. Not much progress, as Begin gave Ezer Weizman and Moshe Dayan very little room to maneuver.
Dec.	LC meets privately with Begin in Begin's Knesset office to discuss ruptured U.S.-Israeli relations.

1979

Feb.	Secretary of Defense Harold Brown travels to Mid-East for Carter. Little progress on peace talks.
Mar.	Begin comes to Washington to visit Carter on stalled peace talks.
	Robert Lipshutz arrives in Israel in advance of Carter. Carter goes to Egypt and Israel on State visits.
	Robert Lipshutz sends Carter word "that if the Egyptians agreed to the same language the (Israeli) Cabinet had approved, everything could be worked out."

Mid-Mar.   Carter tells Bob Strauss that he is to lead the remaining negotiations to carry out the remainder of the Accords.

Mar. 26   Signing of the peace treaty.

Sept.   LC to Vienna to ask Chancellor Kreisky's help with Soviets in freeing Shcharansky.
Robert Lipshutz resigns from the White House; returns to Atlanta law practice.

Nov.   LC and Robert Lipshutz to Vienna to talk to Chancellor Kreisky on alternative ways to free American hostages in Iran.
LC to Israel to discuss with Ezer Weizman the Kreisky proposals.

Dec.   Sol Linowitz replaces Robert Strauss as Middle East envoy.

1980

Jan.-Feb.   Controversial vote at U.N. on Jerusalem and West Bank settlements.

Oct.   Ezer Weizman to U.S. While here he speaks out for Carter for President, and sparks an uproar.

SPECIAL COUNSEL

PRELUDE

The Ceremony

I thought the sun could have displayed a bit more respect for such an historic occasion. The White House lawn gleamed palely in the chilly sunlight of an early Washington spring morning. Together with the other slightly shivering but greatly excited guests, I was witnessing the long-awaited signing of the Israel-Egypt peace treaty under American auspices. It was March 1979.

As I stood at the back, taking in the splendid setting and listening to the familiar, famous voices come over the loudspeaker system, I felt a hard object nudge my back. A TV-inspired fantasy of some kind of gun flashed for a split second through my mind, until it dawned on me that one of the hungry pack of television cameramen was pushing me with his camera.

"Don't push me," I bristled.

He responded angrily. "Look here, kid, I'm trying to record the most important event in the 20th century, and you're blocking the view. For Gawd's sake, I want to get shots of really important people and you're in my way. Why don't you just move to the side?"

Faced with such a persuasive argument, I moved.

I felt very much alone. It was probably the loneliest experience I have ever undergone. For I could tell no one of my contribution that had helped this ceremony to come about.

I thought I could see the tall figure of my collaborator, Robert Lipshutz, Counsel to the President, peering over the heads of the crowd standing at the side of the White House colonnade. In front of him President Carter was seated at a table, flanked by President Sadat and Prime Minister Begin. With some difficulty I discerned my good friend Ezer Weizman, Israel's Defense Minister, in the front row sitting next to the President's mother, "Miss Lillian." Back in the third row I could just pick out the broad shoulders of my Israeli working partner, Israel Defense Forces' chief strategic planner General Avraham (Abrasha) Tamir. He was with the Israeli delegation. I had been invited to join them but deemed it inappropriate. Then again, I did not belong with the American delegation. Nor was I numbered among the packed ranks of official American Jewish leadership. Nor could I take a seat with the big campaign contributors.

My sense of solitariness stemmed from the secretive nature of my role as special counsel. My effectiveness depended on my keeping out of the headlines. Together with Bob Lipshutz, I had fashioned an informal and unpublicized back-door channel connecting the White House and the Kirya, Israeli Government compound. Both sides claimed it had been invaluable in furthering the peace process. But, irony of ironies, no one knew about it beyond the inner circles in each capital.

Still, I felt compensated by knowing that I had been of some help in furthering the cause of peace in the Middle East. I was being paid in a coin better than metal...for I had never sought nor received financial compensation for my efforts toward peace. I felt a sense of completeness, of a job well done. I had performed my duty as an American and a Jew. That knowledge had inspired me to continue when I had felt tired or frustrated. It had pushed me to work harder. Not too bad for a 40-year-old "kid," I thought. Not too bad for the son of immigrants, for a boy from Bayonne, New Jersey.

It was with mounting emotion that I heard President Carter

proclaim: "Let us now lay aside war. Let us now reward all the children of Abraham who hunger for peace in the Middle East." This historic agreement was the first peace treaty between an Arab country and Israel.

After signing as a witness for the United States, the President declared: "We have won, at last, the first step of peace—a first step on a long and difficult road." His Southern accent seemed more pronounced than ever. Is this really finally happening? I thought.

Last-Minute Jitters

Only a few hours earlier, I had heard a less-than-optimistic prognosis for the signing from William Quandt, assistant to the President's National Security Advisor, Zbigniew Brzezinski. We had met by chance in the White House waiting room, and the tall, thin, dour Arab-affairs expert spoke darkly of a threatened Egyptian walkout less than four hours before the signing deadline. He was shaking his head and appeared to be in the grip of a profound depression, talking of obstacles on the final lap to the peace treaty. Judging by my sources of information, I thought him too alarmist. Further, he did tend to view affairs somberly. I recalled how fearful he had been that the President's talks in Jerusalem would turn out disastrously. Instead they proved to be very successful.

I left Quandt and, nodding to the guard, ascended the stairs to the corner office on the second story of the West Wing which was occupied by Bob Lipshutz. I exchanged greetings with Frank Moore, the President's Congressional liaison assistant, whose office was just across the corridor.

I found Bob his usual, even-tempered, courtly self. I advised him of Quandt's alarming news. Then, before doing anything else, I presented him with the gold Parker pen engraved with his name which I had ordered to mark the great day and as a memento of our partnership. I had learned only recently that other colleagues of his in the White House referred to us as The Odd Couple.

Ever the Southern Jewish gentleman, Bob apologized profusely for having to leave shortly. He had a State Department luncheon to attend. He left me a phone number where he could be reached should I need him. Much would hinge on how Quandt presented the facts to the President, I told Bob. "To judge by my contacts with the Israelis earlier this morning, I tend to be skeptical about Quandt's alarm. But of course one never knows."

Bob sat up in his chair tidying his desk. I thought it was one of the tidiest desks I had ever seen, an ingrained habit from his Atlanta law office. He said nostalgically, "We have covered a lot of territory together, haven't we? I know we've made a first-class team." Bob told me how much our work was appreciated in the right places. "You should know that only the other day the President remarked, 'Bob, I really don't know how we would have managed without Leon.'" He watched me, enjoying my pleased reaction.

Not bad, I thought to myself, such praise coming from the 39th President of the United States of America. I had a fleeting memory of my dear, departed father back across the years, in our modest living room in Bayonne, New Jersey. He would make it almost a daily ritual to bring out of the closet his U.S. citizenship papers and fondle them lovingly. It was as if he were making sure that his personal anchor in this vast continent was still secure. I wondered what he would have said about such Presidential praise for his yeshiva boy.

Bayonne was the place where I had lived, but my parents sent me out of town for my education. The dominant passion in those years was basketball, in which I was encouraged by the example of my older brother, Herbert, who was an exceedingly fine athlete. Any free time I had was spent on the basketball courts. One of the traumatic experiences of my youth was associated with that sport, just as was one of my proudest moments. The first happened when I was 14, on a basketball court in a public park in New York's lower east side. I had been part of a victorious squad in what was supposed to have been a friendly game, when a youngster from the defeated side attacked me with a switchblade knife, screaming, "F----g kike!" The internal scar was much longer lasting than the external wound, which healed rapidly. The proudest moment

In my youth, a highly traumatic experience was associated with basket-ball, as was one of my proudest moments.

of my teenage life came two years later. At 16 years old I was exceedingly happy to have been named Assistant Captain of my high school basketball team. (I played the game straight through college.) In the last three seconds of an important game, I shot the winning basket to put our school for the first time in its 30-year history into the high-school-league championship game at the famous Madison Square Garden. Nothing could have been more exciting to a teenager as passionately involved in basketball as I was. The exhilaration of that day and the applause of my schoolmates remain with me over the years.

I lost my father during my first year at college, which necessitated my working and studying at the same time. Thus at an early age, along with my brother Herbert, I was thrust into the role of breadwinner for my widowed mother and my younger sister, Bryna. Since my father left little money I realized that, if I wished to get ahead in life and become successful, it would have to be solely by virtue of my own efforts and capabilities.

Being a good fighter by nature, I set about preparing myself properly for the battle of life.

My thoughts jumped back to the present when Bob asked me to phone Quandt and check on the status of last-minute negotiations. Quandt sounded a bit calmer and more reassured, although he still had cause for anxiety. It appeared that last-minute molehills had assumed the size of the Rockies. The Egyptians were balking at Israel's insistence on inserting the terms *Judea* and *Samaria* in the treaty footnotes. The Egyptians preferred to use the term *West Bank*. There was also some wrangling between the two sides over whether the southern waterway leading to the Red Sea should be called the *Gulf of Aqaba*, as the Egyptians insisted, or the *Gulf of Eilat*, as the Israelis demanded. Quandt said that the unsettled oil-supply issue also remained a rather sticky matter.

I then immediately called Ezer at his Madison Hotel suite in downtown Washington. His wife, Re'uma, answered the phone and said he was with Israeli Prime Minister Menachem Begin.

Later I was to hear a detailed version of the last-minute details from Abrasha Tamir. He is one of my favorite Israeli Generals, as well as one of the most intellectual men I have ever met. He had been working in a suite at the Madison on the final shape of the maps and other crucial details until about 5:30 a.m. the night before the signing. In an adjoining room Israeli and Egyptian translators were also working through the night, readying the Hebrew and Arabic versions in time for the ceremony. The Egyptians reported to their General Magdhoub. The Israelis had brought along their own expert in Arabic to go over the Egyptian version with a fine-tooth comb.

As Abrasha told me in his throaty voice: "Our translators had a fit of zealotry, angering the Egyptians by insisting that the Hebrew word *'sulha'* was a much stronger term for peace than the Arabic term *'salem'* preferred by the Egyptian drafting team. To my mind it was all nonsense," he hurriedly added. "Every civil servant wants to demonstrate his loyalty to the Government line."

"And the Aqaba-Eilat quandary?" I asked.

"That wasn't too difficult," he chuckled throatily. "We wrote the *Gulf of Eilat* on our map and our version of the treaty, and they kept the *Gulf of Aqaba* in the English and Arabic versions."

But the main stumbling block was the timetable for handing back the Sinai oil fields and guaranteeing future oil supplies to Israel. Israeli opponents of the peace treaty had aired their reservations about giving back the country's primary source of energy since 1967 for untested Egyptian commitments. True, the clear U.S. guarantee of future oil supplies had allayed the skeptics' worries, yet the issue remained a sticking point right up to the signing deadline. Indeed it was one of the problems that had almost destroyed the President's mission to Jerusalem and Cairo. As Bob reminded me on the day of the signing, the President remembered appreciatively the working formula we had submitted to him at that critical juncture.

The evening before, Abrasha had left General Magdhoub and the translating teams hard at work at the Madison to meet the Prime Minister in his suite at the Washington Hilton. Menachem Begin had just returned from meeting Anwar Sadat and had agreed to the Egyptian demand to advance the return of the Sinai oil fields by two months—from the original nine months to seven months. Begin quickly obtained the concurrence of those of his Cabinet Ministers who were in Washington for the signing ceremony, and Abrasha was instructed to make the necessary amendments. So Abrasha rushed back to the Madison to instruct his team, especially the map-makers, to make suitable changes in the substages of the withdrawal schedule.

It was then that some kind of misunderstanding took place between the Israeli General and his Egyptian counterpart. It threatened to rend much more than the delicate fabric of trust that had been nurtured between them during months of military commission talks at the Tahara Palace in Cairo and elsewhere. Unlike the political commission, whose Egyptian and Israeli negotiators relied on a calming influence imposed by the U.S. presence, the military had managed to dispense with any need for the Americans. It was a fascinating and indeed rather hopeful sign that these professional soldiers, who had devoted all their lives to planning on how best to destroy each other, should have established a personal rapport that had been beyond the grasp of the civilians.

It may well have been that the huge row that blew up between the Egyptian Generals and their newly found Israeli friends was the result of the mounting tension and fraying nerves brought about by the approaching deadline. At any rate, there had been a screaming match over the schedule for handing back Et-tour and the new advanced timing substage Begin had agreed to with Sadat. Talk of an Egyptian walkout hovered in the air. In fact, one Egyptian officer did stalk out in anger, banging the door behind him. But Abrasha used his rough Sabra charm to calm everyone down, and another Middle East *sulha* was arranged.

Quandt, of course, had gotten wind only of the row and the threats to leave, not of the finale when the Israelis and Egyptians all parted after embraces and ritual kisses.

After Bob Lipshutz left me the morning of the signing ceremony, his assistant, Michael Cardoza, took me to lunch at the White House mess. The stomach at the heart of the world. All 12 tables were occupied. Bob had told me that the Carter Administration had abolished the old distinction between dining rooms for senior and junior staff members in keeping with its populist philosophy. I had eaten in the mess many times before and knew some of the personnel well. They were accustomed by now to my peculiar culinary habits. As I still observed *kashrut* dietary rules, I found myself an expert on the tuna dishes served up by the White House mess. Cardoza, it emerged over lunch, belonged to an old Washington Jewish family. He was an attorney by profession, staying within the family tradition. His great-uncle had been Justice Cardoza, the first Jew on the U.S. Supreme Court. Mike and I had some laughs, and then he told me that his associates referred to me as *007*. I told him the notion was flattering. Mike then went on at some length on how Bob underplayed himself. He wondered whether the courtly Southerner might prove too genteel for the grab-for-the-jugular style of palace intrigues in Washington.

Just before 2 p.m. I saw Bob again and together we walked out onto the sunny but chilly lawn for the ceremony. We parted and took up our places on opposite sides of the lawn, an action that was perhaps symbolic of our relationship.

The Emotion of Peace

It must have been the largest gathering of people ever assembled on the White House grounds for such an occasion. There was an aura of collective excitement gripping the assembly, as all present knew they were being touched by history. There were some unforgettable moments that moved even the most cynical of observers. There was a public celebration of religion not customary in the United States on such official occasions. Pundits might mockingly refer to the Presidential mansion as being flooded with religious rhetoric, but I remain convinced that most of the people there on the lawn, as well as the millions watching on television, were uplifted by this demonstration of the unity of the three great religions. After all, it's not every day that an Egyptian President quotes from the Prophet Isaiah: "They shall beat their swords into plowshares and their spears into pruning hooks."

Emotion got the better of me and many others when Menachem Begin rose to speak. As he stood there, his head covered with a yarmulka, he reminded me of my father in prayer. Especially when he quoted from Psalm 126: "they that sow in tears, shall reap in joy." As his voice soared over the loudspeaker, certain scenes from my life flashed in my mind's eye: as a nine-year-old sitting with my family listening to the radio in Bayonne, N.J., not quite grasping all the commotion as we passionately followed the United Nations vote on partition of Palestine. Less than a year later, watching my mother hang out a blue-and-white flag with a Star of David in celebration of the birth of the Jewish State. In the mid-1950's, the high pitch of drama at a Yeshiva University convocation where along with my fellow students, I witnessed David Ben-Gurion, the first Prime Minister of Israel, proclaiming like a prophet of old: "*Lo yanum ve le yishan shomer Israel* (Neither shall he sleep, nor will he rest, the Watchman of Israel)." My first visit to Jerusalem in July 1967, how my heart beat as I inserted a note in a crack in the Western Wall. It bore a few words: "I wish peace and health on Israel." Then the dread significance of *Yad Vashem*,* and emerging out of the dark depths of the horrors of the Holocaust into the brilliant sunlight. My own personal oath to do all I could so that it would never happen again. And the sickening recollection of the bloated corpses in fraying uniforms lying in the sands of the Sinai desert during my visit at the height of the Yom Kippur War in 1973.

My reveries were interrupted by the cries of Palestinian demonstrators whose protests pierced the police cordons and the White House shrubbery. I remembered reading on the flight to Washington that morning an editorial in *The New York Times*. It referred to the Palestinians as the "absent guests at the ceremony." Not-so-absent guests, I mused. Their problem would now take center stage. I had had indications from Bob of the way things would drift during our short exchange of words before the ceremony. Fresh from his State Department meeting, the Counsel to the President turned to me and said solemnly, "Our next job is to get to work on the West Bank and all of its problems."

I turned my attention to the ceremonial speeches. I must have wept along with many others in that throng when Menachem Begin mourned the "six million martyrs" who had died in W.W. II concentration camps who could not be with us. He certainly inspired me with his impassioned plea: "No more war, no more bloodshed, no more bereavement. Peace unto you. Shalom. Salaam. Forever."

---

* Memorial to the Holocaust victims.

The Celebration

The ceremony was at an end. Everyone was hugging everyone else. I went over to Ezer Weizman, who was standing with
his wife, Re'uma, and their son, Shaul, who still suffered from
a head wound inflicted at the hand of the Egyptians. Ezer had
determined to bring his family despite Begin's insistence that
only Ministers should attend the ceremony. Re'uma was very
excited and embraced me tightly. Ezer was at his most ebullient, beaming at everyone. He called out to me, "Here's Leon,
my legal eagle!" He enfolded me in a huge bear hug, declaring,
"Thanks for everything. Without you we couldn't have done
it!"

Bob called me over. I walked with him into the West Wing
and up the stairs to his office. I managed to tell him how the
Sinai oil issue had been satisfactorily solved. Before we could
discuss Quandt's report, Bob's cousins from New Jersey
walked into the room. He had arranged for them to be invited
to the ceremony. They had a holiday home in Natanya, the
seaside resort near Tel Aviv, and after Bob introduced me as
"Leon, he knows everyone in Israel," they started badgering
me to help them to get a telephone installed. I told them,

"Believe me, it's easier to help put together a peace treaty than to get a phone in Israel."

As Bob showed me to the door, he and I discussed how to get working on the autonomy scheme planned for the West Bank. He stressed that we had to maintain the same working relationship we had established in helping to put together the peace treaty—a behind-the-scenes sharing of information on moods, personalities, realities, possibilities, and alternatives. This was information not available through public officials or channels—and it was vital. I was to act as an informal emissary between Israel and the United States and was to make use of my numerous sources of information both within Israel and throughout the world—a large, loosely knit network which Bob called my "back-door channels."

I strolled across Pennsylvania Avenue to the historic Hay-Adams Hotel facing the White House—a bit old-fashioned, but most comfortable. Shortly after 5 p.m., Don Tanselle, one of my most intimate friends, arrived from Indianapolis. The Indiana banker had already proven his devotion to peace— and to me—leaving his family on Christmas Eve 1978 to fly to Jerusalem with me on one of my missions. He felt honored to hear that the invitation I'd wrangled for him to the State Dinner that night was one of the hottest tickets in town.

When I had spoken earlier that day to Re'uma from Bob's office, she had complained to me of the tremendous pressure that some of Ezer's cronies had put on him to get invitations. Ezer had blown up at one of them over the phone. I had heard that the Israeli delegation had been obliged to drop 30 names from the list of invitees. Abrasha was boiling mad at the exclusion of his aides from the entire celebration. After all, they had done all the detail work on mapping and such. Even Prime Minister Begin had had difficulties getting some of his friends into the overflow dinner at the White House.

After changing into tuxedos, Don and I walked out into the cold evening air to find quite a mob of people already lining up outside the East Wing to enter the largest State dinner party in the White House's history. All was beautifully arranged, from

the huge yellow-and-red-striped tent to the interior arrangements, and hundreds of hurricane lamps cast a cozy glow on
the forsythia branches decorating the place. The torrent of
well-dressed humanity gradually funneled in through a lav-
ishly appointed parlor, and white-gloved Marines in dress
uniform ushered the guests into the dining space. There was a
gala atmosphere. A Marine Corps musical ensemble played,
and a pretty harpist added her soft sounds. Lovely women
with glittering jewelry sauntered inside on the arms of well-
groomed men. There were celebrities galore, and there was an
excited hum as everyone, including myself, moved from table
to table greeting friends.

While Don discussed local Indiana politics with that state's
Senator Lugar, I found myself being introduced to the Soviet
Ambassador, Anatoly Dobrynin, hailed by White House Chief
of Staff Hamilton Jordan and White House media man Gerald
Rafshoon, and bumping into Begin's aide, Yehiel Kadishai—
as usual cracking jokes. He greeted me in Yiddish with the
accolade *"ein gutter Yid* (a good Jew)." On the way back to my
table I spent some time chatting with former Israeli Prime
Minister Yitzhak Rabin. After his term of office, I served as
counsel for Rabin on occasion. He was talking cordially with
his once-and-future party rival, former Defense Minister
Shimon Peres. I wondered whether their sudden conviviality
might not be regarded as the peace treaty's first achievement.

New York Congresswoman Elizabeth Holzman came over
to discuss our joint appearance with Congressman Stephen
Solarz on a TV panel discussion on Middle East prospects. It
had been taped with Bill Boggs for WNEW-TV, Channel 5 in
New York, the previous evening, and had been broadcast
earlier in the day.

The Hoosier State was well represented at our table, what
with Don and his long-time acquaintance Congressman Lee
Hamilton. Bob Lipshutz sat at an adjoining table in deep
conversation with Stuart Eizenstat, the President's Domestic
Affairs Assistant and, along with Bob, a charter member of
the original Georgia "network" the President brought with
him to the White House. I had had very little to do with

Eizenstat, but I knew from Bob that he cared deeply about Israel and its security.

Soon I found myself intently conversing with my immediate neighbor, AFL-CIO chief George Meany. A tough but genial person, he emanated an aura of power and was totally secure in his position as one of the most influential men in America. When he inquired why I was at the state dinner, I told him that I had been invited as a good friend of Bob Lipshutz. Meany grinned affably and knowingly retorted, "It's my bet that you probably did more than you let on if you were invited to *this* dinner." We talked politics and about Carter's re-election prospects. When I emphasized my admiration for Jimmy and his courage, Meany's reaction was lukewarm. He seemed more inclined to support "Scoop" Jackson, with Ted Kennedy as a second choice. I wondered whether the Carter people had neglected to perform an ego massage on Meany, and resolved to check with Bob later. Meany gave me a long lecture on how much he had done for Israel and the depth of his admiration for Golda Meir.

Meany then switched his attention to Don Tanselle, who had been relating his impressions of the marvelous King Tut exhibition then touring the country. We all concurred that it was a very clever Egyptian public relations operation. When the stocky labor leader heard Don was from Indiana, he launched into a tribute to Larry Bird, then the star of the Indiana State University basketball team. Don said, "Believe me, the team is so dear to me, it would have to be a special event like this dinner to get me to miss tonight's big game." This brought Meany's rejoinder, "What's the score right now?" When Don confessed his ignorance, Meany leaned forward and, wagging his finger at him, said, "If you care about the team and about basketball as much as you say you do, you ought to keep track...." Don interrupted, "Well, I guess you've got more clout in the White House than a guy like me. *You* find out what the score is."

Meany looked around, saw a youngish man hovering in the background, and crooked his finger to call him over. "Look, I want to get the score of tonight's Indiana game. Find out for me, won't you?" he said in a quietly commanding voice. We all immediately realized that Meany's messenger was one of hundreds of Secret Service men posted around the tent. The young man nodded and disappeared. He was back a few minutes later, mission fulfilled. Meany's eyes gleamed triumphantly through the thick lenses of his horn-rimmed spectacles as he informed his visibly impressed neighbor that Indiana was winning.

Although some guests demurred, I rather liked the President's opening the dinner with a short prayer. Carter introduced the Palestinian theme into his toast, which did not ruffle Begin, who evoked prolonged applause by mentioning his intention of nominating the President for the Nobel Peace Prize.

The dinner organizers went to a lot of trouble to ensure the evening's success, from placing special heaters at strategic spots in the tent to commissioning abundant kosher food from a Baltimore caterer. The latter courtesy was especially appreciated by guests like myself and my good friends former Mayor Abraham Beame of New York and his wife, Mary. During the meal, Mrs. Beame insisted on going to the head table to shake hands with President Sadat. She remembered that, when the Egyptian leader had been in New York in 1976 for the United Nations General Assembly, her husband had purposely not called on him nor invited him to Gracie Mansion in protest of Egyptian support for the U.N.'s abhorrent resolution equating Zionism with racism. Ignoring the cordon of security men, Mrs. Beame and her husband went up to Sadat and shook his hand. Sadat seemed very pleased with the tribute, and Abe Beame assured him, "If I were Mayor today, I'd put out a red carpet for you." The Egyptian leader laughed appreciatively, and both Carter and Begin waved to the Beames.

The heaters notwithstanding, the cold was getting to everyone, making it difficult to enjoy the superb performances of soprano Leontyne Price, and violinists Yitzhak Perlman and Pinchas Zuckerman.

While others stayed for the dancing, I left with Don and

Ezer's aide, Colonel Ilan Tehila, a highly congenial companion. We entered a cab, asking the driver to take us to the Hilton. As we sped through the cold Washington night, the driver opened up, "I see you've been to the big peace celebration. Well, let me tell you, I'm a Palestinian from Jerusalem." We all exchanged silent glances. No one said a word. There's a symbolism here, I mused to myself.

At the hotel we joined Ilan's colleagues who had not made it to the dinner and, after some desultory conversation, went looking for some drinks to celebrate. But the hotel bar was closed. So instead we sat in the chairs and started to sing, as is traditional in Israel. I launched into one of my favorite cantorial songs, *"Veyiune beit Hamikdash"* (And When the Temple Will Be Rebuilt). Some of the Israeli press corps drifted in—Ari Rath of *The Jerusalem Post*, Ron Ben-Ishai and Eitan Haber of the Israeli Hebrew daily *Yedioth Aharonot* all joined in. I don't know what the hotel management thought, but there was a marvelous harmony in the air of the Washington Hilton bar that night. Then Ezer stalked in together with Yigael Yadin, Deputy Prime Minister of Israel, and Yitzhak Modai, Minister of Energy. Ezer and Modai joined in the singing. Yadin stayed for a bit and then turned in early. The rest of us got to bed around 3:30 a.m.

Five hours later I joined Ezer for breakfast. We were both somewhat subdued. There was a sense of anticlimax.

I turned down Ezer's offer to fly back to New York with him on his special plane for that night's big party. I spent the day as an ordinary tourist and culture-vulture, enjoying the beauty and museums of Washington.

Flying back to New York that night on the last shuttle I drove straight from La Guardia Airport to a party at the Fifth Avenue apartment of Larry and Dalia Leeds. He is President of Manhattan Industries, and she is a former Israeli beauty queen. Ezer was there and, as usual, was the heart and soul of the party. After he introduced me to our hosts as his attorney and associate, I pressed him on the contradiction between Begin's lavish tribute to Cyrus Vance at the dinner and the way Begin had described the Secretary of State as "a coarse man" not so long ago. That started one of Ezer's amusing discourses on Menachem Begin and Israeli politics. But he was interrupted when our hostess came over to introduce me to a rather beautiful Israeli girl. Politics aside, it developed into quite a party.

At one point, the music was turned off and all attention was drawn to our host, Larry Leeds, standing on a coffee table. He offered a toast to Ezer Weizman on the achievement of peace. The guest of honor grew rather somber and replied, "I want to tell you all. I need everybody's help. And I mean everybody in the room. Because what we saw yesterday is only the beginning. We all have to pray that it will not be an end."

PART ONE
BACK-DOOR CHANNELS

1

The Dashing General

I had first met Ezer Weizman seven years earlier. Believe it or not, it was on a movie set. I was acting (yes, acting!) as a Mexican "heavy" in a German TV Western alongside film stars Geraldine Chaplin, Anna Karina, and Thomas Hunter.

How the Bayonne boy who was now a lawyer ended up acting on that hot desert movie set is another story. I'll tell that one first.

In the spring of 1971 I was in Israel discussing legal matters with one of my clients, the director of the Herzliya Motion Picture Studios. All of a sudden a big man burst into the room crying, "That's the guy!" He introduced himself—a West German movie director named Hans Geisendorfer, who was in the process of trying to make a Western out of *Don Carlos*, the classic German play by Friedrich Schiller. When that was explained to me I thought, "Well, if the Italians can make spaghetti Westerns, why shouldn't the Germans try their hands at sauerkraut Westerns?"

Geisendorfer had unsuccessfully interviewed 25 actors for the role before he spotted me. I protested loudly that I was not an actor but a lawyer, whose only experience in this sphere had been to represent show business personalities. "No matter," the director insisted, "you've got exactly the face and build I'm looking for." When he explained the role he wanted me to play, my misgivings grew. "I need a swarthy type that can come across as a very mean Mexican bandit," he explained, his Americanisms sounding slightly comic in his Teutonic accent. Well, I may have put on a bit of weight at the time, but my friends had always assured me that my face was more cherubic than mean. Moreover, I had serious doubts how my clients would respond to seeing me looking mean on the screen. Still, like most human beings I was somewhat intrigued by the idea of engaging in such an adventure. So after hours of the director's cajoling, I decided to check out the matter with some of my clients and friends. Through a series of transatlantic calls, I found they were generally amused and approving. One lawyer friend reminded me that the law practice of Joseph Welch, attorney to the U.S. Army in the Army-McCarthy hearings, had not been hurt by his acting in the movie *Anatomy of a Murder*.

Before committing myself, I insisted on a screen test. A special scene was written in a great hurry, with Charney the brand-new actor spitting watermelon pits at hero Tom Hunter. That's how I got into the movies, and my one and only film was finally called *Carlos*.

So there I was, trying to follow a movie director's instructions on an "instant hacienda" set amidst the 120-degree heat of the desert near Eilat, when Ezer Weizman charged onto the set.

Indeed, my first impression of Ezer Weizman was of a dashing, swashbuckling military hero. He cut a rather romantic figure. Geraldine Chaplin said he reminded her of Douglas Fairbanks, Jr., or of one of those Royal Air Force pilots from Battle of Britain movies. However, Geraldine did not even want to talk to the air hero. As she explained, "He's undoubtedly an exceedingly charming and nice man. But he is a military man and I have no interest in meeting a military man."

But later, in the cool of the evening, Ezer joined us for a

The cantorial singing I learned as a young man has given me joy and others pleasure.

drink at the hotel pool overlooking the waters of the Red Sea glittering beneath summer moonlight. Geraldine said he might have done well in the movies had he opted for Hollywood, rather than building up Israel's Air Force and then going into politics.

Incidentally, I became very friendly with Geraldine, and we spent much time together off the set. Both she and Anna Karina took a liking to my cantorial singing, which I had started as a youth. This is a soulful, tremulous singing that sounds somewhat like Portuguese *fado*. To while away the long waiting periods between the actual shootings, I would take a *siddur* and sing heartfelt renderings of song after song in Hebrew. Anna Karina, a beautiful but rather unpredictable woman, would only occasionally talk of her married life to Jean-Luc Godard, the famous French film director. Geraldine spoke often of her renowned father, Charlie Chaplin. She also referred frequently to her eminent maternal grandfather, Eugene O'Neill. Geraldine totally idolized her father and

I became very friendly with Geraldine Chaplin (right). Both she and Anna Karina took a liking to my cantorial singing.

wanted me to come to Switzerland to meet him, but somehow that plan never materialized. The lovely, fun-loving, and talented actress felt bitterly about America's shabby treatment of her father, who, she said, would never, never return to that country. Her feelings were rather ambivalent toward the United States. She admired it and loathed it at one and the same time. Geraldine was sad because she could not marry the great love of her life, Spanish film director Carlos Saura. Divorce (from his first wife) was still prohibited in Spain. (She had to wait another six years to obtain her wish.)

I recall that one lazy afternoon I asked her, "Tell me, was Charlie Chaplin born a Jew as I've heard?" Her reply was evasive. "I'm not saying he is, and I'm not saying he ain't," she said with a grin and an imitation Cockney accent.

That story about Chaplin's origins was overheard by Noah Klieger, who was both a good friend and a top reporter for the Israeli tabloid *Yedioth Aharonot*. After he printed it, the item received worldwide publicity when it was picked up by news agencies.

Night Memories

I next encountered Ezer Weizman a year later. By coincidence or fate we ended up sharing adjoining seats on an El Al flight from Lod Airport to New York. As our neighbors dropped off to sleep, we talked for hours.

It was from then that I date the beginning of my friendship with Ezer, although some years were to elapse before a really close relationship developed. He spoke and I listened. Ezer talked of his childhood in Haifa; of his parents and his great-uncle, Chaim Weizmann, the first President of Israel; of his happy-go-lucky years as a young pilot in the R.A.F.; of the decades building up the Israeli Air Force; of his overnight rise in the Golda Meir Government as Likud Party Minister of Transport, and of his disagreement with Menachem Begin about the Likud Government's quitting in 1970. Ezer felt frustrated. He had been an executive at the highest level all his adult life and the role of opposition politician did not fit him well. He was a doer, not a talker. He was at that time in business, but it did not greatly interest him. He had had a taste of power and felt he and the Likud Party could do much better than the current Labor Government. I sensed I was dealing with a thoroughbred horse straining at the reins, ready to run, but the owners refused to enter him in the great race. Ezer felt he was fated to be a man of destiny and do great things for his country. But smaller men were keeping him back.

During one lull in our conversation, I said, "I'm sure that as a true egotist you like to read autobiographies." He laughed, and we discussed various books we had enjoyed. We found we had much in common and laughed a lot about the same things. It was on that transatlantic flight that we discovered the special chemistry between us, despite our totally contrasting life experiences and backgrounds. The super-Sabra I.A.F. General and Israeli aristocrat felt immediately at home with the boy from Bayonne, New Jersey, the American Jewish attorney. Ezer was traveling with a former Air Force aide, Peleg Tamir, who looked at me questioningly at the end of the journey, wondering about the sudden intimate warmth he sensed between his old Air Force chief and (for him) an unknown lawyer.

I clearly remember a rather telling anecdote. Ezer had been talking at length of the enigmatic, one-eyed Moshe Dayan, who had been both his brother-in-law and Israel's Defense Minister. Ezer illustrated the contrast between Dayan's coldly aloof personality and matter-of-fact approach and his own warm interest and involvement in people's affairs when he referred to Dayan's response to Ezer's appointment to the Golda Meir Government.

Ezer had resolved to let Dayan be among the very first to know of his impending overnight switch from General to Minister, after he had accepted the Likud offer to quit the I.D.F. and join the Cabinet as one of its six Ministers. He wanted to tell Dayan personally, before the Prime Minister did. He had called his brother-in-law early in the morning to catch him before Dayan left for the Ministry. "I told him, 'Moshe, I'm resigning from the Air Force and joining the Cabinet.' All that

Dayan said in reply was a terse, '*Mabruk!*' 'Congratulations' in Arabic. Then he hung up the phone."

We Meet Again

A year or two elapsed before our paths crossed again. We met at a big party given by Ezer's successor as Air Force chief, Motti Hod. Hod was by then in international business and I was acting as his counsel. The party was in honor of the legendary one-legged British air ace Douglas Bader, and the house overflowed with pilots past and present. It was there I first met Ezer's wife, Re'uma, who was most gracious.

During the next few years I continued to travel to Israel frequently. Sometimes I went on vacation, but more often than not I was on business. I represented numerous American companies seeking to do business in Israel. Further, I was still involved with extricating Soviet Jews from the U.S.S.R.— work I had started when I worked with Senator Hartke. I also traveled there frequently in connection with the aftermath of a scandal of the Israel-British Bank, which started in 1974 and lasted several years. This involved the loss of some $50 million, and American banks were among those that had sustained serious losses. The scandal not only did much to damage Israel's standing in the world financial community, but it might have contributed to the fall from power of the Labor Party, which had dominated the country since its birth as a sovereign state in 1948.

I represented most of the American banks as counsel. Among these was the Merchants National Bank and Trust Company of Indianapolis, my friend Don Tanselle's bank. Don, who was president of the bank, had come to Washington early in 1975 to enlist the aid of his state's senator, Vance Hartke of Indiana, to put pressure on the Israelis to make good on the losses sustained by investors in the I.B.B. I was working with Senator Hartke at the time, and it was he who introduced me to Don. Settlement of the I.B.B. dispute took years, but it increased my contacts among the wealthy and powerful in Israel as well as in the U.S. Congress.

I was in Israel on business in May 1977 and witnessed the final phase of the election campaign. I happened to call at Motti Hod's office the day before the voting took place. He said, "I think you've met my friend and former chief Ezer Weizman, haven't you? Well, he needs an American lawyer to help him sell a book in the United States. He's in the upstairs office now running the Likud campaign. Why don't you go up?"

I went upstairs and found a highly ebullient Ezer in the middle of the final campaign arrangements. He recognized me and recalled our night-long flight together. It appeared that the chemistry was working, as it had on the plane. He asked me to represent him in the U.S. and arrange the American publication of his autobiography, which was also a history of Israeli air power. It was called *On Eagle's Wings*. (The original Hebrew version remains an all-time best-seller.) Ezer conferred on me there and then the power of attorney and title of special counsel. Before we parted, he predicted, "Tomorrow we are going to win the elections. You are speaking to the next Defense Minister of Israel." I looked at him somewhat bewildered. I did not know quite how to react, for there was no sure sign until the very last moment that the Likud would win.

Well, win they did. When we next met two months later, he was Israel's sixth Defense Minister, and I had worked out for him what they call in the book trade a rather "creative" deal. But because he was now a member of the Government, we had to clear this business arrangement through appropriate channels. First, it had to be cleared by Attorney-General Aharon Barak, today an Israeli Supreme Court Justice, whose brilliant legal mind contributed so much to the Camp David peace process. Then, in keeping with accepted procedure, the deal was submitted for the appraisal of the State Controller's office. The style in which Ezer handled his personal affairs contrasted sharply with that of his successor, Ariel Sharon, regarding the ownership and management of an extensive ranch once Sharon became Minister of Agriculture. (It took quite a long time and nearly provoked a public controversy before a satisfactory arrangement was reached in Sharon's case.) Their differences in approach to leadership and government remain to this day.

Forging of a Bond

Then a highly significant incident occurred, which proved to be a turning point in the mutual bond of trust that had been forged between us so quickly, and I might add instinctively. On that same trip to Israel, I came to the Knesset one day to see Ezer. In the members' dining room I encountered some former Labor Party Ministers I knew, rather downcast in their new status, and the brand-new Likud Party Cabinet Ministers. Some of these people I knew from 1973 when I had become heavily involved in the good fight for Soviet Jewry. I went downstairs to Ezer's new office. There were some Army brass waiting to see him. When he finally received me, he had good news. The book deal had been cleared through official channels. That prompted me to tell him, "You know, I don't think I should walk around carrying the Israeli Defense Minister's power of attorney. I don't feel quite comfortable." I proceeded to hand back to him the file containing the document and he nodded his thanks. As we parted, we arranged to meet again the following week at the Defense Ministry in Tel Aviv.

It was nearing my deadline for returning home. Phone calls from New York had advised me of the growing impatience of some of my clients. A few days later, I drove from the hotel to the Defense Ministry complex that dominates the Kirya, the Government compound. En route the right fender of my rented car was bashed in by a swerving car that barreled through a red light. It reminded me of an indictment of Israeli drivers I had once heard from an American correspondent. He was explaining his theory on the source of the swiftness of the Israeli army's advance through Sinai to the Suez Canal during the Six-Day War. He said that then Chief-of-Staff General Yitzhak Rabin had packed the Israeli tanks with Tel Aviv cab drivers and then cried, "Charge!" Before anyone knew what was happening the "cabbies" had plowed through the entire Egyptian army and reached the Canal.

The guards at the Ministry were very polite and directed me to an adjoining public parking lot. (After I became a more frequent visitor, the guards would let me park inside among the Ministry cars.) I was shown up to Ezer's office, and there admired the maps covering the walls and the model planes adorning the cupboards. What I liked most was the photo of a black Spitfire that Ezer kept in working condition. It was reportedly the only black Spitfire still in commission anywhere in the world. It certainly added to Ezer's image as a dashing pilot. One might even say it formed part of the living legend that separates the star from the masses.

The Minister was in high good humor and it was the first time I heard him use the nickname he had picked for me. "Ah, here comes the legal eagle," he declared. Then, becoming more business-like, he said, "You know what? I've decided to give you back the document. It's because I like you and trust you. So you still have my power of attorney." We chatted a bit and I left, musing to myself, "Well, so I'm counsel to the Israeli Minister of Defense." I heard him call out, "And don't forget to keep in touch."

Enter Sadat

Ezer had been Defense Minister only a few months when he had a road accident that seriously injured his leg—and this just on the eve of the earth-shaking arrival in Jerusalem of Egyptian President Anwar Sadat on his historic visit to Israel in November 1977. I was in Washington at the time, and a very worried Ilan phoned me to tell me about Ezer's accident. I immediately put through a call to the hospital and was connected with Ezer. He was cussing and complaining, but he reassured me, "It isn't all that serious. But of all times to be so unlucky. Even if I have to bend all the hospital rules, I'll get to meet Sadat." And he did. Overcoming his agonizing pain with the help of painkillers, Weizman forced himself from his hospital bed to meet the Egyptian leader in his hotel suite. Henceforth, the two former sworn enemies would establish a warm friendship that helped keep the vessel of peace afloat, even as it appeared to be floundering on the quicksands of suspicion resulting from decades of war. As Sadat's "good friend Ezra," Weizman became the driving force inside Israel for peace with Egypt.

2

Sadat the Charmer

Ezer Weizman held firm to his course for peace with Egypt despite the roller-coaster shifts in Israeli national mood—from the total euphoria immediately following Sadat's journey to Jerusalem, through a gradual descent into the doldrums of disenchantment, to an eventual "cold peace." As it was explained to me, the disenchantment was natural. A sea of blood and a mountain of corpses separated the two countries. These could not be crossed as easily nor erased from collective memory as quickly as some well-intentioned American diplomats or journalists might wish. On my visits to Israel throughout early winter, I discerned signs of the shifting mood. Just after Sadat's visit, I remember noticing a rather tacky clothing store near Tel Aviv's Carmel market calling itself the "Begin-Sadat Peace Store," with a large sign depicting the smiling faces of the two leaders entwined in the flags of Israel and Egypt. But then I began to hear sounds of anxiety and concern from even the most moderate Israeli acquaintances. Even Hanna Semer, the editor of *Davar*, the Labor daily, one of the most level-headed persons I have ever met, was prompted to ask Sadat whether the overwhelmingly friendly welcome extended to visiting Israelis immediately following Sadat's Jerusalem trip might not change back to enmity overnight. That was at the Ismailia summit in December 1977, when the Egyptian hosted Begin and his entourage.

In trying to understand Israel and Egypt and how the leaders of each might respond, one must always keep in mind the vast differences between the two societies. Israel is a Western Parliamentary democracy, and a rather quarrelsome one at that, while Egypt, since the days of the Pharaohs, has always been a one-man show subject to the dictates of a single leader. Indeed, what remained in my memory from the televised reports of the Sadat visit to Jerusalem was not only his arrival at Ben-Gurion Airport, his Knesset speech, and meeting with Golda Meir, but above all the scene of his return home to a tumultuous reception by millions of Egyptians. A triumphantly beaming Sadat was waving to his rejoicing subjects, standing up in his limousine with his Nilotic profile etched on the TV screen, like any Pharaoh of antiquity drawn in his chariot through ancient Thebes.

The Ismailia conference ended in an impasse. However, it did define more clearly the yawning gap between Egypt and Israel and the differing concepts that were prevalent among the Israelis themselves—between the Labor opposition and the governing Likud—and even within the Cabinet.

It may be considered the greatest irony of Israeli history that Menachem Begin, the man considered the most extreme of all Israeli political leaders and a feared symbol to the outside world, became the first Prime Minister to sign a covenant of peace with the largest Arab country. Gallons of ink have been poured onto tons of paper by political specialists trying to fathom what they regard as Begin's transformation. Yet as his followers pointed out, he had already outlined his plans for peace on the eve of his electoral victory.

Was it because he wished thereby to confound his widely feared image as a warmonger, which was cultivated by Labor propagandists during the 1977 election campaign? And did

Begin pick Moshe Dayan, the legendary former Labor Defense Minister, to be his Foreign Minister because he knew that Dayan would abandon party and principles in order to rescue his name for posterity from the sands of Sinai where it had foundered on Yom Kippur in 1973? These are questions for future historians to answer.

The Secret Meeting

What is not widely acknowledged is that Sadat came to Israel already holding an Israeli commitment to hand back all of Sinai—oilfields, airfields, settlements, the lot. Sadat's journey to Jerusalem had been preceded by a top-secret meeting in Morocco in September 1977—four months after Begin became Prime Minister—between one of his senior aides and Dayan. At Begin's behest Dayan offered Sadat the whole of Sinai in return for peace. This was done without the knowledge or consent of any other member of the Government, and it obviously rankled Ezer that the Prime Minister and Foreign Minister kept their Defense Minister in the dark on such a dramatic and important move. In later years Ezer was to remark that Begin and Dayan spent the ensuing peace negotiations doing all they could to amend the far-reaching concessions they had made at the outset. There was much talk at that period of breaking down psychological barriers, and the critics at home alleged that most members of the Begin Government were psychologically ill-prepared for such a revolutionary turn of events. Yet it may also be argued that, considering the recurring cries of *Jihad*—the Arab Holy War against the tiny Jewish state—and the refusal of the Arab world to accept Israel, accompanied by four attempts to wipe Israel off the map, that the fears and suspicions were most understandable. What was remarkable was not only the readiness of Begin the superhawk to change his feathers, but also the swiftness with which a hitherto equally famous hawk like Ezer Weizman was willing to grasp the outstretched olive branch.

An American Dream

But anyone expecting smooth sailing for the ship of peace was in for a rude awakening. Anwar Sadat's charismatic appeal and his canny management of the American media made him the most popular foreign statesman in the United States. He won over all Americans, from President to the average person, with his charm and easy-going manner, which contrasted sharply with Israel's Prime Minister Begin, who was not one to please for the sake of pleasing either the U.S. Administration or the general public. Begin's old-world East European manners and formalistic style did not endear him to Americans. Many Israelis began to see in Sadat the cunning crocodile of the Nile rather than the great peace-maker, and accusations surfaced that Egypt was using Israeli leverage to open the gates to American aid and arms, without offering true peace in return.

Others in Israel recognized that Sadat's historic gesture of stretching out his hand in peace was not diminished by being motivated by self-interest. There was also the desire to end the chain of hostilities and war, even at the price of temporarily isolating Egypt from the Arab world. Labor leader Shimon Peres once related that Sadat had told him in all seriousness that his visit to Jerusalem was on a par with such awe-inspiring historical events in the area as the exodus of the children of Israel and the birth of Jesus.

Star-Quality General

The only Israeli who could balance the impact of Sadat on the American scene was "my friend Ezra" (as Sadat referred to him). Ezer Weizman's dashing film-star qualities were (and remain) admirably suited to the medium of television.

It is of interest to note that at the outset of the peace process a major disagreement between Ezer and Dayan was over the Foreign Minister's almost obsessive insistence on involving the United States in all phases of the negotiating process. Ezer, on the other hand, wished to maximize the opportunity

of direct negotiations with the Egyptians. After all, it had
been the primary objective of Israeli policy for years to get the
Egyptians into face-to-face discussions. Ezer sought to reduce
to a minimum any dependence on a third party. To Dayan's
mind only a *Pax Americana* would ensure a durable peace,
with Washington committing itself out of the United States'
own interest. Ezer feared such a course might end in Israel's
being faced with an American-Egyptian coalition, with all
that implied. Ezer's view at the time was that the over-
readiness of Dayan and other Ministers to have American
involvement in the negotiations was indicative of a colonial
mentality.

As things turned out, both approaches prevailed at the
Ismailia summit. Sadat and Begin agreed to split the negotiations between a military commission and a political commission. The military negotiations were more or less Ezer's baby;
they had relative if limited success. At least they survived the
exigencies that beset the political commission. The military
group's Israeli side was led by General Tamir, and the
negotiating-team members stayed at the Tahara Palace in
Cairo. There they established a fairly decent working relationship with their Egyptian counterparts. Indeed only after
Sadat dispatched Tamir and his team back home in January
1978 did Ezer change his view. He saw that, along with other
elements, a serious impasse had been reached in the negotiating process. Not one to cleave dogmatically to any concept
proven to be outdated, he reached the conclusion that the
peace process would best be pursued through the good offices
of the "friendly super-power across the Atlantic."

And that was where I came in. Fate often appears haphaz-
ardly, and though I didn't know it then, fate would soon link
me up with an American who would become Israel's first—
and most important—"back-door channel" in the search for
peace.

3

The White House Connection

I met Robert Lipshutz through my good friend Wolf Blitzer, an American who is Washington correspondent of *The Jerusalem Post*. I had known Wolf since the early 1970's when I served as counsel to Senator Vance Hartke of Indiana, and had been close to Wolf and his family. For a number of years I commuted to his hometown of Buffalo, New York, during the High Holy Days to serve as cantor for his parents' congregation.

I had asked Wolf to introduce me to the President's Counsel after I had read a slur against Lipshutz in an Israeli tabloid. It quoted Begin's aide, Yehiel Kadishai, as labeling Lipshutz "a Jewish anti-Semite." Knowing the affable Kadishai well, I was absolutely convinced that he would never say such a thing. Moreover, I thought it palpably unfair to cast such a vile aspersion against someone who enjoyed a long-standing reputation as a pillar of the Atlanta Jewish community and as a most honorable man. So I asked Wolf—who knew everyone in Washington—to arrange an introduction so I could personally dispel any bad feelings that such a misquote might have evoked. No one had asked me to do this. As an American and a

Jew I felt duty-bound to do what I could to alleviate any harm
that such a fabrication might cause between two key persons
in the two countries.

It appeared that Bob was as eager to meet me as I was to be
introduced to him. That emerged after I was obliged to cancel
our original appointment. I had been summoned urgently to
Jerusalem to confer with officials of the new Government
there about various aspects of the aftermath of the Israel-
British Bank scandal, which had happened under the previous Government. I was still striving my utmost to ensure
Israel's standing in the world banking community and simultaneously contain, if not cut, the multimillion-dollar losses
sustained by the group of American regional banks which I
represented—especially the Indiana bank of my friend Don
Tanselle. The fact that the White House Counsel accepted my
apologies and agreed to a further appointment was an indication to me of his eagerness to establish our acquaintance.
Apparently he had inquired about me and learned of my
extensive contacts in Israel on both sides of the political spectrum. Even at that stage he was weighing how best to use his
high position to serve the President in the search for peace in
the Middle East, a cause which was very close to his heart.

My first meeting with Lipshutz occurred on a rather rainy
Washington day in mid-November 1977—just after Sadat had
completed his trip to Jerusalem. Wolf and I had been checked
through by the White House security guards on our way to
Bob's West Wing office. In previous years, while counsel to
Senator Hartke, I had called at the Executive Office Building
next door on more than one occasion, but I do confess that my
initial encounter with the White House was an awe-inspiring
experience. For me this was the very heart of the mystery
which I had observed from afar during my years with the
Senator. I think that this is true for most Americans, even the
most hard-headed and irreverent among us, that being inside
the White House is almost a religious experience. There seems
to be something special and different even about the oxygen
one breathes within its precincts. There is the magic aura of

power about the place that affects even the most cynical members of the permanent press corps.

A foreign visitor once told me of his slight disappointment after a tour of the public rooms of the White House. He thought it should have been grander. He had been accustomed to the pomp and splendor of the palaces that house the Governments of Europe. I told him that rather comfortable, country mansion feeling is precisely what is so attractive about the place, and so inherently American.

It would be untrue if I did not confess that my heart missed a beat or two as Wolf and I mounted the stairway on my first visit to the second-floor office of the White House Counsel. Even such an experienced Washington hand as Wolf confessed to a similar sense of mounting excitement. After all it was not every day that he was invited beyond the limits of the press room, which had become a routine part of his daily rounds.

When we arrived at Bob's office, we had to wait until he completed a previous engagement. His secretary, Caroline, was as pleasant to me on that first visit as she was to be during my frequent incursions in the coming years. Soon the door to Bob's room opened and out came his visitor, a tall, imposing man talking in a booming British-accented voice. Later I learned it had been Marcus Sieff (soon to become Lord Sieff), head of the giant British chain-store network, Marks and Spencer. He was prominent not only in British politics but also as a leader of the Anglo-Jewish community, and he was deeply involved in everything to do with Israel. I never learned whether his visit had concerned either Britain or Israel or neither. Bob, as usual, was totally discreet about such matters.

I liked Bob's office, with its fine view of the city, the trees, and the Washington Monument tapering into the sky. What made me feel immediately at ease was the fact that Bob prominently displayed the model of a *shofar* (the ram's horn used during the High Holy Day services) which a Washington Jewish organization had presented to him. That he did not choose to hide his religion, as others in his position might have done, but rather displayed one of its most ancient symbols, was to me a firm indication of the man's ironclad integrity.

My thoughts briefly flashed back to my first job after graduating from law school. My employers—who were Jewish—insisted I remove my Yeshiva University diploma, fearing it might scare away clients. I chose to quit instead.

The conversation during the first meeting focused almost entirely on the intensely exciting subject of Sadat's epoch-

The bonds strengthen—Leon Charney with his "White House connection", Bob Lipshutz.

making visit. The dramatic scenes from Jerusalem had covered television screens and the front pages of America's newspapers.

The Bonds Strengthen

As our relationship grew, Bob asked me to visit him at the White House whenever I came home from one of my frequent trips to Israel. Naturally, he was most interested to obtain a firsthand impression of top-level Israeli thinking from an eyewitness with extensive connections. After all, I invariably met friends in Israel among the Labor opposition leadership, such as Yitzhak Rabin and Chaim Barlev, so I did enjoy a broad perspective on Israeli affairs. From Bob's responses to what I had to say, I would intuit what the prevalent thinking was around the White House, and when I was back in Israel I would pass this information along to Ezer. Both men knew that the other was getting the information.

As time passed I found myself drawn willy-nilly into a kind of pattern—when I was in Israel I would seek to ascertain the views of the Israeli Defense Minister and the opposition leaders. (Once, in an early phase of our friendship, when Bob did not wish to appear to be pressing me for information, he responded to my plans to spend some time swimming at an upstate New York resort hotel with the supposedly innocent query, "And there's no swimming in the Mediterranean?")

I had no way of knowing then, but as the movement toward peace escalated, my role as a back-door channel would evolve from being a friendly visitor to Lipshutz's office, to being a sounding board against which possible proposals and impressions of leaders in each country could be tested. Gradually, I became a major and important conduit of information and messages that were deemed too private or tentative to be trusted to public or official channels. I was used increasingly as a private emissary. This enabled the leaders of the two Governments to avoid the twists and turns that can color negotiations when the good-sized egos and vested interests of some career diplomats and military professionals get between the message and the ear for which it is intended. Finally, when my discretion, accuracy of information, and judgment had been tested, my advice and counsel were sought directly by the heads of the two countries to which my heart owes allegiance: the President of the United States and the Prime Minister of Israel. In the later stages of negotiation Carter, in particular, placed great store in what I said.

I was to pay a heavy price for my role in history although I regard the financial cost as minor. I contributed my time and paid for all my expenses simply because I felt it my duty as an American Jew. My early grounding in ethics and instruction in Talmudic law instilled in me a value system that has guided my life. I have always put loyalty above business and traditional values above material aspirations. A friend of mine once spoke of Jews as possessing special psychological antennae which alert us to other Jews in need. Perhaps that explains my instinctive responsiveness to calls to come to the aid of Jews in distress—often at great personal expense and sacrifice. (When I served as counsel to Senator Hartke, I interceded on behalf of hundreds of Russian Jews at the request of Prime Minister Golda Meir. But more on that later.)

A more pertinent and exacting toll was the price in personal pain and loneliness. I could tell *no one* of my role, for my efficacy depended on my silence. I could tell *no one* what I knew or why I had to fly off to strange lands in the middle of the night. I could tell *no one* what I was doing.

The pressure and responsibility were so great that I gained 40 pounds. I broke up with a girlfriend. I even argued with my own mother. I was labelled and even hissed at by some American Jews who thought, at best, that I was naive; by Israeli Jews who were jealous; by middle-level diplomats who were threatened. I was never able to convey my inner thoughts to my two major colleagues in the back-door channel—Weizman and Lipshutz—because each was part servant of his own constituency and country. I was a middleman, with no constituency. Of necessity I had to maintain my *silence* to all, about all, above all. But I continued on because the goal was so tempting. If we were successful, if Egypt and Israel could settle on a permanent peace, then we would be transforming the Middle East and perhaps saving millions of lives in the future. It may sound arrogant, but I believed that destiny had picked me. I was in a unique position in the history of American-Israeli relations, as no one before had ever performed the role that I did: I was the President's silent advisor on Israel.

Carter's Growing Involvement

During his second year in office, Carter benefited domestically from the move toward a peace treaty between Israel and Egypt. Increasingly, as 1978 progressed, he shared headlines and space on the evening news with Begin and Sadat. Indeed, at times the anchormen of the three main American TV networks became the catalysts of Middle Eastern diplomacy, trading on the mutual passion for publicity of the three leaders. Curiously, while lower-level officials in both Governments were sworn to secrecy, their leaders would use audiences of millions as confidants.

Initially, Carter who was a novice in international affairs, really seemed to believe that open diplomacy would produce results. Carter began to earn a reputation for naiveté in foreign affairs. For example, he told correspondents on Air Force One returning from Europe in January 1978 that the United States would accept an interim solution for the West Bank, including a limited form of self-determination for the Palestinians that would lead to an ultimate referendum in five years' time. This came as a bombshell and led people to question whether Jimmy Carter wished to distance himself from the secret diplomacy so earnestly pursued by Henry Kissinger under the previous Republican Administration. As the months slipped by and the momentum toward peace slowed, the chief protagonists began to learn the hard way that, when policies are spelled out in too much detail in the mass media, it inevitably leads to a hardening of formal positions, making subsequent compromise much more difficult.

The President, too, began to appreciate the advantages of pursuing his goals away from the bright lights of television. For example, he once admitted to me that he had ordered public opinion polls to be conducted in Israel just before the Camp David summit meetings. He wanted to gauge the readiness of the Israeli public to make concessions in return for peace. It may well be that his advisors thought he could spring some surprise on Begin should an impasse be reached. On the other hand, it would appear much more valid to surmise that the President wished to ascertain how far he could go with the Israelis. As the months passed, I fervently wished that, by our joint efforts, Bob and I could somehow help improve matters and promote a greater understanding of the situation.

"Nu, Sing!"

Business took me to Israel in the early months of 1978. By this time Ezer and I had become the best of friends and would spend hours together discussing a wide range of subjects—from world politics to personal matters. On numerous occasions, he invited me to official ceremonies or cocktail parties that he was obliged to attend. At one party I met the visiting Defense Minister of Ecuador, who wore the most colorful collection of medals I have ever seen on one uniform. Other occasions were really stirring, like Air Force Day, when I was Ezer's guest at an Israeli Air Force base "somewhere in Israel." Israel's best pilots performed a thrilling display of air tricks—with Ezer beaming like a proud father, excited by the antics of his favorite sons.

One time Ezer even thrust me to the fore. It was at a Purim party held in February 1978 for the Ministry personnel. All the top officials attended, including Deputy Defense Minister Mordechai Zippori and his wife. My pal, actor-singer Mike Burstyn, had just given us all some first-rate entertainment, when Ezer cried out, "We've got another musical number here," and pulled me to my feet. He pushed the microphone into my hand and in a mock commanding voice, said, "*Nu*, sing!" (Well, sing!) So I rendered some of my cantorial songs, and apparently the audience liked them. I hope it was my voice and not my Ministerial sponsor that inspired their applause.

Undoubtedly, by this time people were beginning to wonder what this American was doing around Ezer, but such questions were to come out into the open only later.

Israel Grows Leery

The feeling began to grow in Israel that the United States Administration was leaning toward Egypt. These apprehensions appeared to be confirmed following Sadat's highly successful visit to the United States in February 1978.

In March tension between Jerusalem and Washington deepened. The President, who never concealed his personal predilection for the Egyptian leader, even invited Sadat to Camp David where, it emerged, he promised Egypt a supply of sophisticated United States offensive weaponry which the United States had never supplied before. About that time he also promised Saudi Arabia advanced F-15 fighter-bombers. The fears were further heightened in Israel when the President invited a group of prominent figures in the American Jewish community to dinner at the White House. There he sought their assistance in pressuring the Israeli Government to make more concessions to Cairo. That they were not prepared to do, except for the World Jewish Congress leader, Philip Klutznick of Chicago, who later became Commerce Secretary in Carter's Administration.

Hence the rather sour atmosphere in which the Carter-Begin talks took place in Washington late in March. Near the end of their discussions in the Oval Office, the President took out a notebook and listed a batch of "no's" in connection with the Israeli negotiating stance. The Prime Minister protested that his host had presented the Israeli Government's position in a negative rather than a positive light. After all, Israel was willing to hand over all of Sinai and extend autonomy to the Arabs of the West Bank and Gaza.

The Administration's view of Israeli negativity soon filtered through to Congress and the general public, dismaying the Israelis. They argued that, although it was Sadat and not Begin who had earlier suspended the political commission's negotiations in Jerusalem, the President insisted on calling Sadat "the world's foremost peace-maker." I had heard that Carter was strongly advised at that time by State Department officials who advocated an independent Palestinian state.

Talk of an independent Palestinian state evokes the deepest of fears among most Israelis, who regard it as a threat to their very existence. In such a quarrelsome country it is one of the few issues on which there is a consensus. Especially at that time, Palestinian autonomy meant having a Soviet surrogate right next door and giving the PLO a legitimate base for its designs against Israel.

If Carter hoped to tackle the thorny Palestinian problem during the late March 1978 visit of Menachem and Aliza Begin to Washington, a PLO atrocity on March 11 canceled that notion, at least for the time being. Thirty-five men, women, and children, including an American woman nature-photographer, were murdered in cold blood by a group of PLO terrorists who hijacked their holiday bus on the Tel Aviv-Haifa coastal highway. Once more Arab fanaticism fueled the extremists of Israel, burying the hopes of the moderates. This was but a small repetition of the great historic error of the Arab leaders in 1947, when they rejected any accommodation with the Jews after the United Nations General Assembly voted for partition of Palestine under British Mandate into Jewish and Arab states. Instead, a fanatical Arab group thought they could push the Jews into the sea, compelling the emergence of "Fortress Israel" and creating the Palestinian Arab refugee problem. War followed war in the ensuing decades, until Anwar Sadat came forth offering the olive branch.

Weizman Comes to Talk

Just before the Begin visit in March, President Carter met with Ezer Weizman for the first time. Ezer was in Washington on his first trip to America as Defense Minister. Carter took to him immediately. Ezer's charm and level-headedness left a good impression. The Chief Executive was interested to hear Ezer's assessment of the Egyptian leadership and what could best be done to resolve outstanding differences between the two countries.

I do not know precisely what role my relationship with Bob Lipshutz played, but it was let out from the White House that the Administration perceived in Weizman the one Israeli leader whom Sadat liked and trusted, which was a prized asset in the then sour phase of relations.

From Bob I learned that the President liked Ezer's pragmatic grasp of things and what he regarded as an unusual degree of objectivity for a Middle Eastern leader. The President's positive view of Weizman was speedily disseminated throughout the media, with headlines soon proclaiming, "U.S. Views Weizman Role as Crucial." The Administration regarded Ezer as Begin's heir-apparent at that time and held him to be much more flexible on the troublesome settlement issue than his colleagues. If in the past Washington, D.C. had pinned its hopes on Dayan to bring Israel around to a more "moderate" position, now the spotlight was focused on the dashing silhouette of Ezer Weizman.

I was in close contact with Ezer during his stay in the United States that bitterly cold March. During the first half of his United States visit in Washington, we talked daily on the phone. When he moved to New York I was at his side in his suite at the Regency. He spoke of his meetings at the Pentagon as fairly successful, and of how he had broken through the somewhat icy facade that Defense Secretary Harold Brown presented to the world. Ezer spoke of Brown as a painfully shy man, short on small talk and rather awkward in establishing contact with other people. Just the opposite of Ezer's extro-

verted personality. But the Israeli's famous charm managed
to thaw even Harold Brown's frozen wall.

A major issue in their discussions had been the Administration's decision—in the wake of Sadat's February visit—to
insist that the supply of new arms to Israel be linked to weapons deals with Egypt and Saudi Arabia. Ezer tried to take the
broader view as far as Egypt was concerned, believing that it
was preferable to cement Egypt's new alliance with America
by replacing its Soviet arsenal with Western arms. Yet he too
grasped the widespread anxieties back home in Israel about
the likely use of advanced American weaponry in some future
conflict. It was widely asked in Israel at that time, "What will
happen if and when Sadat goes?" As for the Saudis, they were
regarded as a confrontation state and paymasters of Israel's
most active enemies, including Syria and the PLO.

When Ezer arrived in the United States, he became rather
upset about the negative image of Israel projected in the
media, with the settlement issue the prime focus. This negative image was especially evident after the President had
termed the settlements "illegal." Ezer put part of the blame on
the American Ambassador to Israel, Samuel Lewis, for having too zealously highlighted Israeli activity on the West
Bank, to the detriment of Begin's Government. But he was
most critical of his own colleagues, accusing them of not having risen to the occasion presented by Sadat. They in turn
accused him of being naive and of having let Cairo take him
for a ride. In Ezer's strategic view Israel and Egypt were
natural allies of the United States in blocking the expansion-
ist designs of the Soviet Union in the Middle East. Thus it was
all-important to reach an agreement with Egypt, but without
sacrificing Israel's basic interests. His first flight to Egypt in
December 1977 through what eventually came to be known as
"the Weizman air corridor" had shaken his outlook. He began
to discern that the ideological dogmatism of some of his fellow
Likud leaders, especially concerning the West Bank, might
hamper the peace process.

In February Sadat had taken America by storm and had
gone home with a lovely weapons package, among other

promises. But Dayan had come and gone during the same month, returning empty-handed. Interestingly, it was this visit that signaled the turning point in Ezer's approach to American involvement in the peace process. It also prompted Begin to decide to attempt to break the impasse and save the situation by coming to the United States himself. He asked Dayan and Weizman to join him. As Ezer was already in New York, about to return home after completing his talks with Harold Brown, he stayed on, pondering the world from the ninth floor of his Park Avenue hotel.

It was there that word reached him that President Carter wished to meet him in person. That was quite an honor. Visiting Defense Ministers, including those from NATO allies, rarely got invitations to meet the United States Chief Executive. Soon he began to get negative reaction from the Dayan entourage. It appeared that the Israeli Embassy in Washington was highly perturbed at not having been the channel for arranging the meeting. Indeed, the Embassy had learned only by chance from a private source that Carter intended meeting the Israeli Defense Minister in person.

However, two mornings before he was to return to Washington from New York, Ezer found himself in the midst of a near crisis in the Cabinet and on the verge of resignation. I happened to be there at the time, and Ezer's military aide, Colonel Ilan Tehila, rushed in with the news that Sharon and Dayan had persuaded Begin to permit preparatory work on a new settlement site in the West Bank. Ezer's face turned almost purple. "I can just see Walter Cronkite, John Chancellor, and others denouncing another Israeli provocation, with their cameras zooming in on every shovel of earth the bulldozer shifts. It'll become the most famous bulldozer in the world," Ezer roared.

Ezer indicated his wish to make official phone calls, so the ever-loyal Colonel Tehila and I moved to the outer room of Ezer's hotel suite. Suddenly we heard Ezer's voice bellowing in anger through the closed door. The conversation went on for some time, and Ilan and I gazed at one another in great consternation. Then the door was flung open and Ezer stalked into the room. He was quite livid with rage, and paced the floor as if to reduce his inner turmoil. It emerged that this extremely angry exchange had been with the Prime Minister. Ezer had served an ultimatum: either the bulldozers be removed or he would resign. He had tried to explain the precariousness of Israel's position with the United States at this delicate juncture, and had said that such an action would only serve Israel's detractors. A most persuasive point, apparently, had been his warning that under such circumstances Begin's forthcoming meeting with the President would be disastrous.

That irate telephone conversation, I was subsequently told, was a turning point in Ezer's relations with Begin, who never forgave him for his tone or for pressuring him by threatening to resign. Ezer henceforth was high on the famous Begin grudge list, for which the Likud leader was notorious. At any rate, the tenor of that exchange soon made its way into the Israeli media, compounded by disparaging remarks from Ezer's many political rivals. They endeavored to drive home the image of an impetuous shooter-from-the-hip, who should never be trusted with affairs crucial to the fate of the nation. The moment the American media started talking about "Ezer Weizman, the next Israeli Prime Minister," all the other would-be heirs-apparent began to sharpen their knives and set their aides to work on their press contacts. Moreover, the fact that Ezer had been called to the White House gave his adversaries the opportunity to spread nasty rumors about his "selling out" to the Americans.

Ezer was slightly discomfited by his White House visit, because Israeli Ambassador Simha Dinitz had been left outside the room. This could well lead Ezer's Cabinet colleagues to misconstrue the entire proceedings. After all, if he had to fight against slanders of "selling out to the Americans," he needed another Israeli source to provide a report. At first a number of Presidential advisors and Cabinet Ministers were included in the meeting, but soon Ezer was left sitting alone with the President and the Vice President.

As the reports that subsequently emerged from that meeting intimated, the participants discussed how best to get the peace process moving again. Ezer pleaded Israel's case, while Carter sought to allay any fears about the American commitment to Israel's security, if not to its territorial acquisitions since the 1967 War. Carter expounded on his warm regard for Sadat; Ezer tried to match him by talking of the personal relationship that had developed between him and Egyptian Defense Minister General Gamasy.

As Ezer was to relate later, the view of the world from the office of the President of the United States looks different. Like all other guests he had been suitably impressed with the furnishings and atmosphere of the Presidential office. As to the state of United States-Israel relations, well, as he said to a reporter waiting outside the White House, indicating the gloomy weather, "The atmosphere in our relations is like the weather in Washington. But I can tell you there is a silver lining to the clouds."

Reprisal and Respite

I came over to the Regency as soon as Ezer phoned me that he was back in New York. He intended spending the weekend in town to wait for Begin's arrival for the official talks in Washington. I met Re'uma in the lobby downstairs. She was off to see some friends; Ezer wanted to rest. I agreed to help Ilan find his way through the mysteries of Bloomingdale's and Macy's. By the time we got back, laden with the fruits of Ilan's shopping expedition, we found an extremely anxious Ezer Weizman. After he phoned Jerusalem to report directly to the Prime Minister on his meeting with the President, he had intended to rest for a while. But a friend telephoned from Tel Aviv, giving him the dreadful news about the terrorists' hijacking of the Israeli tourist bus. As we came in carrying Ilan's shopping bags, the phone began ringing incessantly. The casualty rate began to climb—10, 15, 20, 30, 35. Ilan had already returned to his room and, as if by instinct, began to pack.

Ezer kept saying, "Peace is under attack." He mentioned how once again Israel's concern for sparing civilians had worked to the terrorists' favor. Some weeks earlier military intelligence had gotten wind of unusual activity at the little port of Damour, just south of Beirut on the coast of Lebanon. It had been a thriving Christian community until the PLO forces had taken over during the 1976 Civil War, massacring as many Christian inhabitants as they could get their hands on, and leaving a pile of corpses in the gutted church. After that it was a PLO base. An Israeli Defense Forces commando unit had raided the place but refrained from going further inland so as to avoid civilian casualties. It was from there the perpetrators of the atrocity had come.

Ezer decided to fly home, especially on learning that the Cabinet in his absence had decided to launch a large-scale reprisal operation. (The reprisal developed into the "Litani operation.") What he feared above all was that through their atrocity the PLO might succeed in derailing the peace process. That, above all, he had to save.

4

"Get Me Charney!"

In May 1978 Begin and many of his Cabinet Ministers came to the United States to attend the White House bash the Carters were throwing in honor of Israel's 30th anniversary. Although Carter's aides claimed that they had issued invitations to only 200 leading rabbis across the country, more than 1200 festively attired people turned up at the White House gates. A stroke of organizational genius made it possible to shift the celebration to the South Lawn. There the President and the Prime Minister had the opportunity to shake hands with each and every guest before taking the podium to deliver emotional speeches.

I had brought along Gerald Green, author of the teleplay for "Holocaust." We had appeared together on a TV show in New York. A fascinating man, Green had also written 17 books, including *The Last Angry Man* and *The Lotus Eaters*. Even he had not expected the kind of tremendous impact that "Holocaust" made.

Green was thrilled to be at the White House for this occasion. He had lunch with Stu Eizenstat, the President's Domestic Affairs Advisor, whose office was a few doors away from that of Bob Lipshutz. Whether it was an outcome of their conversation or the result of the impact of the TV series on the general public, the fact remained that the President announced in his speech that day the formation of a commission to establish an American memorial to the victims of the Holocaust.

Shake Hands with the Great

Not until June 1978 did I meet Jimmy Carter in the flesh. It was at a benefit dinner held in the lavish surroundings of Lincoln Center. Carter had flown in from Washington to signify his support for my good friend Mayor Abraham Beame. The dinner, a black-tie affair, was aimed at raising enough funds to help the Mayor wipe out his campaign debts. It was quite an experience for me to sit in the Presidential box, where Abe Beame introduced me to President Carter and Jack Watson, who was to succeed Hamilton Jordan as Chief of Staff. I spoke to both of them at length. Carter and I hit it off from the first moment when he leaned across to me and said, "Hi, Leon. Bob sends his best regards to you." Despite the hubbub around us, the President and I still managed to have a meaningful discussion about the Middle East.

Senate-Hopeful Bradley

In mid-June 1978 I found myself being used as a back-door channel in a different kind of "peace" negotiation. My friend, Phyllis Schmertz, urged me to help a friend of hers extricate himself from some political trouble. That friend was the former basketball star Bill Bradley, who had just won the New Jersey Democratic primary for the United States Senate contest. In the course of a lengthy profile on the aspiring candidate in *The New York Times* Sunday Magazine, the reporter had attributed to him pro-PLO views. Not unexpectedly, Phyllis told me, the Bradley campaign headquarters had been deluged with protests and questions from members of New Jersey's Jewish population. Would I be Bradley's special counsel? My reply was that I would do my best, as long as the *Times* had indeed misquoted him.

So Bradley came to see me, tall, personable and deeply unhappy over the whole incident. He showed me the offending article. It attributed to him the view that "the PLO should be accepted into Middle East negotiations." He swore it was untrue and asked me to help him compel the *Times* management to print a correction. I phoned the *Times*, advising them a letter was following and insisting on a retraction, otherwise the candidate would avail himself of his legal rights to sue. Under my guidance Bradley then issued a statement to the press, which was taken up by other media in the tri-state area, criticizing the *Times* for inexact reporting of his views. He stated that his position was that "Israel should not negotiate with an organization which has as its doctrine the destruction of Israel." He described the PLO as "a murderous group."

That was on the Monday. By Thursday the *Times* had agreed to our demand and we were negotiating the type and size of the correction. On Friday, Bradley was in my office relishing the speed with which I had helped to extricate him from that mess, when the phone rang. It was Ezer calling me from Israel to wish me "a good *Shabbos*," and saying he hoped to see me in Israel soon. Bradley was impressed on hearing the identity of my caller...a sign of the growing recognition of Ezer Weizman as a star in the international firmament. Ezer was becoming one of the most popular Israelis in the United States since Golda Meir.

Personalities and Leaks

I spent a good deal of the 1978 summer going back and forth to Israel, some of it on business, some on pleasure, and some consulting with Ezer. He would ask me frequently to come over so we could discuss specific approaches and strategies, problems and personalities involved in the peace negotiations.

I got to know Ezer's key aides better, in particular his genial military aide, Ilan Tehila, and his brilliant National Security Advisor, Abrasha Tamir. General Tamir had been conducting

the Israeli side of the military commission talks with the
Egyptians, until Sadat ejected the Israelis from Cairo, largely
because of a leak. The leak caused Ezer a lot of trouble.

Ezer and Sadat had met in Salzburg, Austria, at Sadat's
invitation. Sadat liked Weizman. The military commission
talks were simultaneously going on in Cairo and Jerusalem.
The Egyptian leader made some requests, including the
immediate return of the El Arish area of the Sinai. In return,
he had assured Ezer that no PLO state would arise to threaten
Israel. Later, some of Sadat's proposals leaked from Ezer's
confidential report and the Egyptians angrily sent General
Tamir's team home. Begin mistakenly blamed Ezer. (A friendly
newsman told me the leak came from another Cabinet Minister.)

That's when Ezer learned what it was like to be a lone wolf
in politics—a style that poorly suited his gregarious personality. His Cabinet colleagues poured cold water on his hot pursuit of peace.

The main Israeli players in the peace game had distinctly
different character traits that were reflected in their negotiating. Begin adored legalistic details; Dayan preferred a step-by-
step approach, which he claimed was more easily digestible.
Ezer—the fighter pilot—went in for the blitz approach. (In
that, we are very similar. Both of us, sensing an opportunity,
like to go for it without delay.) There also were fundamental
differences in the backgrounds of Begin and Ezer (and Dayan
for that matter), which certainly colored their outlooks. Begin
grew up in Eastern Europe between the two World Wars as
part of an oppressed Jewish minority, while Ezer had always
lived in a free Jewish society—even if under British rule—and
had never personally suffered from anti-Semitism. Hence his
attitude toward the non-Jewish world was more tolerant and
flexible than that of Begin.

The leak gave Ezer's political adversaries an opportunity to
hurt him as much as possible. The country was still reverber-
ating with the story of Ezer's emerging from a rather harrowing Cabinet discussion, noticing a Government peace propaganda poster on the wall, and removing it forcibly, grumbling

aloud that it did not appear this Government was actively seeking peace. Newspapers, radio and television blew that impulsive action out of all proportion.

"Keep the Channels Open"

By this time Ezer had already overtaken Dayan's position and advocated what he called "using the American tow truck" to pull the country toward peace. Earlier in the summer Dayan had apparently shocked the Egyptians into a more flexible position by advising them at a conference held at Leeds Castle near London that Israel might cancel its readiness to withdraw from Sinai and instead concentrate on the West Bank and Gaza issues. Ezer's former brother-in-law joined with him now in an active search for peace.

Before I left, Ezer said to me in an earnest tone, "Listen closely, Leon. When you go back to America, I want you to

Photo by Tim Boxer

Before I left, Ezer Weizman said to me in an earnest tone, "Listen closely, Leon. When you go back to America, I want you to keep the channels open for me."

keep the channels open for me. I want you to keep in contact with the right people, in case we have problems with the Americans." I promised I would do my best.

On my way out of the office compound I popped into Abrasha's room. "You know, Leon," he said in his throaty voice, "I don't think things are as desperate as some of my colleagues do. I know that some believe we are once again on a collision course with Egypt. That's because my team and I were sent home after some idiot in Jerusalem leaked Sadat's request to get back El Arish now. I'm optimistic about the negotiations and, believe me, I've had lots of experience in them. I am convinced that people on both sides don't want another war; they want peace, and they don't want any more casualties. We have enough bereaved families on both sides of the border. Also, I believe that the Egyptians appreciate that, after 1973, when they had the initial advantage and we turned things around, it is now doubtful that they will ever get rid of us by military force."

This clever man made a brilliant point about negotiating. When talking of hesitations in both countries about the negotiations, he remarked, "The negotiating process is like entering a tunnel. You have to move on, and more often than not you find yourself emerging with a different position than the one you went in with."

As he accompanied me to the door, shaking my hand, Abrasha said, "You know, Leon, you must be one of the few close friends Ezer has who is not a pilot. You have become very important to him, because he trusts you. Don't think that we who work with him don't appreciate that although you are in his confidence, you have not leaked a thing to the press in all this time." I interjected, "It's because I'm not an Israeli politician, Abrasha." He laughed and continued, "Do you know when he comes to the office and faces some problem, and he has to talk to someone, preferably you, he gets restless and shouts to Ilan or to his secretary, 'Get me Charney!' Some of us think you've become his closest confidant." I knew this was an exaggeration but the notion amused me all through the night flight back home.

Years later, I was told by Mark Segal, a reporter for *The Jerusalem Post* who had interviewed Ezer, that perhaps the closeness of our relationship had not been exaggerated. Ezer, said Mark, had spoken of me as "one of my closest friends, if not *the* closest. If I had to pick someone with whom to go on a round-the-world cruise it would be Leon. I never get bored in his company. He is one of the very few people I can sit and talk with for hours on end." He went on to say, "He is certainly the most Jewish American I have ever met. I remember that when we were once in Atlanta, Leon got me out of bed at 6 a.m. on a rainy morning to go to synagogue for the prayer service in honor of his late father. I would say he was the only person able to do such a thing. He is very American and very Jewish but possesses a wide-ranging world vision.... Leon gave me a different perspective on things. I was drawn to [him], perhaps, because in my background was the influence of my Weizman grandfather, with whom I spoke only Yiddish. I grew up in a home with a father who had been to *Heder* [Hebrew School]. I personally had no religious [education]. For us, after all, Zionism was to break away from Eastern Europe. We rejected the Diaspora but not Judaism. Thus I had an affinity with Leon from the moment we met."

5

The Viennese Road to Cairo

Late in the summer of 1978 the back-door channel was ready to move into high gear. By now the world knew of President Carter's invitation to both President Sadat and Prime Minister Begin to join him at a Camp David summit. Both had accepted unreservedly, and the diplomatic train had begun to move out of the station and gain momentum.

One evening just after I had arrived in Israel, Ezer called me at my Tel Aviv hotel inviting me to come to his Ramat Hasharon suburban villa to meet "someone you'll find intriguing." Upon arriving, I found an elegantly dressed European sitting in a chair on Ezer's lawn. His dress was particularly noticeable among the casually attired Israelis. He was introduced to me as Karl Kahana of Vienna, and he turned out to be a truly sophisticated man of the world with meticulously good manners.

When Ezer and I were by ourselves, he described Kahana as the son of a wealthy, assimilated Jewish family; however, he had become a multimillionaire in his own right. He was very close to Austrian Chancellor Bruno Kreisky and on friendly terms with Anwar Sadat. I learned later that Kahana had had a hand in Sadat's decision to invite Ezer to Salzburg, where he entertained them all in a princely manner. On that first encounter with Kahana and on subsequent ones, he treated Ezer as one aristocrat would another. As for me, while he was most cordial, it was obvious that he was wondering what this informal American in jeans and T-shirt was doing in their company.

I found Kahana to be an interesting and stylish person, traveling from one place to another in his own plane, and he was stimulating to be with, although he was still an unknown quantity to me. Later I formed an acquaintance with him which eventually proved to be extremely helpful.

Following our meeting, I made discreet inquiries about him. I learned that, like many of his class, he enjoyed dabbling in politics. He had been doing business in Israel for some time and had even tried to sell Israeli-produced Kfir warplanes to the Austrian Air Force. (Supposedly Kreisky vetoed the scheme.) My dear friend Chaim Barlev, Secretary General of the Labor Party, a man of impeccable integrity, vouched for Kahana's credibility and good relations with Israeli labor. But Kahana's prime involvement was with Kreisky's Social Democrats, which obviously did not harm his business affairs in Vienna. I also learned of his connections with the Socialist International, an international consortium of socialists in which Kreisky was very active.

A day or two later Ezer asked me to join him, Ilan, and a few others for lunch in Jerusalem in Kahana's suite at the King David Hotel. It was a large, sumptuous suite on the top floor. We sat on the veranda overlooking the Old City, with the summer heat shimmering off the gleaming golden dome of the El Aqsa mosque. It must be one of the most stupendous views in the world, with all the beautiful old churches, cemeteries, and holy sites—all bathed in that special Jerusalem light. We had a splendid lunch with lots of wine, and I noticed Kahana at the end of the meal produce an elegant silver box and take a mint powder from it which he put into his coffee. Kahana's attitude toward me altered dramatically after Ezer had explained my White House connections. He began to treat me as an equal despite my jeans and T-shirt.

Kahana thanked Ilan effusively for having arranged special landing rights for his private jet at the sleepy Atarot Airfield in Jerusalem. The Austrian talked at length about Egypt, where he had been just before Israel. He spoke glowingly of Sadat, not forgetting to let us know of the kingly welcome the Egyptian leader had extended. The conversation gradually turned to how best to lower tensions between Jerusalem and Cairo. Kahana mentioned that Ezer might find it useful to utilize a channel to the Austrian Chancellor, who was on very good terms with Sadat. Kahana assured us that he enjoyed Kreisky's absolute trust. At one point he even dropped a hint about his connections to the so-called moderate wing of the PLO. I was thankful he did not expand on the subject, otherwise Ezer might have lost his temper.

After the luncheon table was removed, we settled into a game of diplomatic simulation—each of three of us representing one of the parties to the peace talks—Kahana-Egypt, Ezer-Israel, and I-the United States. Ilan was an interested onlooker. Ezer dwelt at length on points Israel could and could not concede, and could and could not accept. It especially could not accept a Palestinian state. That had to be ruled out, if the negotiations were to get anywhere. I ventured that the talks had to succeed for the United States, for if they failed, it might make it difficult for President Carter to govern. Kahana spoke vehemently, "You people don't seem to realize what Sadat is risking. He is taking his life into his hands. It's your Prime Minister Begin who does not want peace." He gesticulated in Ezer's direction. He then said how much easier it would be to reach peace if only a Labor Government were in power. Ezer interrupted him to remind him mildly that it was to Begin's Jerusalem that Sadat had come, and that it was with the Likud Government that the Egyptians had to reach an agreement.

Kahana changed his tone, leaned over the table, and said in

a low voice, "What would Israel and America say if Sadat agreed to accept Sinai now as part of a peace treaty and leave the fate of the West Bank to the future?" There was a thrill of excitement in the air. What we had just heard sounded like a signal, albeit secondhand, but still a real signal from Cairo. Kahana mentioned the possibility of a separate peace once again, with "the fate of the West Bank being settled by mutual agreement, taking into consideration the cooperation of the Palestinians and the security needs of the State of Israel. Such a Palestinian entity would be linked to Jordan."

As for Jerusalem, the knottiest problem of all, Kahana spoke of "a united city, with its municipal administration patterned after that of Paris or London, with self-governing boroughs."

As he elaborated on these and other ideas, I hurriedly wrote them down on the first piece of paper in sight, a hotel paper napkin, and afterward tucked it into the back pocket of my jeans. I was sure these proposals had come from the Sadat camp. As an afterthought, Kahana said he was sure that Sadat would be amenable to trying out autonomous rule first on the residents of the Gaza Strip, leaving the troublesome West Bank for future deliberations. I quickly wrote that down too on a clean edge of the napkin.

Before we parted, Kahana spoke directly to me. We exchanged our home and office phone numbers. He mentioned the advantages to my White House contacts of a connection between us, because of his direct access to Kreisky.

When we left his suite, Ezer and I pondered Kahana's love-hate relationship with the Jewish State, and to what extent Vienna might or might not be useful as an opening to Cairo.

I sensed that Kahana's information was of major importance, so I decided to catch a plane to the States as quickly as possible and present the information in person to Bob for the President's attention.

I was sure that Kahana's supposed bargaining chips in our "game" of negotiation had been real possibilities from Sadat. Kahana had, after all, made a point of letting us know how warmly Sadat thought of him and trusted him.

As soon as I reached JFK Airport in New York City, I booked the next flight to Atlanta. I had learned by phone before I
set out from Israel that Bob was home on vacation for the last
week of August. I arrived bone-weary from the long hours
spent cramped in airplanes and took a cab to Bob's office in
town, which had served as the Carter Presidential campaign
headquarters. He was his usual courtly self, and took meticu-
lous notes of my report. He thought my reading from the hotel
napkin was pretty funny, jesting in mock-Churchillian voice:
"Never has such important information been recorded on
such a nondescript piece of paper in such an indecipherable
script." I also asked him to recommend that Sadat invite
Begin to Cairo after the Camp David talks. An appropriate
ceremonial welcome might work wonders with the Israeli
Prime Minister and help move the peace movement forward.

Bob was intensely fascinated by my report and kept ex-
claiming, "Leon, are you sure? Are you sure? If all this is true,
it will be a big breakthrough to bring to Camp David." I
reassured him, "I'm not a prophet. But my instincts and my
insights tell me that it's reliable material. It's my considered
counsel that the President should arrange his agenda in such
a way as to include such possibilities. Of course, I can't guarantee anything; you know that. But in betting lingo, I'd give
nine-to-one odds." The White House Counsel looked at me for a
moment, and then said: "I'm going to communicate this to the
President immediately. I trust to heaven that you are not
wrong."

I took the next flight back north. A few days later, just after
the Camp David summit had begun, I talked with Kahana by
phone. He offered to come to Washington to be available if the
White House thought he could be of assistance. I conveyed his
offer to Bob. I was subsequently informed that the information had been passed along, but the White House was not
interested.

I learned later that Bob thought my information was so
important that he wrote the following to the President by
hand, not wanting to waste time to have it typewritten.

Administratively Confidential
Sept. 4, 1978
To: The President
From: Bob Lipshutz

On August 31, 1978, an American citizen (Leon Charney, New York attorney) personally conveyed to me the following information. He came to Atlanta (where I was vacationing) for the sole purpose of giving me this information, immediately following his return from a trip to Jerusalem.

Charney advised that, at a meeting with Ezer Weizman and an Austrian Jewish businessman, Karl Kahana (who *presumably* is close to both Austrian Chancellor Kreisky and Egyptian President Sadat) [Kahana] said that Sadat's "secret deal" would be as follows:

(1) Permanent West Bank borders will be drawn by mutual agreement of Israel and Egypt, taking into consideration aspirations of the Palestinians and the security needs of the State of Israel.

(2) A Palestinian entity linked to Jordan.

(3) Jerusalem a united Israeli city patterned after London or Paris (city borough type), with a Moslem square (Temple Mount) flying a Moslem flag.

Other information presented by Charney as a result of his trip to Israel last week is:

—Sadat definitely wants a signed paper out of Camp David.

—The Israeli delegation *is* authorized by its Cabinet "to sign a paper, such as a declaration of principles."

—Begin's *first* specific proposal will be to obtain a definite agreement to resume negotiations following Camp David; apparently Begin would very much like to be invited to Cairo.

RJL

6

Messages from "the Gilded Cage"

The back-door channel was thus in business, and Bob was to inform me later how much the President appreciated our input at that critical juncture. As a private citizen, and as an American and a Jew, I felt a sense of satisfaction that my perceptions and connections had become so very useful in furthering the cause of peace at that historical turning point. On a personal level, though, it was a rather lonely period for me, because I could not share my experience with my nearest and dearest; my silence was an essential element of my usefulness.

The eyes of the world were soon on the Camp David conference site. One could hardly imagine a place more remote from Middle East tensions than that aerie perched high in Maryland's Catoctin Mountains, a 75-mile drive from Washington. There had been a magical aura about the place in the public mind since the days when Franklin D. Roosevelt called it his Shangri-La hideaway. He had planned D-Day there with Winston Churchill. It became synonymous with the ending of the cold war after it had hosted the summit meeting in the late 1950's between Dwight Eisenhower and Nikita Khrushchev.

The Americans, and President Carter in particular, may have found Camp David an idyllic place, but as I was to hear firsthand, two of their Israeli guests did not share their enthusiasm. Begin felt claustrophobic, while Ezer reported that the place was gloomy and damp. The working press was gloomier still, so I heard from journalist friends who were kept at a distance from the camp. They had to stay outside the encircling fence.

Even before Carter, Begin, and Sadat reached the place, the media began to put the burden for the conference's success or failure on the Israeli Prime Minister. I remember one evening hearing on a TV newscast a fairly typical comment of that time: "Unless the heart massage the President will administer to the Mideast talks here works, Sadat's initiative of last November will be as dead as a beached mackerel.... Begin must yield most...the September meeting is truly the last chance. If Begin muffs it, then no matter that Israelis support him now, he will be remembered in time as the man who killed the Peace...." *Time* magazine quoted a senior British diplomat as predicting that "there's no chance of a Middle East peace as long as Begin remains Prime Minister of Israel."

Ezer feared that should the conference fail there would be a rift between Israel and the United States, and even with the American Jewish community. The West Bank issue came to the fore, with Dayan—in the preparatory discussions—urging that enough room be left for the Jordanians to come in eventually. But Ezer argued that the Americans should be persuaded to leave King Hussein out for the time being—Israel should reach an agreement with Egypt first.

Thirteen days later white smoke was seen to rise metaphorically over Camp David as a rejoicing world celebrated the American coup. Carter had managed to get Begin and Sadat to concur on the framework agreements. My good friend Abrasha Tamir, who was at Camp David as Ezer's official aide, later explained the winning formula to me in his wryly succinct way: "The United States pushed, Israel made the concessions, and Egypt got the real estate."

Yet it took some doing to get Begin to make the big leap.

Some who should know say the Prime Minister was influenced by three crucial telephone conversations he held from his cabin. The first and second were to Jerusalem—with Deputy Prime Minister Yadin, when Begin assured himself of the moderate wing's backing, and with Ariel (Arik) Sharon, in order to secure his ultraright flank over handing back Yamit and the Sinai settlements. The third, and some say the most decisive call, was to Denver. There his firstborn, Benjamin Ze'ev Begin, was engaged in further studies in his specialty, geology. They say that the younger Begin proved a major influence on his father.

For my part I stayed in New York keeping my end of the channel open. Ezer was in a "Get me Charney!" mood as a result of being cooped up in the mountain retreat and he phoned constantly to relieve the tension by telling funny stories and gossiping. Ezer also told of the movies being screened around the clock (perhaps someone knew of Begin's passion for the cinema?) and of the Carter people's jokingly looking forward to their hoped-to-be-made movie epic *How the West Bank Was Won*.

But the main purpose of our long-distance conversations was serious. Ezer wanted certain messages and signals to get through to the Americans. After I had mulled over our conversation I would sort out exactly what should or should not be passed along. If I determined the situation called for it I would dial the White House number and speak to Bob. Bob, in turn, would call Camp David on a secured line to convey to the President whatever information I had passed along to him, usually via Bill Quandt.

Ezer's intent was to soften the American position and make the Administration more amenable to an understanding of Israel's stand. Not only then, but before and after Camp David, Ezer and I created concepts ultimately utilized in the official diplomatic process.

During those 13 days we talked almost daily. Ezer felt it important that the Americans be cognizant of the Israeli mood and of those points beyond which no concessions would be forthcoming. I think—although I have never discussed this with him—that he was using me to try to influence Carter's attitude toward Israel. I suspect he thought of me in his Air Force jargon as a kind of targeted missile aimed at softening the United States position. Years later I discovered that the President thought our communication had been very helpful to his search for peace because it gave him an extra insight into the Israeli mood.

Months later, when I received a personal letter of thanks from the President, I felt content that my insights and communications had proven so vitally important at that historic juncture.

From the first day that Ezer arrived at what he called "the Camp David gilded cage," the fluctuations of the mood inside "the gilded cage" may be gleaned from some of the notes of my reports of conversations with Ezer jotted down by Bob on his White House memo block. I learned of them only some time later.

THE WHITE HOUSE
WASHINGTON

Tuesday—Day One—Sept. 5

Long Discussion

—(...)* "workable with the other side"
—Get W. [Weizman] & S. [Sadat] together as much as possible
—But (...) has not moved much.

---

* For reasons of confidentiality and the protection of numerous sources, some portions of the entries have been omitted; the brackets denote editorial amplification.

THE WHITE HOUSE
WASHINGTON

Thursday—Day Three—Sept. 7

—Begin's Secretary, Yona [Klimovitzky] is in New York.
—Begin definitely leaving on Sept. 13.
—*TODAY* is the crucial day.
—But Leon has feeling that things are going to be O.K.
—Ezer coming to New York next weekend.
—Under *NO* circumstances American troops on West Bank. *BUT* would enter into military defense pact with the U.S.A.

(Above phoned to Bill Quandt at Camp David on secured line 9/7/78 3:00 p.m.   RJL)

THE WHITE HOUSE
WASHINGTON

Friday—Day Four—Sept. 8

—Leon is talking to "my friend" three times a day.
—E.W. plans to be in N.Y. to sign some contracts on Wednesday (13th) and he plans to be back in N.Y. that weekend (16th & 17th).
—L.C. reports "good vibes." Thinks this will continue after the Summit. Other "lower people" have an upbeat attitude. Except for a cold, he (E.W.) feels good.
—Dayan not getting much play, but E.W. arranged for Dayan to see Sadat.
—Begin's secretary planning to see RJL next week. Begin says "everything is going beautifully. President has treated me with great cordiality & warmth. The President couldn't have treated me better." He and Sadat have repaired their relationship.

(Phoned to Quandt 9/9/78.)

THE WHITE HOUSE
WASHINGTON

Wednesday—Day Nine—Sept. 13

—L.C. spoke to E.W. 3 or 4 times today. He is very upbeat.
—E.W. plans to leave Camp David on Friday 15th Sept. He had a very good meeting with the President.
—Ezer comments: "My uncle told me, tough things take a long time—and the impossible, a little longer."
—Ezer going home to Israel on Sunday 19th Sept.
—E.W. asked L.C. if L.C. had been in touch with RJL, & L.C. said "yes."

(Phoned to Bill Quandt 9/14/78 2:45 p.m.)

THE WHITE HOUSE
WASHINGTON

Thursday—Day Ten—Sept. 14

—A call from E.W. Very unhappy today. "Worst mood of my life."
—E.W. probably will not come to N.Y. on Friday...maybe not Sunday.
—L.C. reports (...) is "pissing mad." His mood is frustration.
—L.C. says Ezer told him, "Keep your fingers crossed. Today is a tough and very important day. We do not have any idea how long we will be up here."

THE WHITE HOUSE
WASHINGTON

Friday—Day Eleven—Sept 15

—(...) called this morning. They are at the crossroads. President meeting often with E.W. IT IS NOW OR NEVER!
—Mood today somewhat better, but still somewhat frustrated. Apparently there is a lot of intensity, probably a snag—but *everybody* still is working in good faith and *wants* to make a deal.
—E.W. probably will stay over in New York Monday.

THE WHITE HOUSE
WASHINGTON

Saturday p.m.—Day Twelve—Sept. 16

E.W. to L.C.: Tell RJL "Seeing some sunshine."
Later: E.W. says, "All sounds O.K.!"
E.W. asks: "Do (...) have anything to say to me?"

THE WHITE HOUSE
WASHINGTON

Sunday—Day Thirteen—Sept. 17, 9 p.m.

(Call to RJL via secured line from Camp David)
"Much greater results than we had reason to anticipate. Two agreements signed:
  (1) Overall peace agreements/Israel & Egypt
  (2) Sinai-2-year phasing; Egyptian sovereignty—Subject to Knesset approval of it—applying to removal of all settlements in Sinai (2 weeks)...Begin, neutral....
  (3) Complete restoration of all peace elements...."
—Israelis very happy.
—Cy Vance: "Dream of a lifetime...!"
—There will be a 10:30 p.m. White House telecast; all 3 present.
(Very DRAMATIC!!)
—Call: Leon Charney,
        Max Kampelman,
        Arthur Goldberg,
        Phil Klutznick, etc...

The Good News

While Bob was listening to his "very dramatic" news from Camp David, I was driving across Central Park to a party given by my friend Phyllis Schmertz at her apartment, with its marvelous view of the Metropolitan Museum of Art and Central Park. About 100 guests were there when I arrived, half of them from Red China, all dressed in Mao uniforms. Phyllis had previously advised me that it would be "an interesting diplomatic party, and do be a darling and circulate," but I was not prepared for the solid body of Chinese, all standing close together. The word *uniformity* took on a new meaning for me. A woman I was talking to said quietly, "Why, they even all eat in exactly the same way!" They were mayors of Chinese cities on a goodwill tour of the United States. It might have been fascinating circulating among them, but none appeared to speak English. With all their smiling politeness, there was something forbidding about them *en masse*, as if they carried their own Great Wall of China with them.

Just then Phyllis rushed over and whispered, "There's a call from the White House on the study phone. It's Bob Lipshutz, and it sounds urgent." Excusing myself, I hurried to the phone and heard the familiar Southern inflection, and this time Bob was really excited. "We've made it, we've made it!" he exclaimed. "There's going to be a White House telecast at 10:30 p.m. Carter, Sadat, and Begin will all be there. The President will announce that Camp David was an historic success." Then he added in more measured tones, "Now, Leon, this is in strict confidence. Please don't tell anyone yet." So there I was, bursting with this tremendously exciting news, and I couldn't share it with anyone. When Jim Jensen of WCBS-TV saw me emerging from the study, apparently with a starry look in my eyes, he made a beeline for me. All I could tell him was that a big story was about to break later that night, and perhaps he should call his studio to check. He did exactly that, and soon enough he received word of the historic telecast. Phyllis' Chinese guests had left by then, and the few of us who remained gathered around the TV set in the study to watch the announcement from the White House. It was a thrilling experience, and I think some of us cried. Phyllis produced some good champagne and we drank to peace.

I must have reached home around midnight and shortly after I had settled in the phone rang. It was Ilan Tehila, trying to talk against a very noisy background. They were celebrating at the Washington Hilton. I managed to hear him say, "Leon, *mazel tov*, *mazel tov* [good luck]. We've done it. The Minister wants to talk to you." Ezer came on the line. He was quite transformed from the man who had been letting off steam over the phone from "the Camp David gilded cage" for the past two weeks. He was totally elated. "Leon, I want to thank you for everything. You've been wonderful. By the way

I've just had an interview with Barbara Walters. Thanks for everything. I'll see you in New York shortly. I'll call you again. I kiss you and love you." As I heard later, it was quite a party and it was going on in Begin's suite. Barbara Walters was one of the few Americans there, along with the United States Defense Attaché at the United States Embassy in Tel Aviv, Colonel Bruce Williams, whom Ezer had befriended. Appreciative of the American veteran officer's warm regard for Israel and for himself personally, Ezer had asked Ilan to invite him to join the Israeli celebration. By the time the Colonel had reached the hotel, they were all in Begin's suite. As soon as Ezer sighted Williams' stocky figure, he cried: "What are you drinking?" When he heard "scotch and water," Ezer grabbed Barbara Walters' drink, much to the TV star's amusement and handed it over to the rather flustered Colonel. Everyone had a good laugh and the party lasted until the small hours.

In my office the next morning, it was difficult to adjust to business-as-usual. Friends kept calling, excited at the news. The one truly memorable call came at noon. It was from Bob at the White House. Even that sober Southern attorney could not suppress the excitement in his voice. After we chatted for a while, he said, "Leon, as you know I'm not a loquacious man. The main reason I'm calling you is to convey to you the President's expression of gratitude. I also want to add some thanks, on this occasion, on my own behalf. But don't forget we've still got quite a job cut out for both of us."

7

After Camp David...Giving Peace a Chance

As September wore into October the Carter Administration attempted to produce a concrete peace treaty out of the framework agreement that emerged from the 13 days at Camp David. Even the Carter people were brought to laud Prime Minister Begin publicly as well as privately for the way he fought his own lifelong right-wing comrades in the Knesset to push through the agreement. The Foreign and Defense Ministers of Egypt and Israel were invited to Washington to flesh out the details of the new relationship, but it soon became apparent that Begin had given Dayan and Weizman little negotiating room in which to maneuver. The back-door channel worked overtime in that period. Bob Lipshutz would summarize my frequent input for the President's eyes.

Thus on Tuesday afternoon October 10, 1978, he jotted down on his White House memo pad: "Things could explode. ...Do not know what the Americans want to do...Begin figuratively has been under shock treatment. All the juice is out of him. Difficult for an American to get to his roots. ...Speed is crucial!! E.W. is very much for this indirect line of communication ...and he is pivotal...." At 9:30 p.m. that day he wrote again:

"Leon has been called over there" (to the Madison Hotel, where Weizman was staying).

A week later, Wednesday October 18th, he learned from me, "Everything is going well, except for intramural battling ...between Dayan and Weizman.... The former feels things going too rapidly vis-a-vis home consumption...." On the same memo is a recorded query from Bill Quandt's secretary to Caroline, Bob's secretary: "Dr. Brzezinski is not asking to meet with Weizman—he is asking if Weizman thinks it would be productive. Dr. B. is willing but is not pushing for the meeting." A few phone calls between Bob and me and Ezer and me, and Bob could record: "Meeting set for Friday a.m. between Z.B. and E.W."

In the next few hours things began to get hectic and the back-door channel began to buzz. Hence the ensuing communication for the President from Bob on Friday:

CONFIDENTIAL

THE WHITE HOUSE
WASHINGTON

October 20, 1978

MEMORANDUM FOR THE PRESIDENT
FROM BOB LIPSHUTZ (RJL)*

Following is a summary of the information which I gave you and Dr. Brzezinski orally earlier today. This reflects information and suggestions given to me on Thursday evening by Leon Charney, the American attorney for Ezer Weizman, who was speaking on his behalf in a private and confidential manner. He met me here at my office in the White House on Thursday evening immediately after spending about an hour with Weizman at the Madison Hotel; Charney had come to Washington from New York at the urgent request of Weizman earlier in the day.

---

* President Carter added his initial, C, to the memo.

The most emphatic part of the message was that the President needs to intervene intensely in the current negotiations for the next 48 hours. Weizman *implores* the President not to leave things "to the lower guys," and states that the President must put his foot to the burner and his brain to it during these next 48 hours.

The *real problem* is the "linkage language." While Weizman himself would prefer to go back to the Camp David language, he recognizes that the Egyptians may need something more than that. Apparently, the issue of "peace implementation" is not a major problem. Furthermore, the military side is under control, including the missiles matter.

One of the major reasons for the urgency is that there is talk about either Dayan or Weizman being called to come back to Israel for the purpose of briefing the Cabinet. Apparently they have agreed that neither "should go back to the wolves alone." Weizman feels that if either, or both, goes back to Israel at this time it could have a *domino effect*.

Begin apparently is getting "snappy," and he is surrounded for the most part at this time by the "Judea and Samaria" type of people, and doubts could begin to build up with him about some of the major agreements. Furthermore, Begin is still taking an enormous amount of heat on the Sinai settlement issue.

There is some feeling among the Israelis that in the current negotiations Israel has given up much more than the Egyptians and therefore it is suggested that at least something symbolic should be given by the Egyptians to offset this feeling.

One of the major concerns of Israel is that it has no money. This of course plays a big part in the discussions about bases, etc.

A second *major request* of Weizman to the President is that he and the others in the American delegation cease talking about the history of the illegality of the West Bank settlements and the Sinai settlements, because this creates additional political and emotional pressures on Begin and others (e.g. Sadat).

The Israelis in the delegation apparently agree that, in addition to their own problems, delay also creates additional problems for Egypt because of the pressure building up on Sadat from the other Arab countries.

Apparently the mood within the Israeli delegation is one of exhaustion and frustration, but certainly not one of despair.

Within the next hour or so I will supplement this memorandum with responses to the various questions which I posed to Weizman through Charney, and which I mentioned to you earlier.

CONFIDENTIAL

THE WHITE HOUSE
WASHINGTON

October 20, 1978

MEMORANDUM FOR THE PRESIDENT
FROM: BOB LIPSHUTZ

This memorandum supplements the memorandum which I gave you earlier today regarding my discussion with Leon Charney...Charney spent a long time with Weizman last night and earlier this morning following his meeting with me at the White House about which I have already reported to you. He also spoke with Weizman again this morning. Weizman again emphasized the importance and urgency of intensive involvement by you at this time. Apparently this feeling is not only because of the fact that the delegation was brought to Washington at your personal invitation and, consciously or subconsciously, there is some reaction that they now have been "dumped" on middle-level and lower-level officials for the negotiating process. Whether this feeling is rational or not is probably immaterial.

Weizman also feels that Vice President Mondale can play a major role at this time, perhaps alternating with you personally in these intensive negotiations.

Concluding on this point, Weizman is convinced that unless you involve yourself intensively in the negotiations at this time, perhaps alternating with the Vice President, that he and Dayan probably will have to go back to Israel next Tuesday for briefings and consultations with Begin and the Cabinet. It is Weizman's thinking that this step would be retrogressive and perhaps even dangerous to the negotiations.

With reference to Barak [at that time Attorney General of Israel], there is encouragement. He apparently is in fact concentrating on the question of trying to come up with the appropriate language on the linkage question. Charney interjected his own opinion relative to this point to the effect that at some point you personally might have to say that "this language is fair to both parties and satisfactory and should be adopted."

Apparently Dayan and Weizman do have sufficient authority to conclude a treaty, with the obvious caveat that it is subject to ratification by the Government.

As to a final question of logistics, which relates to the Sabbath (sundown today through sundown tomorrow) and the last day of *Succot* (sundown Sunday to sundown Monday), I believe that it would be satisfactory for Dayan and Weizman to meet with you here at the White House provided they walk from the Madison Hotel to the White House.* However, considering the devastating political experience of an earlier Israeli Government, this question might have to be submitted to Jerusalem for approval before Dayan and Weizman would "talk public" in such an open and formal manner. The other experience to which I refer relates to the Prime Minister having met a delivery of badly needed military planes from the United States, but on the Sabbath, and which resulted in a major contribution to that Government's downfall because of the intensive opposition to the Religious Party. I hope to have further clarification of this later on in the day.

Bob later told me that as a direct result of that communication the President did decide to intervene. But his ensuing involvements did not always please Israel. Tension began to build up in Jerusalem and Washington over the settlement issue. The situation was exacerbated by the visit to Amman of

---

* Jews observing strict religious custom do not travel or work on the Sabbath. The policy of the Israeli Government is that no one should conduct business on the Sabbath.

Assistant Secretary of State Harold Saunders, who was sent to sound out King Hussein's position on possibly joining in the peace process. The negotiations were at a low point now—the Israelis were very upset at what they saw as a definite tilt toward the Arabs. Sadat was under growing pressure from other Arabs to indicate that he really would take the Palestinian question into peace treaty negotiations. As a result of my meeting with Karl Kahana of Austria and Ezer a few months earlier, I had been able to advise the President through Bob that Sadat regarded the West Bank issue as a fig leaf with which to cover his position on the Palestinian problem to the rest of the Arab world. However, as the months elapsed, the fig leaf appeared to have grown into a fairly sizeable fig tree, which might not only block the road to peace, but produce some rather bitter fruit.

Carter felt Begin had let him down on the settlement issue when the Israeli Cabinet decided to enlarge the West Bank settlements. Carter let his displeasure be known. Thus on October 26th, United States Secretary of State Vance issued a statement rapping Israel. From Cairo there was talk of recalling the Egyptian delegation from the talks in Washington. At the heart of the talks was the question of linking the future of the West Bank to the actual Egyptian-Israeli treaty, and the need to find suitable language for the appropriate documents. But overshadowing the proceedings was a statement attributed to Assistant Secretary of State Saunders that East Jerusalem would become part of the Arab West Bank, thereby raising the specter of Jerusalem, the capital of Israel and the heart of Jewish history, being divided once more.

The Israeli negotiators were perturbed. I conveyed these feelings to Bob, who for lack of time put them down in a handwritten note. As far as I knew in such instances he then would descend to the President's office and present the material by hand. Immediate access of this kind was accorded to very few in the Presidential inner circle—Bob, Hamilton Jordan, Jody Powell, Dr. Zbigniew Brzezinski, and Stuart Eizenstat. Here is the communication:

THE WHITE HOUSE
WASHINGTON

October 27, 1978

MEMORANDUM TO THE PRESIDENT
FROM: BOB LIPSHUTZ

RE: My conversation today with Leon Charney

Reflecting the statement and opinions expressed to him personally today in Washington, Charney emphasized to me:

(1) That the current conflict regarding the West Bank settlements question was aggravated greatly by the *timing* of the Saunders trip—i.e., giving so much attention to our response to Hussein *before* conclusion of the Israel-Egypt peace treaty.

(2) That each deal is a separate emotional situation for Israelis (Sinai, West Bank, and Golan), and that Israelis are quite fearful of permitting the basis of the agreement regarding Sinai settlements [to] become a model for West Bank settlements.

He urged that everybody try to cool things off and encourage Israel and Egypt to finalize the agreement regarding the West Bank item vis-a-vis their peace treaty.

He also suggested a joint statement by Israel and the United States, including perhaps:

(1) "Clarification" that the current Israeli "thickening" involves only about 200+ people (*if* Begin will make this public).

(2) Restatement of the Camp David language plus whatever Israel and Egypt agree upon vis-a-vis the West Bank settlements issue.

(3) Tie in the Nobel Peace Prize in some manner.

I gave this report initially to Zbig this afternoon, along with some other background data, and I am giving him a copy of this memorandum.

However, Bob omitted from his memo some sharp comments I had conveyed to him during those tense days. For example, I wrote to him:

> "Israeli Government and Egypt can make an agreement *re* West Bank language. But why did U.S. have to send Saunders over and not send the response to Hussein through Embassy ...Begin has been personally and politically 'squeezed out' at this time...No Israeli Government can make a West Bank deal at this time. Why is U.S. apparently pushing it so hard at this time...The *problem* in Israeli minds: that the Sinai settlement removal not be a model for either West Bank or Golan. Timing of Saunders's effort was bad—couldn't this wait until the Israeli-Egyptian treaty is signed (nothing personal about Saunders)?....
>
> "This morning Ezer was 'livid' but later this afternoon he was in a good mood. Ezer says: 'Israel is wall-to-wall on the current position regarding the West Bank....' Ezer and others feel 'they are creeping into Jerusalem.' Saunders might have said privately some of the things which he said but he created the problem by going public."

I also asked one or two pointed questions such as:

"In the negotiations the American representatives have been much more aggressive about the West Bank issue than the Egyptians. If that is accurate, why is that so?"

The questions went unanswered.

On October 30, I was able to report to Bob, "It looks much better; Dayan upbeat. A lot of meetings going on." And on November 2, "All positive...Ezer going home tonight. Very good meeting with Vance. President had lunch with Begin. Aid converted to a loan..." On November 5, the Israeli Cabinet met on the treaty, and by November 8th, Weizman was due to return to America with an initial agreement.

My first report for November 11th, 1978 read, "Both E.W. and M.D. went to Toronto to speak with M. Begin. Tamir and Sharon giving them a hard time...Poll in Israel—Likud would lose by two seats. Ezer Weizman: 'If we can't live with open borders—if we have a ghetto mentality—we cannot survive as a nation.' "

The second report at 4:30 p.m.: "Ezer became a grandfather for the first time—his daughter's son."

The Israelis were not to know that Carter had instructed Vance earlier in the week to pull out of the negotiations. Carter even accused Israel of using the settlement and East Jerusalem issues to prevent the involvement of the Jordanians and Palestinians.

As the talks appeared to founder at this stage, my input to Bob increased, with the following result:

THE WHITE HOUSE
WASHINGTON

Tues. November 14, 1978

ADMINISTRATIVELY CONFIDENTIAL

MEMORANDUM FOR THE PRESIDENT
FROM: BOB LIPSHUTZ

RE: *My conversation today with Leon Charney*

This memorandum supplements the oral report which I gave to Dr. Brzezinski late this afternoon, and a copy of this memorandum has been given to him also.

At Weizman's request Charney came to Washington late yesterday, and he has talked with me here at the White House several times during the past 24 hours, and between his visits with me had been with Weizman.

The meeting of the Israeli Cabinet later this week obviously is quite important, and Weizman feels that it will be most helpful for the peace process if he is able to attend. However, since Prime Minister Begin had left him here to continue the negotiations, he was having a difficult time figuring out a basis upon which he could return for the meeting. He has also the personal interest in being at the *B'rith* of his new grandson on Friday.

Apparently he has felt the need of some significant message to take back to the Cabinet meeting, in order to justify his returning at this particular time.

In addition to the linkage question, about which I received very little information, the thrust of the message which he sent related to financial matters. [...] apparently...the total financial package which has been presented of about $3.3 billion is a great deal higher than is really needed to carry out the essential elements of the peace process relative to the Egyptian agreement... [...] suggested that the sum of $1.5 billion, spread out over three to four years, would be sufficient to take care of the essential elements such as the construction of the two new airfields, the building of roads and infrastructures in the Negev, and additional...equipment. Little mention was made of the form of such financial assistance but I get the impression that long-term, low-interest loans would suffice.

(As a personal observation from me, it is my understanding that whereas direct loans by the Federal Government would constitute expenditures under the budgetary process, loans from other sources with Federal Government guarantees might only cause a budgetary impact of the differential between total interest costs and the interest charged on such loans.)

Weizman had expressed some concern as no contact had been made with him during these current negotiations by our Defense Department, but I understand that this evening he is meeting with some representatives from the Pentagon.

Concerning the type of expression of financial support which Weizman thinks could be adequate for the purpose of getting the Israeli Cabinet to overcome a sufficient amount of its concern about this factor is a message which includes language such as: "the United States Government will consider," or "the United States Government acknowledges this financial need," along with a caveat such as "subject to the review by the United States of the actual needs, and subject, of course, to Congressional approval." Along with such language, some indication of your understanding and general support for such financial assistance should be sufficient.

• • •

Charney came back this evening after having been with Weizman following Weizman's meeting here at the White House. Weizman apparently is anxious to be here to meet with the Egyptian Vice President when he comes on Wednesday. Presumably Secretary Vance called Weizman and urged him again to go back to Jerusalem in time to attend the Cabinet meeting, and Weizman apparently agrees that it is very important. Also, Weizman has invited the Egyptian Defense Minister to have dinner with him either tonight or tomorrow night; it was not clear to Charney which night he is doing so.

Regarding the question of financial aid, Weizman states, "The President did not tell me 'no'" and apparently Weizman received this response in a positive way.

c.c. Dr. Brzezinski   *"I made no comment at all. J"**

Later that month headlines such as "Are the Peace Talks Floundering—and Is Carter to Blame?" began to appear in American newspapers. Some Middle East experts were speculating that the President did not comprehend the slow and intricate nature of these negotiations. In Israel, Prime Minister Begin spoke of "Egyptian proposals being inconsistent with the Camp David agreement," and his officials began to talk of the "American tilt to Cairo."

Carter's position was not eased by the fierce attack on him that month in *The New York Times* by columnist William Safire, who accused the President of threatening the peace agreement by his attempt "to force the Israelis to give up the West Bank and thus to establish a homeland for Palestinian

---

* President Carter added his handwritten retort in the side margin.

Arabs that Israelis see as a knife at their side." He charged Carter with having dispatched Saunders to reassure King Hussein that his hope for the ultimate removal of Jewish settlements was not misplaced. He wrote: "News of the Saunders-Hussein meeting...caused the Israelis to announce the thickening of their settlements, as they had every right to do...." The columnist blamed Carter for having brought the Egyptians to adopt a tougher stand on the linkage issue, claiming that "insiders hint that the reason for the linkage pressure is to placate the Saudis, who have turned thumbs down on Camp David; this leaning on Israel is supposed to be in our interest."

Further, the Carter Administration found itself in the embarrassing situation of having to issue firm denials about secret guarantees supposedly given by Carter to Sadat at Camp David, as revealed by King Hassan of Morocco in an interview. The King revealed that Sadat had told him during a visit on his return home from the Camp David talks that Carter had guaranteed that "East Jerusalem will be returned to the Arabs, and the West Bank and Gaza will eventually become independent."

By early December 1978 the drive toward peace appeared to be losing momentum.

8

The Drive Toward Peace

Both Bob and Ezer feared that the momentum toward peace was being dissipated. Ezer repeatedly said, "Time is of the essence." They continued using the back-door channel, with phone calls going back and forth between Israel and my Manhattan office and Bob's office at the White House. Even while I was on a West Coast business trip, both were calling me at my San Francisco hotel.

News about Israel had been filling the television screens— Begin's and Sadat's journeys to Stockholm to receive the Nobel Peace Prize, Golda Meir's state funeral.

When I returned to New York, I received a surprise phone call from the Prime Minister's office in Jerusalem. Begin's secretary, Yona Klimovitsky, told me in her pleasant voice that her boss had asked her to call. He was looking for some way out of the current impasse in relations with the United States. Perhaps it could be accomplished through Vice President Mondale, whom Begin considered Israel's best friend in the Administration. At any rate, as Yona said, "The Prime

Minister thinks that you might be the right person from whom
to seek counsel. Will you come over?" I expressed my willingness to do anything to help. Yona promised to call again on the
following day and connect me directly with the Prime Minister. I then called Ezer in Israel and found him highly supportive of the idea. "Everyone is so down here," he said. "Perhaps
a fresh face might help matters."

At noon the next day, December 19th, Yona's voice on the
line was soon followed by the familiar soft tones of Menachem
Begin's voice. He sounded pleased that I could come over. "...I
know I can trust you, but really, those people in Washington
...really awful...." The line was not very clear, but I could
gather that he was extremely irate at some recent statements
emanating from Washington about Israel.

As I told Bob the next day in his West Wing office, all I
sought was to keep the spirit of Camp David alive and assist in
any way I could to improve relations between the two countries to which I felt love and allegiance. The main thing, I said,
was to avert any repetition of the Yom Kippur War. The sight
of the corpses rotting in the Sinai still haunted my dreams.

Quandt then joined us. While I quickly demolished a late-
afternoon fish luncheon prepared by the mess, he expounded
on the situation in the Middle East and the mixed results of a
visit there by Cyrus Vance. Quandt appeared genuinely mystified by Menachem Begin. It seemed to me that he could not
plumb the man's character. My concrete advice was that
someone in the White House, preferably the President, should
send Begin warmly worded Hanukah greetings. Meeting
Quandt's rather skeptical gaze, I contended that it might
prove to be an icebreaker.

At this point I suspect there was still some "trepidation"
toward me at the Presidential level about my advice, information, and intentions. So Bob chose to send me on my way to
meet the Prime Minister and Defense Minister of Israel with
the statement that, while "they" were most interested in keeping my informal channel open, I should appreciate that I was
not being given any formal recommendation from the United
States Government. Naturally, I would be briefed in detail on

the factual situation and the state of the negotiations, etc., but I would not be asked to "carry the water for the Administration," as he put it. Nor, for that matter, he continued, should I ever express the Administration's position.

Fine, I thought, that's exactly how I want my role to evolve. Bob's words, in effect, accorded me the kind of independent course of action I desired. While continuing to be part of an informal diplomatic effort, I would remain unencumbered by formal bureaucratic obligations.

My good friend Don Tanselle agreed to accompany me on my voyage to the Holy Land. Although I departed only two days before Christmas, the Indiana merchant banker agreed with alacrity to be my traveling companion. We had been to Israel together a number of times in the past, primarily on business related to the Israel-British Bank scandal. Don saw in the Israelis' struggle to build a modern society in the wilderness a clear parallel to the experience of his Huguenot ancestors who had pioneered on the American frontier and helped found the state of Indiana.

Israel seemed so full of light and sunshine after the wintry darkness of New York and London. After checking in at my Tel Aviv hotel, I phoned in my arrival to Yona and drove over to see Ezer at his Ministry office. The Minister was in a gloomy mood over the future of the peace process and the fate of the Government. He had not enjoyed ordering troops to remove the unauthorized settlements set up by the zealots of the *Gush Emunim* (Camp of the Faithful) extremist movement. The settlements had enjoyed the patronage of Arik Sharon, Minister of Agriculture.

Ezer was also unhappy over the apparent lack of American interest in the Middle East. He believed that the United States had put the area on the back burner now that Carter was totally preoccupied with China. Ezer was also concerned at the spill-over of Iranian revolutionary ferment into Egypt and its likely effect on the stability of Sadat's regime and his margin for maneuverability. That's why to him time was of the essence.

By this time we had moved to the King David Hotel in

Jerusalem. As evening approached, I stood looking at the view of the Old City and Mount Scopus. The special quality of light in Jerusalem is particularly poignant in the waning hours of the day.

Ezer kindly arranged transportation for Don to go to Bethlehem for Midnight Mass to celebrate Christmas. I paid a late-night visit to the floodlit Western Wall. I stood there entranced by its majesty and the aura of sanctity it radiated. As I prayed I could hear the rustling of pigeons nesting in its upper reaches. Legend has it that they symbolize the restlessness of the souls begging the Almighty for forgiveness at the only surviving relic of His Temple.*

Don arrived back in the hotel in the early morning hours after the Midnight Mass at the Church of the Nativity. He had been thrilled by the richness of the pageantry and the procession which preceded it. The candlelit service and the thousands of pilgrims had left an indelible impression on him.

My friend from Indiana was a good listener, and I told him of the impressions I had gleaned from Israeli friends—how the mood was shifting in the country after the so-called moderate Arabs had lined up behind the Rejectionist Front and denounced the very notion of peace with the Jewish State. On the Israeli side extremists on the right were becoming increasingly militant, as evidenced by the recent Herut Party convention, where the Israeli version of the Rejectionists had split off from the Government party. The Prime Minister had been subjected to a cascade of personal vilification. One right-winger had denounced him as a "false prophet." Worse still, he had even come under physical attack from the militants. One of them had splattered his limousine windshield with a shower of eggs and tomatoes when he arrived at the convention.

And yet, many other Israelis were asking whether Begin might not do more—much more—to push for a comprehensive peace settlement. Ezer Weizman was among many of my Israeli friends who were asking that question.

---

* The Western Wall, sometimes called the *Wailing Wall*, is held by Jews to be the remaining wall of the Temple of Jerusalem.

A Sense of Destiny

My appointment with the Prime Minister was scheduled for 5 p.m. at his office in the Knesset. I walked through the winding streets of the Rehavia quarter, with its stone-faced houses and well-tended gardens, down across the valley containing a marvelous 12th-century monastery, and up to the Parliament building. As I reached the Palombo Gate I met Mike Wallace of TV's "60 Minutes" program. I knew him from my days as counsel to Senator Hartke. I later heard that he had caused quite a ruckus with a highly hostile program about Begin's Israel.

As I reached the Prime Minister's office on the lower level of the building, I encountered the jolly, affable figure of Finance Minister Simcha Ehrlich. He had just completed his weekly tete-a-tete over tea with Begin, in which they both would settle accounts with political troublemakers. (With Erlich's death Begin lost one of his most trustworthy lieutenants.) Yona greeted me warmly and, as I waited in her office, she dwelt on her beloved boss's tribulations and the way the Americans were leaning away from Israel and toward Sadat.

I was lucky in having made a number of friends in the Prime Minister's office over the years—including his jovial chief of staff, Yehiel Kadishai, and particularly his long-time private secretary, Yona. Whenever we met in Tel Aviv or Jerusalem, she was always gracious to me. When she had visited New York on a speaking tour that fall I was more than happy to guide her through the sights of Manhattan. Later, Bob Lipshutz arranged for her (at my request) to get V.I.P. treatment at the White House.

It was also fortunate that I had established friendships on both sides of the political divide in Israel—partly because I always stayed impartial. Having friends across the political gamut afforded me the extra perspective so necessary for evaluating trends and developments in that beloved and turbulent land. At one point during the Israeli-Egyptian talks I had an insightful conversation with Labor's last Prime Minister, Yitzhak Rabin. (He became a friend and a client.) I also had a detailed discussion with Labor's Secretary-General, Chaim Barlev.

To this day, I retain a high regard and deep respect for Likud Prime Minister Begin—despite, I might add, the occasional disapproval of his policies by my good friend Ezer Weizman.

I consider Menachem Begin to be one of the great Jews of our age. From our very first encounter in 1977 I felt an immediate rapport. He reminded me very much of my father in his conscientious observance of the outward ritual of Judaism— *Yiddishkeit* as my father liked to say. My father's family came from Poland and my mother's family from Lithuania, so there was something very familiar about Menachem Begin to me. I sensed that he responded to my feelings toward him. Unlike his Sabra predecessor in office (Yitzhak Rabin) he was most articulate about his Jewishness in his encounters with the Gentile world. Perhaps he was too articulate for some tastes. My yeshiva training also helped me to understand the workings of his mind and his passionate addiction to legalistic details. Once when in Jerusalem I was told, "Begin may be a little condescending to many people, but not to you."

I recall one visit to the White House when I encountered Bill Quandt. He discussed various ideas on how best to get through to Menachem Begin. I recall advising him half-jestingly, half-seriously, "Perhaps you should go to a yeshiva. You'll be able to tackle him best after studying Talmud for 18 years. For, if anything, Begin has a Talmudic frame of mind."

When I was 24 years old, our neighborhood synagogue in Bayonne went up in flames. The firemen urged everyone to keep back, but according to Jewish precepts, a Jew must do everything in his power to prevent the sacred Torah Scrolls from burning. Acting against all rules of logic and self-preservation, I fought my way through the blazing building to rescue two smouldering Scrolls of the Torah. I tell this story about my personal response to a dangerous situation, based on early training in tradition and Talmudic Law to point up a fact about Menachem Begin: a man who believes in his faith must follow the dictates of a greater imperative.

Photo by K. Weiss

Prime Minister Menachem Begin (left), and one of his oldest and closest confidants, Chaim Landau (right) in the Prime Minister's office in the Knesset.

Part of the Prime Minister's trust in me undoubtedly resulted from my original introduction to him by Eitan Livni, a member of his inner "fighting family" circle since the time of their struggle against the British in the Irgun underground in the 1940's. Livni was one of the top Herut Party organizers and had asked me to help them raise funds among American supporters. He not only introduced me to his party leader, but also established contact between me and one of Begin's few really close confidants, Chaim Landau (with whose untimely death Israel lost one of its veteran figures).

Shortly after the Likud came to power in June 1977, Landau arrived in New York and immediately called on me. I willingly gave him the run of my office, and he was soon establishing suitable connections across the country. Both Landau and Livni, as well as Weizman, had explained to me how Israel's raging inflation and other factors had caused the party's *Tel Hai* fund, used for charitable and political causes, to balloon its debt into intolerable dimensions. While in Israel, I had been told confidentially that vocal pressure from some party creditors had brought on one of Begin's heart attacks. I had made a contribution to help out.

Here I might add, however, that I always remain impartial in Israeli politics. I subsequently contributed to the Hapoel sports club—a Labor Party sports organization—in the Tel Aviv suburb of Ramat Hasharon. My not-unsubstantial contribution to Israel's other leading political organization was solicited by Re'uma Weizman, who is equally non-partisan when it comes to charitable causes.

On a number of occasions, Landau phoned Begin at the Prime Minister's office in the Jerusalem Kirya directly from my office. During one such phone call Landau explained to Begin where he was calling from, and I could hear the soft, modulated voice of Begin asking him to thank me for coming to the party's aid with a sizeable contribution. On a subsequent visit to Jerusalem, the Prime Minister received me most cordially and repeated his thanks for helping his party. Thus my credentials were established among the "fighting family" as *"ein gutter Yid,"* as Kadishai would say.

Finally, Yona ushered me into Begin's presence. He was all smiles and greeted me with his usual Old World courtesy. I sipped tea as he finished one glass after another. We were alone for over an hour. Mostly he spoke, and mostly I listened; that is, after I told him about my mother and sister setting up a home near Tel Aviv. That pleased him, and his eyes gleamed through his thick lenses.

There was a sense of destiny about him. He spoke of Jewish fate, exemplifying his remarks with historical anecdotes. He talked at length about his lessons of the Holocaust, and reiterated his desire to retire from public life and write a monumental work on the contemporary history of his people, focusing on the twin themes of Holocaust and Renaissance.

He then turned to relations with the United States, claiming that there was a tilt in Washington toward the Egyptians. "No one there seems to appreciate the kind of sacrifices we are making. They don't seem to realize what it means to hand back Yamit and all the northern Sinai settlements. Don't they realize in the great American capital that in effect it means that we are rolling back Zionist history by turning the flowering land back into wilderness?" he asked with passion. "No one there realizes the kind of abuse I have been enduring here. But I am ready and willing to accept these trials and tribulations for the sake of achieving peace—even if it means that I have to be the butt of criticism from within my own party and the Government coalition."

He ceased his harangue to sip a fresh glass of tea that had been brought in, and then spoke of how upset he was at United States pressure. He deplored recent American conduct as coarse, denouncing the behavior of Cyrus Vance on his recent trip to Jerusalem. "He came straight from Cairo with unacceptable proposals and tried to force them down our throats. We cannot accept such behavior," he declared. Begin took care, while calling the Secretary of State "coarse," to rain praise upon President Carter as "a truly wonderful man," and to remark on "how fair" he had been at Camp David. Speaking of Vance, he said, "I can only judge people by their deeds, and not by what they say." He mentioned in passing having received a personal letter from Vance a few days earlier containing Hanukah greetings from Vance and the President. I mentally smiled my delight that my input was immediately acted upon and was having a positive effect. All I said to the Prime Minister, however, was, "Isn't that a nice gesture."

Begin reiterated his passionate desire for peace with Egypt, but said it must be arrived at through the proper negotiating process. When I told him of Quandt's prognosis that the United States might simply pull out of mediation to allow for direct contact between Israel and Egypt, Begin shook his head and said it would be counterproductive at that stage. He went on at length about "the regretful misunderstanding" with President Carter over the settlement-freeze timetable.

When I asked what he meant by the autonomy scheme for

Arabs in the West Bank and Gaza, he stressed, "We do not wish to impose sovereignty over them." When I asked him about the mood in Israel and whether he might have difficulties getting the peace plan approved, Begin gave a steely smile and declared as a parting shot, "I'm not worried about the Government not accepting the peace plan. I am fully confident that the people are behind me in this respect."

Before I returned to the hotel, I went to the dining room for Knesset members and was invited to join Rabin and Barlev for coffee. They were waiting for a late vote in the chamber. An old acquaintance, Energy Minister Yitzhak Modai, came over to greet me. I arranged to meet each of them separately in the following days so that I could add their views to my "input."

That evening over dinner with Don I spoke of Menachem Begin. Don had some interesting insights to offer. He had just finished reading Begin's book, *The Revolt*, and expounded his theories over an after-dinner brandy in the hotel dining room. "Those people in Washington should read that book. It's all in there. He's got one agenda and it's in that biography. He's not changed since he was 19 years of age, and he'll stay that way until he's 900. I doubt whether any pressure could budge him. Why our Government doesn't understand the man, who is so predictable, is hard for me to grasp."

For my part, I offered the thought that too often the policy-making apparatus is manned by experts who have all the academic learning in the world at their fingertips, but who lack any firsthand knowledge of the countries and leaders on whom they are advising.

Shortly after we returned to Tel Aviv, I was on the phone to Bob and made my report in our agreed code. Referring to Begin as "my new girl friend" and Ezer as "my old girl friend," I advised Bob that a United States shift to the Arabs was perceived in Jerusalem. I then informed him, as much as I could on an open phone line, of the general tenor of my conversations with my two "girl friends." Above all I stressed that the "new girl friend" was very much in control of the situation "at home"—no one should make any mistake about that. I also cautioned Bob not to pay too much attention to any ominous-sounding statement that might emerge from the forthcoming Israeli Cabinet meeting.

I let it be understood that, complaints of a pro-Arab tilt notwithstanding, the invitation to me to come to Israel had been intended as a signal of the desire—via the back-door channel, in as informal a manner as possible—of my "new girl friend" for "a renewed courtship." Bob almost whooped out loud over the transatlantic phone, quite out of character for such a restrained man, over the quality of my "input." He told me, "I'm truly glad that 'the avenue' is working so fast"—his initial reference to our channel of communication. Now he had some material of value to offer the President before he left for Camp David to spend the New Year holiday pondering the world situation with Cyrus Vance.

Time for Reflection

Just at that time Ezer underwent a harrowing personal experience. His son, Shaul, who still suffered from head wounds he sustained during the War of Attrition, was hurt in a road accident. But still, Ezer managed to organize for me a special expedition to the Gidi Pass in Sinai, and for Don and me a joint visit to the Allenby Bridge over the River Jordan. The Gidi Pass, with its strategically significant lunar landscape, has some of the most awe-inspiring scenery on the globe.

En route to the Jordan, Don kept repeating, "It's such a tiny country! What a tiny country!" He remarked on the contrasting landscapes within such a small territory. We arrived at the Allenby Bridge, one of the few chinks in the curtain of sand erected around Israel. A two-way traffic of people and commerce passed across it. Don pointed out the Israeli and Jordanian soldiers fishing peacefully together on the banks of the river. "That's the kind of sight the formal negotiators never see from their conference rooms," I said. I expressed the pious hope that, once peace was established between Israel and Egypt, that would become commonplace.

I stayed on a few more days. Before I went home I gave Bob

some more information. The Israeli leadership was ready to renew the negotiating process, I said, preferably in Washington. I quoted the words of an unnamed source close to Begin, "The Prime Minister is waiting for the buzzer to ring"—which meant that the initiative had to come from America.

When I got home, I went straight to Washington. Bob welcomed me warmly. Once more I cautioned him about the internal pressures on Begin. "He is not De Gaulle," I said. "The strains he has sustained with so many of his old friends make life exceedingly tough for him." As to a United States initiative, Bob told me Quandt's comments. "There won't be an imminent call from us," Quandt had said. "When we get them together we need to do it the right way, and we haven't quite figured out how to do that."

That night on the shuttle flight back to New York, I thought about the policy-making process and the gap between the public image and the private reality. Most people think of policy-making flowing like quiet water, with sober men smoothly producing wise and clear-cut decisions. But from what I had heard and discerned during my association with the White House—and even earlier when I was counsel to a senator—there was frequent confusion as well as indecisiveness.

9

A 50-50 Chance

I had become a constant traveler during the early months of
1979. My flight mileage began to equal that logged by some
Air Force pilots. I became a full-fledged expert on the subject of
jet lag. But my psychological queasiness resulted less from air
pockets than from the ups and downs of the Middle East
diplomatic roller-coaster.

Aside from conveying reports on the hectic shifts in the
Israeli Cabinet line and counseling my friends back in
Washington, D.C. on how far to push the various Israeli protagonists, I was able to gauge for Bob the extreme volatility of
the national mood in Israel. One scholar with whom I discussed the psycho-political aspect took me back to my Talmudic studies, quoting the scriptural phrase "from the dust to
the stars" to describe the fluctuations in public opinion toward
the prospects of peace. Ezer talked to me often of his concern

that the seige mentality that had prevailed for so long among much of the Israeli public might create a fear of peace.

After the initial euphoric welcome to President Sadat and the soaring expectations of a near-miracle, there had come a considerable letdown, caused partly by Egyptian actions, but partly, one must admit, by the shrill cries of warning from a minority hostile to any accommodation with the Arabs. Ezer was not beyond charging that this minority even gained encouragement from some members of the Government. The sense of insecurity that comes to any group that is thrust into an entirely new situation might cause a crisis of identity among a people compelled to live for decades with the imminent threat of war.

In the quiet of the evening, Ezer would evoke his great uncle, Chaim Weizmann, whose vision of the Jewish State was that of a model society that would turn into the Switzerland of the Middle East. Meanwhile, in reality there were strong forces pulling in opposite directions away from the ideal of an open society: from ultra-nationalists to those favoring a religious society dominated by Orthodox clerics. Ezer, I could sense, had moved far from his dogmatic party comrades. The unspoken question hovered in the air. Who would provide the healing leadership that the people of Israel so required?

Business Picks Up

Business through the back-door picked up markedly during the early months of 1979. Bob asked me to use the secure line from the United States Embassy in Tel Aviv to the White House when I called him, and he dispatched appropriate instructions to the officials there. The actual "scrambler" was in the Ambassador's office. I doubt any other civilian had been permitted to use it before—or since. Most of the times I used it Ambassador Samuel Lewis was away, and filling in for him was Deputy Chief of Mission Richard Veits, a very shrewd Yankee who later was appointed Ambassador to Tanzania and then to Jordan. He befriended me and we had lunch together on a number of occasions at the Embassy commissary. He also tried to sound me out on my opinions of Menachem Begin and other Israeli political personalities.

However, lower-level staff members were relatively open in displaying resentment. A United Stated diplomat friend of mine later told me their attitude was, "Who the hell is this guy coming out of nowhere? Why don't they leave diplomatic work to the full-time diplomats?" Curiously, they shared the same attitude toward me as did their counterparts in the Israeli Embassy in Washington. The Ambassador's Secretary seemed the most disturbed; to her I was an enigmatic outsider, almost an intruder.

The mystification of the Embassy staff at the sudden appearance of this private American citizen using top-secret facilities was vented in various minor discourtesies. I imagine that it did not ease their sense of discomfiture that this private American citizen would often appear in T-shirt and jeans, not in the tie and seersucker suit which was almost the Embassy uniform.

Through association with Ezer and other Israeli Generals I became friendly with the United States Defense Attaché, Colonel Bruce Williams. He occasionally ran interference for me through the recalcitrant Embassy staffers. He was a tough, seasoned Army veteran who had served his country with courage and distinction for more than 20 years. He had served in places like Lagos and Addis Ababa but it seemed that Tel Aviv, where he had been for many years, was most like home. Moreover, he enjoyed his professional duties, especially with the honeymoon existing between the defense establishments of the United States and Israel. Bruce used to say that, to succeed at this kind of post in Tel Aviv, one needed not only good professional credentials, but also lots of patience and a very good sense of humor.

In late February and early March 1979, the diplomatic momentum picked up. Sadat visited Washington, followed shortly by Moshe Dayan. The back-door channel was very much in business.

Bob's handwritten communication on February 25, 1979, read thus:

THE WHITE HOUSE
WASHINGTON

ADMINISTRATIVELY CONFIDENTIAL
Feb. 25, 1979

TO: THE PRESIDENT
FROM: BOB LIPSHUTZ

RE: *The Middle East—Israel/Egypt Negotiations*

[In the top left-hand corner it bore the following addendum: Delivered by RJL to the President personally at 1:40 p.m., just before his meeting with Dayan, [Egyptian negotiator] Khalil, and Vance.]

This memo conveys statements from Leon Charney to me via long-distance telephone calls from Israel during the past 24 hours...Leon went there presumably on business for other (non-political) clients, but also at the urging of Weizman.

Until about 10:00 a.m. EST today Leon's words were upbeat and optimistic, such as "Brown's trip was wonderful...he spoke with Weizman on Friday...the Brown visit to the West Bank had a big and very positive effect on Israel.... Ezer has again become very strong politically...."

But at the same time the hope was expressed that we (the U.S.A.) would "go very slow" the next two or three days.

Then, in two calls this morning (10:00 a.m. and 11:30 a.m. EST)—immediately after the Israeli Cabinet meeting—Leon's tone and words changed to anxiety, urgency, and concern, such as:

"It may be too late to go slow.... They may be running into a minefield (at Camp David)...."

Leon says he was briefed about the situation but that, insofar as talking over an open phone line, his lips were sealed and he could not say a word. *But* he added that I (RJL) should find out what is going on and that "I hope a *big blunder* is not being committed." He emphasized this!

Bob's memo concerned the Israeli response to President Carter's invitation for an Israeli delegation, led by Prime Minister Begin, to come over for a three-way discussion. In Israel, the feeling was that the Egyptians had hardened their position because of an American shift in the Arabs' direction. Strong suspicions were spreading throughout Israel regarding Egyptian intentions; even Labor politician Yitzhak Rabin attributed a "withering away of Israel through peace" theory to Egyptian Minister of State Butrus Ghalli. He said that Ghalli had advocated, in his former capacity as head of a Cairo strategic studies center, that "peace be reached with Israel in order to lead to the Jewish State's falling apart, because the only cause for its coherence is external enmity." In addition, I had reported to Bob from Tel Aviv sometime in February that "the unfurling of the PLO flag over the former Israeli Embassy in Teheran is very, very unsettling to Israel." I added at a further date, "Today the President's prestige in Israel is down...because of Iran." I also reported the fears in Israel for Sadat's Egypt in the wake of the Iranian revolution, noting Ezer's concern "...since hunger, sickness, dissatisfied poor, etc., exist in Egypt as they [do] in Iran."

The phone lines between Israel and Washington were humming. Time and again I would return to my hotel and find a message like, "Will you please call the White House and ask for operator 181" or, "Mr. Lipshutz is awaiting your call." I ran up a record phone bill at my hotel; still, I would sometimes make collect calls to the White House. I think there must have been few instances where White House operators would take collect calls from non-members of the Administration. They usually recognized my voice. I once suggested half-jokingly that they be sent over to Israel to teach the telephone operators how to talk correctly to people. The all-pervading egalitarian atmosphere in Israel has its drawbacks where such services as telephones are concerned. Some operators seem to think they are working Army switchboards. They sound as if they are doing you a favor. An English friend of mine once quoted a saying attributed to Winston Churchill that the British

Empire would be defeated, not by the Russians or the Germans, but by messengers and telephone operators.

Bob would call me when I was on the West Coast for business, or in Paris for a few days and, of course, during my various trips to Israel. He insisted on knowing where I would be. One weekend in February 1979 I drove out through one of the most beautiful parts of Israel, the Valley of Jezre'el. It was after the rains, and the scenery was glowingly green and bright with the colors of flowering shrubbery. This ancient landscape, frequently mentioned in the Bible, has some of the best Israeli farmland and the most prosperous rural communities—*kibbutzim* and *moshavim*, the different cooperative farms for which Israel has become so famous. It was difficult to imagine that before the Jewish pioneers had settled there so few years ago it had all been swampland and wilderness. That kind of history makes for the common experience and values shared by Americans and Israelis. I was on my way to visit General Peled in Nahalal, one of the most famous of the *moshav* cooperative farm villages, which had produced some famous sons—particularly Moshe Dayan. When I reached the Peled's homestead, I was told by his young daughter, "You've just had a call from the White House, they're asking for you." Her tone was slightly incredulous. After all, it must have been the first time that a White House operator ever put through a call to Nahalal. I made an appointment with Bob to phone him back via the scrambler in Tel Aviv.

The result of my communication was as follows:

THE WHITE HOUSE
WASHINGTON

ADMINISTRATIVELY CONFIDENTIAL
MEMORANDUM FOR THE PRESIDENT

FROM: BOB LIPSHUTZ   February 26, 1979

RE: *Israel-Egypt Negotiations*

Leon Charney telephoned me on a secure line from the American Embassy in Tel Aviv at about 9 a.m. this morning. He apparently has been spending a great deal of time with Ezer Weizman and others, specifically with reference to the proposed meeting at Camp David later this week. He [Charney] clarified the earlier statements to me, which I related to you yesterday.

Apparently,...feels that there has been a great deal of momentum toward getting the necessary backing of the Israeli Cabinet for a major effort to conclude the peace negotiations, anticipating that the "original team" of Begin, Dayan, and Weizman would be able to come to Washington to meet with sufficient backing from the Cabinet to take the necessary decisive action. The earlier request for an additional two or three days apparently had this in mind. As a result of the invitation yesterday to Begin to come to Camp David this week, there is some concern that the meeting may not permit...the opportunity to conclude such a consensus among the necessary majority in the Cabinet. Nevertheless, Charney states that [there are intense efforts to fight this]. I anticipate that I will get a further "reading" on this situation during the day.... The Israeli Cabinet is going to meet tomorrow morning Israel time to hear Dayan's report and presumably vote on Begin's response to your invitation. I gather that Dayan has not yet conveyed much detailed information to the Government in Israel....

Charney reports that immediate press reaction to the invitation includes such statements as, "Khalil is not the equal of Begin"; "Including Begin and excluding Sadat from the meeting is a sign of the United States' plans to put pressure on Israel." However, since this is a very sketchy and early report on the press reaction, we probably should wait until the Embassy gives a more comprehensive report.

Charney spoke with [Ambassador to Israel] Sam Lewis' Deputy, Veits, and quoted him as saying that he felt that Ezer Weizman was *pivotal* to the successful conclusion of these negotiations. Veits also presumably told Charney that he thought the meeting was proposed at this time because of the Saudi trip being postponed.

Charney also said again that if it seemed worthwhile, he would fly back to Washington with more detailed information....

THE WHITE HOUSE
WASHINGTON

February 27, 1979

ADMINISTRATIVELY CONFIDENTIAL
MEMORANDUM FOR THE PRESIDENT

FROM BOB LIPSHUTZ

RE: *Israel-Egypt Negotiations*

I wish to report to you on three telephone calls which I received during the early hours today from Leon Charney in Israel....

Leon first called me at 3:00 a.m. EST (10:00 a.m. Israel time) when the Cabinet meeting apparently was getting under way. He stated that things were going very good and that [some Ministers were] pushing for Begin to accept your invitation to come to Camp David.

He added that it appeared Begin had "come around" and that if Begin made the step of coming here we should be able to close the deal. He added that it would be important under these circumstances for the United States to close the deal now.

Four hours later Charney called back to say that something had developed and that as of now it was 99 percent certain that Begin would not be coming. Things turned around during these four hours. He [L.C.] suggested that possibly Weizman would come (not indicating if it would be with or without Dayan).

An hour later Charney called again to say that the Cabinet definitely had rejected the idea of sending Begin to meet with you and Khalil, presumably on the rationale that if he did come and then did not reach an agreement, the results for Israel would be catastrophic. Charney added, however, that it was clear that the fault for this breakdown was on the Israeli side. He added that if there is an attempt to place blame on us he would do everything to dispel such allegations.

I probably will receive a further call from Charney later today. Should you decide to recommend that you meet bilater-

> ally with Begin, I suggest that you give serious consideration to
> including both Dayan and Weizman in such a meeting.

Where Do We Go from Here?

There was surprise in Israel when Carter announced through
the media his intention of convening a mini-summit. Only
Weizman and Dayan voted for Begin to go, while the Prime
Minister and the rest of the Ministers claimed that the Egyptians would have to "climb down." The Camp David mini-
summit thus was stillborn. Instead, plans went ahead for
Begin to travel to Washington to confer with the President.

Meanwhile Ezer came out in a newspaper interview with an
optimistic view on peace with Egypt. He blamed the Americans for precipitating the Iranian revolution by letting down
the Shah. He held that the crisis in Iran highlighted further
the need for a peace agreement. The record of my transatlantic
reports from the secure line at the Tel Aviv Embassy read
thus:

> *Feb. 28, 1979/9:40 p.m.*: There is a 50-50 chance Begin would
> sign an agreement. Specific proposals: If Begin had agreed on
> Khalil meeting with Dayan...and then backed down...[L.C.
> thinks] E.W. then would be very disturbed. [L.C. believes] E.W.
> does not want to embarrass the President of the U.S. If Begin
> had *not* agreed, then President made a mistake in inviting
> Begin. NOTE: No heavyweights are coming with Begin.
>
> Possible plan. It is a process. But Begin thinks Vance is
> coarse and that Quandt is an Arabist. He reveres President *but*
> believes there is an Egypt-U.S. conspiracy.
>
> Gaza autonomy—proposal by President—might be sold to
> Begin. Dayan left E.W. out of discussion between Begin and
> Dayan about the Khalil-Begin proposed visit. Question of
> Israeli credibility is at stake. Everything has to be plugged into
> Begin psychologically. Begin *can* conclude an agreement *if* he
> wants to do it...very concerned about the danger of loss of

credibility of Israel with the President. Assume: (1) Autonomy in Gaza...less military, self-rule, (2) less autonomy for the time being for the West Bank.

Feb. 28, 1979/1:40 p.m.: Keep Begin as much as possible with the President. See notes earlier today re other(s) in the Administration. Yona [Begin's secretary] says: "Object of this exercise is [only] to have a discussion with Carter."
L.C.: 'Begin is a better bet by himself than with his group!'

THE WHITE HOUSE
WASHINGTON

February 28, 1979
ADMINISTRATIVELY CONFIDENTIAL

MEMORANDUM TO THE FILE
FROM: BOB LIPSHUTZ
RE: *Israel-Egypt Negotiations*

The President called me today at about 2:00 p.m. in response to my earlier memorandum which he had just read.

In response to my specific inquiry, he said that I could convey to Charney and Weizman that the handling of the recent events by Dayan and the Israeli Government did raise some concerns with him. He reviewed the sequence of events and key elements of the invitation to Khalil and Begin. Khalil and Dayan prepared the President's statement, with the concurrence of Secretary Vance. They showed it to the President, and from the discussion the President concluded that both of them had the authority to speak for their respective Governments. Further, the President asked both of them if they wished to stand next to him when he read the statement to the press in order to show their concurrence, and they did so.

The President does not know whether or not Dayan actually discussed this invitation with Begin or, if so, what Begin told

Dayan. He relied upon the fact that Dayan was here for the entire meeting as the representative of the Israeli Government.

The President, obviously, is quite concerned about "where do we go from here."

The President advised me that the Israeli Ambassador in the United States has assured Secretary Vance that the reason for Israel's declining to attend the summit meeting this time *was not* that Sadat was not going to attend and that Khalil would be representing Egypt. I told him that the information given to me did not seem to be consistent with that representation and that further inquiry should be made to ascertain the correct information.

The President said that the information that I have been giving him as a result of my contact was very valuable but called my attention to the fact that he was not sharing it with others. I told him that I had been keeping Dr. Brzezinski informed by having him read the memoranda which I have been giving the President, and the President felt that was good. (Note that an earlier memorandum, in which I referred to the level of financial aid contemplated after the peace agreement, was distributed, and so indicated by the President, to both Secretary Vance and Secretary Brown.)

I also told the President, as stated in today's memorandum, I was going to meet with Bill Quandt today and give him the tentative additional details concerning the current situation.

10

Begin, One-on-One

Prime Minister Begin arrived with his wife, Aliza, in Washington on March 1. His subsequent talks with Carter at the White House were less than satisfactory to both sides. Carter did not respond to Begin's warnings of negative Egyptian intentions against Israel, but rather emphasized Sadat's concessions over those of Begin. The atmosphere was not warm.

Meanwhile, Bob and I were whisking important data in through the back-door channel.

THE WHITE HOUSE
WASHINGTON

Thurs. March 1, 1979

ADMINISTRATIVELY CONFIDENTIAL
MEMORANDUM FOR THE PRESIDENT

FROM: BOB LIPSHUTZ
RE: *Israel-Egypt Negotiations*

Leon Charney telephoned me this morning at 10:00 a.m. EST (4:00 p.m. Israel time) on an open line. Apparently [he is]...a little concerned about communicating through the Embassy phone, even though it is a secure line, and [decided]...to use the regular open lines. Leon tried to talk somewhat in "code" but his expressions are pretty easy to understand.

He emphasized that *the most important factor in the pending visit is that you personally, and as much as possible alone, handle this negotiation with Begin*. It is not only based upon an apparent exclusive trust in you [but also] on a lack of respect and trust in anyone else with whom he has dealt. Charney...emphasized this and repeated it several times.

On the substance of the negotiations, he said that Begin not only can act decisively for Israel and sell an agreement which he makes to the Cabinet and Knesset, but also that Begin still is anxious to make the deal. Specific suggestions which Charney conveyed were:

(1) That Egypt's proposal for Gaza autonomy separate from the West Bank is pretty good and probably can be accepted by Israel in most of its aspects; and the position of Jordan regarding the West Bank makes this distinction easier to sell to both parties.

(2) The language in Article 6 is a minor problem and either the language can be worked out or the Article even stricken. The word "arbitration" was mentioned as a suggestion. Charney conveyed the clear impression that this particular item of dispute should be minimized as a serious obstacle. (I discussed this with Bill Quandt and he believes that, even though this is Weizman's perception, it is not Begin's; and to the contrary, that Begin considers this to be a very important sticking point.)

(3) Begin must come back to Israel with something which would enable him to claim that he had obtained some results for Israel from his visit and from this overall final settlement. Thus far the only specific suggestion advanced is that you arrange for Sadat to agree on a definite date for exchanging Ambassadors, such as nine months. Charney described this concession as Begin's "fig leaf."

Finally, he stated that it is extremely important to remember the psychological importance of Begin's pride, by the manner, substance, and public perception of the negotiations.

Charney stated further that these ideas reflect not only his thoughts but also a consensus among several political leaders in Israel, including key persons in the Labor Party.

What Bob omitted reporting from our phone conversation was how far [Israeli Ambassador to the U.S.] "Evron [had] screwed himself up terribly with Israeli principals in the past three days. Evron [was] in trouble with Dayan."

The Carter-Begin talks were bogged down, with the President even talking in despair of abandoning the entire Middle East peace effort. He was egged on by Sadat, who phoned him to announce that he would like to come over and blast the Israelis before the American public. Efforts were made to try to find a formula to save the talks. They included the following ideas recorded by Bob as follows:

THE WHITE HOUSE
WASHINGTON

Fri. March 2, 1979

ADMINISTRATIVELY CONFIDENTIAL
MEMORANDUM FOR THE PRESIDENT

FROM: BOB LIPSHUTZ
RE: *Israel-Egypt Negotiations*

I have discussed with Bill Quandt the following report of my telephone conversation with Leon Charney at 5:30 p.m. EST on Thursday in which he states that he is reflecting the ideas of...the Israeli Government.

The main thing that he talked about was the possibility of working out the Gaza-West Bank matter by implementing basically the Egyptian "Gaza" proposal but giving it the appearance of a new proposal. He states that philosophically on the issue of Gaza and the West Bank, Israel and Egypt are very close together.

He states that the Gaza agreement could be implemented by Israel, Egypt, and the Gaza Arabs, with the five-year period running separately. With reference to the West Bank matter, there would be two possibilities:

(1) If Jordan did not join in, then the five-year period would

never begin to run and Begin would not be faced with the Judea-Samaria question at the end of the five-year Gaza transitional period.

(2) If, on the other hand, Jordan did join in along with the West Bank Arabs, that would be consistent with the Camp David agreement, avoid the sovereignty question relative to this area, and (whenever Jordan joined in) permit the full five years for "transition" vis-a-vis the West Bank.

Charney says that this would be *de facto* the same thing as the Egypt proposal but would give the apparent change that Israel might prefer so that the question of "linkage" thus would only apply relative to Gaza. Bill Quandt pointed out that up until now Begin himself has been unwilling to treat Gaza and the West Bank as separate matters, but his current attitude would have to be determined by the earlier discussions. However, Charney states that Begin has no difficulty accepting the substance of this proposal but has been concerned about the public opinion reactions to it because it is an Egyptian proposal; and he feels that if it can be presented as Begin's or your proposal, Begin would be prepared to and able to handle the public relations and political aspects.

Summarizing this matter, Charney states that these are the projected assumptions:

(1) Judea and Samaria would remain together and with Israel until and unless Jordan joined in.

(2) If Jordan joined in, then this would implement an agreement to which Israel's Government already has given approval.

(3) The autonomy in the Gaza area would be implemented without delay. If necessary, he states that the parties probably would play around with the timetable relative to the matter.

In essence, Charney says that such a proposal would have to look like Begin was bringing home a big thing but at the same time would be very close to the proposal which Sadat has already made.

One other item he noted is that the November deal involving the exchange of Ambassadors and the El Arish transfer might well be revived.

As Carter and Begin labored on in Washington over the various draft treaties, with Sadat eavesdropping, so to speak, we tried our best to offer a suitable way out of the Article 6 quandary, as evinced by the following:

THE WHITE HOUSE
WASHINGTON

Sat. March 3, 1979

ADMINISTRATIVELY CONFIDENTIAL
MEMORANDUM FOR THE PRESIDENT

FROM: BOB LIPSHUTZ
RE: *Egypt-Israel Negotiations*

Regarding the Article 6 sticking point, and based upon my discussions with Leon Charney earlier today, ...I would like to recommend that the following language be carefully considered:

"Where not in conflict with prior *legal* agreements, the parties agree that this agreement shall supersede.

"The parties agree that in the event of any disagreement with respect to the intention or interpretation of this provision, the law governing the relationship of nations, as defined in Article 103 of the United Nations Charter, will prevail.

"Disputes by the parties with respect to the interpretation or application of this provision shall be submitted for binding arbitration to the President of the United States."

As a matter of explanation of the foregoing recommendation, it is our understanding that a major item troubling Begin greatly, relative to Article 6, is the definition of "what is an act of war" and "what constitutes an act of defense." Apparently, Egypt and Israel have different legal positions concerning the interpretation of the agreements now existing between Egypt and other Arab nations, insofar as those agreements relate to Israel. Egypt insists that they are defensive agreements and therefore legal under international law; and Israel insists that they are war agreements and therefore illegal under international law.

With respect to the Gaza West Bank matter about which I wrote you in detail yesterday, I wish to reiterate that recommendation. It is my understanding that the change in this particular recommendation, as compared with other similar ones, is "splitting the clock." I am not certain that that was clear in the earlier memorandum.

I wish to emphasize the importance of your negotiations with Begin being, as much as possible, "one on one."

Finally, I was just told that *October* magazine, which I understand to be the official Egyptian publication, is coming out with an article tomorrow in which it states that Sadat is coming to Washington on Tuesday to sign a peace treaty!

Begin had some sleepless nights at Blair House over the language of the draft peace treaty, but dispatched it to Jerusalem for approval by his waiting Cabinet Ministers. Meanwhile, Carter sprang on Begin the surprising news of his intended journey to Cairo and Jerusalem in the coming week.

A Trip for Peace

Our telephone connection was very busy. On March 5th, at 10:00 a.m. EST, I called Bob at the White House to inform him ahead of the news agencies that the Israeli Cabinet had approved the peace treaty draft, promising details later.

At 11:30 a.m. Bob called me. He sounded excited about something but stayed mysterious over the cause of the excitement. All he would say was that I should listen to the news during the next hour and that "you will be pleased about what you hear." He also told me, "Don't plan on coming back to Washington in the next few days." After hearing of the planned Presidential trip on Israeli radio I called back and alerted him to details of the Cabinet vote—nine for, three against, and four abstentions, minus the absent Prime Minister. I quoted Ezer's comment to him, "Things are terrific, but as a fighter pilot, I am never satisfied until the landing." I further advised Bob that "Begin will still have a tough road ahead of him, and that you should come. We are going to need you." Later—at 6:05 p.m.—I conveyed concern about a possible anti-Sadat uprising in Egypt. I again mentioned that it was very much desired that Bob accompany the President on his trip. The dialogue went as follows:

> *"I trust that you are coming,"* I said.
> *"I'm not on the list,"* Bob replied.
> *"You have to come!"* I insisted.

It emerged later that Dr. Brzezinski had drawn up the original list of passengers for the official mission, which was then approved by the President.

A Talk with Peres

It was my intention and working style always to keep channels open to both sides of the Israeli political spectrum. This was helped by my personal liking for Labor Party Secretary-General Chaim Barlev, the slow-speaking, quick-witted former Chief-of-Staff and ex-Cabinet Minister. On the morning of March 6th he called me at my Tel Aviv hotel and invited me to Labor Party headquarters. It's about a five-minute walk down Rehov Hayarkon.

Barlev welcomed me warmly to his second-floor office and immediately introduced me to Labor Party Chairman Shimon Peres, a dark, intense man. Peres asked me to sit in his office, which is dominated by a huge photographic portrait of Peres' mentor, David Ben-Gurion, looking like a prophet of yore. Peres then asked whether I knew if Carter might be bringing any kind of plan with him. I told him that I knew very little about the subject, and what I did know I could hardly divulge—in fact, I could not even convey a hypothetical answer—due to my delicate position between the Americans and the Israelis. I told Barlev and Peres that I was sure the visit would have a positive outcome.

Peres talked about his ideas on peace. He emerged as a highly intelligent, credible politician. I wondered why he never managed to project this image to the Israeli public. His most telling remark was that Labor would support the Begin Government's efforts to bring about peace, even if it meant having to form a grand coalition Government. The Labor leader pointed out that the main threat in the Knesset vote would come from the Likud's own ranks, and the irony would be that the Labor opposition would save Menachem Begin from his own party zealots.

I decided to convey what I had learned from my various sources via the scrambler at the Tel Aviv Embassy. When I arrived there, the United States Marine guards as usual looked at me askance. I asked for Colonel Williams, and when he warmly welcomed me to the Embassy, the Marines' attitude altered. The result of my conversation with Bob that day was the following:

THE WHITE HOUSE
WASHINGTON

March 6, 1979

ADMINISTRATIVELY CONFIDENTIAL
MEMORANDUM FOR THE PRESIDENT

FROM: BOB LIPSHUTZ
RE: *Israel-Egypt Negotiations*

A few minutes after I spoke with you this morning, Leon Charney called me on the secure line from our Embassy in Tel Aviv, following his discussions with (...)* during the day.

I want to relay the most emphatic part of his call, even though it may seem self-serving. Leon states that it is extremely

---

* Name(s) deleted.

important that I be available in Israel in order to maintain the line of communication...to you.

Charney states he does not feel comfortable in conveying information, or his ideas, through other channels (and I assume that it even would be difficult because of protocol for him to have much, if any, direct and private communication with you personally, even though you are there.)

Charney relayed the following information at this time:

That the debate in the Cabinet on Begin's recommendation was very tough, and that Weizman and Yadin were strong advocates for Begin's recommendations, and that Dayan "acted like a child" because it was not his deal, and that Tamir* (who abstained) tried very hard to sabotage the matter with legalities—Charney described Tamir as "an operator." Presumably Begin is quite grateful to Weizman and Yadin for their efforts, and Charney believes that the relationship between Weizman and Begin is improving tremendously. Apparently, there is a good bit of speculation in Israel, both privately and publicly, about the purpose of your trip, even though it obviously is creating a great deal of excitement there. Begin presumably did not discuss the trip with anybody until after it was broadcast on the news and has not conveyed even to the Cabinet very much of his discussions with you with reference to the trip itself. Among the ideas and interpretations being expressed there are:

(1) That Sadat is in very serious trouble—of an unspecified nature—and that this trip is a "last hurrah" for him.

(2) That no deal has yet been "clinched."

(3) That there still can be a minor political crisis within Israel with the Cabinet, such as some of the hardliners leaving the Government—but that it can be handled by such means as people like Meir Amit, former Minister of Mossad, coming into the Government and by support from the Labor Party, which presumably is being given; if some of the hardliners leave the Begin coalition, there is even renewed talk of a broad coalition Government.

---

* Shmuel Tamir, Minister of Justice.

11

A Presidential Visit

The next day we were on the phone again. At first I could not get Bob. His secretary, Caroline, said, "Sorry, but he's with the President, and I really can't disturb him." She said I should call back again later, which I did. The White House operator recognized my voice, and before I could ask for Bob she told me he was looking for me. He came on the line, sounding very excited, telling me that as a result of my pressure, he was coming to Israel. However, he was not flying in with the Presidential party via Egypt; he was coming straight to Israel, so I should expect him a few days earlier. Amidst the excitement I also managed to convey to him information about the Israelis "keeping a very sharp eye on the north."

Meanwhile, unprecedented security planning for the Presidential visit moved into full gear. In charge was my pal Bruce, who was overburdened handling all the people from the various branches of Government. He had to coordinate between the Israeli security and police authorities and the complicated security setup on his own side. Days before Air Force One landed at Ben-Gurion Airport Bruce was busy juggling advance parties of Secret Service men, the White House and Pentagon staff, and State Department personnel. Two nights before the visit, at 10:45 p.m. Israel time, he was informed from Washington of the impending descent onto Jerusalem of a sizeable chunk of the United States Government, and he had to find accommodations for them all. So he picked up the phone and dialed the King David Hotel in Jerusalem, asking for one of the managers he knew. The dialogue went something like this:

"Hello, Colonel Williams, what can I do for you at this late hour?"
"I want your hotel."
"When do you need the rooms for?"
"In two days' time."
"How many rooms do you need?"
"The whole hotel."

The manager gasped, but he delivered on hearing who the guests would be. All the tourists staying there were cleared out.

Bruce, it later turned out, was as mystified as other United States Embassy people about my use of the red phone. But, as a military man, when he received an order from the Counsel to the President to afford me free access to the phone, he naturally followed instructions. But there are ways and *ways* of carrying out orders, and the fact that we had grown to like each other certainly helped. Later on he told me, "Of course, you never told me exactly what you were doing, and I was somewhat mystified; about all I knew was that you were with the Counsel to the President."

To prepare for the visit, I had a long discussion with Barlev regarding the Labor Party's positions. I had previously ascertained the Likud's positions from my sources. In summation, Labor was ready and amenable to compromise on the West Bank; the Likud most certainly was not. Labor was very

committed to holding on to the Jordan Valley rift as a protective security zone against terrorist incursions across the river,
which had been a regular occurrence in the late 1960s. Both
parties agreed that the status of Jerusalem was not a point for
negotiation. After subsequent talks with various Likud leaders I confirmed an earlier evaluation: that Labor would save
Begin in the peace treaty vote in Parliament; many Likud
votes would be missing.

A Welcome Fellow Traveler

I was really glad to welcome Bob at Ben-Gurion Airport and
was interested to hear from him that my prodding indeed was
responsible for the President's decision to include him in the
entourage. He told me how our input had been utilized to
overcome a mini-crisis with Begin the previous Sunday night,
which had proven highly dramatic. Of particular use was our
recommendation on "splitting the clock" on the Gaza issue.
He went on to say how grateful the President was to me for
what I had been doing.

I then took Bob on a two-day tour of Sinai with Ezer's active
cooperation. We used military planes for part of the journey,
and we rode in army jeeps across bumpy desert roads for the
rest of the way. My friend Mussa Peled was well known in the
area and he arranged a special itinerary for us. We were
turned over to the faithful Brigadier General Yossi Peled,
another good Army friend of mine and an Israeli Defense
Force commander in Sinai at the time. We even visited a
United States' surveillance point in the desert, where American soldiers in distinctive uniforms were stationed (under an
earlier disengagement agreement between Israel and Egypt).
Our Israeli military escorts had to wait outside the area. To
balance the isolation of this wilderness, the Americans had
very comfortable living quarters. It was quite something to
find Holiday Inn-style accommodations in such a forlorn
place. The soldiers got quite excited on hearing who Bob was.

As we headed back toward civilization, both Bob and I

agreed that we were just plain city boys, who liked softer scenery, preferably urban.

I knew Bob would love Jerusalem as much as I did. It was for him, as it has always been for me, a place of solemn wonderment, representing as it does the millennial continuity of our faith. Bob checked in at the King David and I, walking distance away, at the Plaza. I made a few phone calls and learned of trouble heating up in the north; my Israeli friends were concerned lest the Syrians distract from the diplomacy of the President, who was arriving in Cairo at about that time.

Over dinner, Bob related that the President had cast him as his Israeli specialist because he was so pleased at the kind of input received through our back-door channel. He assured me that we would be in close touch for the duration of the President's visit and that he would settle the matter of my getting a security clearance immediately—usually a time-consuming process. He called Bruce Williams, who was "keeping his cool" despite the pressures on him, and somehow my clearance was quickly arranged. After the President had returned to Washington, Bruce told me over a drink what had happened. "I got this call from the Counsel to the President, who said to me in his soft, persuasive Southern voice, 'Would you help me out, Bruce? I need Leon Charney. Will you be so kind as to arrange the security clearance for him? Good, I knew you would be helpful.' " As Bruce told me, it was the kind of approach he could hardly resist, especially as he was well acquainted with me already.

Meanwhile, news reached us from Cairo of the tremendous welcome extended to the Presidential party. Sadat's people were pulling out all the stops, with millions of cheering Egyptians lining the roads and railway routes. This was the first part of what came to be known as "The Six-day Odyssey of Jimmy Carter." Serious questions were raised in Washington about the sagacity of the United States President engaging in such personal diplomacy. If the diplomacy failed, the entire effort could backfire, damaging his international and domestic standing. However, before setting out on his "Odyssey," Carter had had in his pocket the Israeli Cabinet's approval of the draft treaty and its conditions, plus Prime Minister Begin's all-important personal commitment on three American compromise proposals. These dealt with the "linkage" between the treaty and the West Bank autonomy scheme; Article 6 on the "priority of obligation" clause defining the relationship between the treaty and Egypt's previous defense pacts with other Arab states; and the connection between the treaty and a comprehensive Middle East settlement. What was left unsettled for Carter to deal with was the question of the exchange of Ambassadors and future Sinai oil supplies to Israel. The latter was a sticking point for many Israelis, because it comprised, apart from the abandonment of the Sinai settlements, the most tangible sacrifice made for peace. Hitherto Israel had had an independent source of oil. Under the treaty's terms, the oil would be transferred to Egypt.

It was an exciting time for my journalist friend Wolf Blitzer, who was part of the press corps accompanying the Presidential party from Washington to Cairo to Tel Aviv. He had some amusing stories to relate when he reached Israel. For example, the Egyptian Railways brochure brought out for the Carter journey to Alexandria was entitled, "The Itinerary of the Special Train of Mr. G. Carter, President of the United States." That caused Jody Powell, the White House Press Secretary, to quip, "That's Jimmy's cousin, George. We've kept him hidden until now." He also told me that the President had been quite fascinated with the problems of constructing the pyramids. The engineer in the Chief Executive was coming out. Finally Carter said, "I'm surprised that a Government organization could do it." Everyone laughed, Wolf had been told, even the Egyptians.

One highlight of Wolf's visit to Egypt was his attending the Sabbath eve service in the surviving synagogue of Cairo. That city once had had numerous synagogues and a thriving community of 100,000 Jews; now only about 200 Jews were left, mostly elderly people. Having been to Egypt while Abrasha Tamir was still in charge of the Israeli military negotiations, I was able to compare notes with Wolf. We discussed the poverty that Egyptians seemingly endured with good-natured acceptance, along with the country's other perennial problems. One of my Egyptian hosts explained to me at that time that one reason Sadat enjoyed popular support for his efforts toward peace was that the Egyptians hoped that some of the money spent on arms and the Army would be diverted to tackling important domestic problems. Anyone who has seen Cairo, a city built for three million inhabitants overflowing with 11 million people, can appreciate the tremendous problems its Government must cope with. I vividly recall seeing only a small portion of the hundreds of thousands of people who actually live among the tombs of Cairo's vast cemetery, called "The City of the Dead." Whenever I read about housing shortages in our country I think of those poor people living—if that's the word for it—among gravestones.

Awaiting the Chief

Even before Air Force One touched down at Ben-Gurion Airport, there was news that irritated the Israeli public. The State Department press kit, distributed to the accompanying press corps, specified that the Carter mission would be visiting three places: Egypt, Israel, and Jerusalem. The press was also informed that the leader of Egypt was President Anwar Sadat, the leader of Israel was Prime Minister Menachem Begin, and the leader of Jerusalem was Mayor Teddy Kolleck. The world was once again reminded of Washington's long-standing refusal to recognize Jerusalem as the capital of Israel, and that this American ban applied even during this historic mission of peace. This added to a negative impression of Jimmy Carter growing among Israel's supporters in America.

That Saturday night the Presidential party was due to arrive in Israel. During the morning I spent two hours with Barlev in Tel Aviv and another two hours with Ezer discussing various problems coming up for discussion. I returned to Jerusalem and had a long chat with Yona, Begin's secretary. Then I went to see Bob, who recorded the following:

March 10, 1979
4:40 p.m. (Israel time)

Questions to be asked: can Israel really adjust to living with peace. Re: peace negotiations: (1) no problem and 100 percent support if Sadat accepts proposals as agreed to by Begin, (2) if minor changes (but no changes in substance), Begin can get Cabinet support, (3) if major changes...??? (But even here *the process* would probably not be broken.)

Re: exchange of Ambassadors...if Egypt insists on the original concept, Begin would go back to the [18 months instead of the 9 months and 3 years to 6 years] withdrawal timetable. Begin told this to the Knesset Foreign Affairs and Defense Committee (as per General Barlev).

(...) thinks that:

(*A*) With a peace treaty there is more chance of war within six months with Syria, Iraq, and Jordan.

(*B*) Without...less chance during that time.

Begin's behavior and goal now are clearly toward a peace treaty. He is geared to the point of wanting to make this thing *happen.*

My input was converted by Bob into the following hand-written communication, which he presented to the President on the latter's arrival that evening:

THE KING DAVID HOTEL

March 10, 1979

TO: THE PRESIDENT
FROM: BOB LIPSHUTZ

During the past two days I have received the following observations from both the source with which you are familiar and Israeli General Barlev (through this same contact).

If Sadat accepts the same proposals to which the Israelis have now agreed, or is asking for only "minor" changes (form and/or language but not substance), Begin can and probably would accept and get Cabinet approval. If the changes were substantive, then that is an open question. (However, even if the requests were substantive, the Israelis probably would not want to interrupt "the peace process.")

Of much concern to Israeli leaders is the problem of Israelis actually adjusting to peace itself!

Re: the exchange of Ambassadors...if Egypt insists on the original timetable and concepts, Begin would probably accept it if the parties also went back to the original withdrawal timetable (18 months instead of 9 months for phase 1 and 6 years instead of 3 years for the final phase). Begin apparently told this to the Defense Committee.

Begin's present behavior and goal now clearly are toward a peace treaty. He is geared to the point of wanting to make this thing happen.

Bob and I prepared to meet Air Force One. Bruce Williams explained the procedures and protocol to us and, armed with appropriate badges, we drove to Ben-Gurion Airport to be on hand for the welcoming ceremony. The security boys had shut down the highway for three hours, and it was an eerie sensation to have the road all to ourselves except for an occasional police vehicle. At the airport I met an old acquaintance, Andrew Meisels, a fine American journalist who has made his home in Israel. He was surprised to see me there, especially with the distinctive United States top-level security clearance badge pinned to my shirt pocket. He knew of my close association with Ezer, with whom he had a good relationship.

The majestic airliner landed, the trumpets sounded, the red carpet was rolled out, the well-turned-out honor guard welcomed the second United States President to have visited Israel. (Nixon was the first in 1974.) Carter added a special touch of near-theatricality by quoting from the *Midrash** in

---

* A commentary on the Torah.

his arrival statement: "Peace is important, for God's name is *Shalom*."

In the wake of the motorcade we drove back to Jerusalem along the deserted highway. Crowds lining the streets warmly welcomed the Carters. But there was a hostile minority; one man brandished a placard for TV consumption that read, "President J. Carter, don't treat us wrong. We won't be weak but strong."

The King David Hotel was overflowing with security people, Americans and Israelis. I met Ezer in the bar, along with Bruce Williams, Ilan Tehila, Abrasha Tamir, and Barbara Walters. From there we went to a welcoming party attended by Weizman, other Israeli Ministers such as Moshe Dayan, and the entire United States contingent—Vance, Brown, Quandt, and so forth. Bob, Ilan, and I sat together, as good a demonstration of United States-Israel amity as could be found.

Bruce was extremely busy on Sunday morning. The Carters had decided to go to church before proceeding to *Yad Vashem*, the great memorial to the Holocaust located on the outskirts of Jerusalem. The Carters picked the charming Scottish church, St. Andrews, on a hilltop facing the Old City, in keeping with long-standing official American policy of not crossing into the former Jordanian (Eastern) part of Jerusalem.

I had begun to hear fears as early as Saturday that something might go wrong. Bickering had flared up over minor issues, which drove the Americans up the wall. For example, at an earlier stage Carter and Begin had agreed that the autonomy plan would be implemented "as soon as possible." Sadat's people wanted the phrase altered to "expeditiously." Further, the Egyptians wished to postpone their Camp David commitment of "full diplomatic relations" until after the autonomy scheme had been implemented instead of establishing relations after the interim withdrawal from Sinai nine months after the treaty was signed, as Israel had agreed. Above all, there was the issue of Sinai oil supplies. This had become even more significant with the loss of Iranian oil, which had hitherto provided 60 percent of Israel's oil needs. I heard from all sides that the atmosphere was rather cold, and this was reflected by the somber tones of both Carter and Begin at the State Dinner held at the Knesset in honor of the United States President. The Americans felt Sadat had made sufficient concessions, and they wanted to fly back to Cairo with full Israeli agreement on the remaining issues.

Ezer was very upset. He thought that the Government should not treat the President in such a cold, distant manner. He felt that the entire operation could explode. Bob sounded depressed. In the Plaza Hotel lobby I met Abrasha Tamir, who told me that everything had to be finished up the following day. He feared for the worst, which was unusual for such a naturally optimistic man.

Monday morning I breakfasted with Bob. My sources had conveyed to me the view that Ariel Sharon was creating the logjam by blocking a compromise on the issue of the Egyptian liaison office in Gaza. Sadat had told Carter the liaison was of the utmost importance *to him*, as it would demonstrate to the Egyptian people that Begin was sincere about the autonomy scheme. The Americans felt that the Cabinet was swaying toward Sadat's direction.

Bob asked me to see Ezer as early as possible. I had a Foreign Service car available and went to the Hilton on the other side of town as speedily as possible. Ezer was in a bad mood. He was very edgy, having been at the Cabinet meeting throughout the night. He got to bed only at 5:15 a.m. and was still in his pajamas.

The Israelis had accepted Egyptian demands on word changes, but not on the formulations regarding Gaza, the Ambassadorial issue, and oil supplies. Ezer disagreed with the American evaluation—Arik Sharon was not to blame—but there were four Ministers who *were* a roadblock to peace: Shmuel Tamir, Zevulun Hammer, Eliezer Shostak, and Chaim Landau. Ezer was upset. Shaking his head sorrowfully, he mourned, "This is no way to treat the President of the United States." I told him that my sources felt the Americans were upset at Begin, and that they had heard such phrases as "things will never be the same between Carter and Begin."

That afternoon Carter spoke to the Knesset. He pledged

eternal support for Israel and said that the Americans would guarantee Israeli oil supplies. Abba Eban wrote in *The Jerusalem Post* that he delivered the most supportive statement in favor of Israel ever made by an American leader. But this message was almost drowned by the heckling from both the right and left of the chamber. The Americans drew the conclusion that Begin had very difficult domestic political problems. Later the President appeared before the Knesset Foreign Affairs and Defense Committee and gave what Barlev told me was a most impressive performance. However, Secretary of State Cyrus Vance's session with the Israeli Cabinet, with Begin presiding, proved to be much less successful, and Vance reported to his chief that he was dejected.

A kind of war of nerves was starting to develop between the United States and Israeli delegations, with the press corps being manipulated by both sides. The Israelis issued optimistic statements; the Americans were consistently gloomy. Press Secretary Jody Powell was already preparing the media for an announcement of failure of the Presidential mission, and Begin's Israel would be blamed. (Powell was later roasted in Washington for giving an extremely pessimistic briefing to the press as part of the media war of nerves.)

During this time, PLO terrorists committed another outrage, and some Israeli military men were itching to strike back. However, I was able to report from my Israeli sources that Israel would not strike into Lebanon. Bob, whose room was two doors from the President's in the King David Hotel, hurried to pass on my message. Later he told me that this information proved to be the bright spot in a day otherwise marked by pessimism among the White House staff over the outcome of the President's mission.

Bob Lipshutz was depressed. The Americans felt that Begin had put a lock on the talks by insisting on Knesset approval of the treaty, rather than taking the responsibility upon himself. The Americans feared that the wording and contents of the draft would not be settled, and they were very worried indeed about Sadat. They felt his position as Egypt's leader would be endangered unless he got what he wanted.

I pressed Bob to write a memo to the President urging him to insist on taking a signed paper back to the States with him; further, the Americans and Israelis should agree on what had been previously agreed upon and let time settle the outstanding matters.

The Americans were talking of departing, even if it meant leaving empty-handed. (Bob was convinced they were leaving that night.) Deadlines kept shifting. I heard that even veteran TV reporter Walter Cronkite was predicting that Carter would leave for home the following day without an agreed settlement.

I was to learn that late Monday afternoon, after his Knesset speech, the President had convened a meeting in his hotel suite. After consulting with his aides he had decided to stay an extra day. He would use the time to try to finalize matters. Bob said the Americans' strategy was to pin Begin down on everything he had agreed to, recognize what the remaining outstanding issues were, and agree to disagree on them for the time being.

Bob outlined for the President the ideas we worked on earlier in the day. The memo read as follows:

KING DAVID HOTEL

March 12, 1979
10:00 p.m.

TO: THE PRESIDENT
FROM: BOB LIPSHUTZ

Based upon our understanding of the status of negotiations, I would like to pass on a suggestion which might be useful if the unresolved problems cannot be agreed upon at this time.

A memorandum of agreement could be initialed by the parties in which the agreed items would be set forth, but the agreement would be effective only if within a very limited time period the parties settled the (three) remaining issues:

(1) Exchange of Ambassadors.

(2) Egyptian liaison office in the Gaza Strip.

(3) Oil supplies for Israel.

To get the parties to initial such an agreement might move the process forward in such a manner psychologically as to enhance the opportunity for them to resolve these last items.

And it would codify the items of agreement and perhaps limit the items of disagreement for subsequent negotiations.

A Sprint for Peace

As Bob dashed off the memo, I dashed across town. Ezer wished to see me urgently. The "Get me Charney" signal was up again. As I was leaving the King David Hotel, I met an unusually depressed Bruce Williams. "Leon," he said, "something has to be done to save things. It's all falling apart. Do something. Only you can keep it together." I assured him I was trying my best.

Speed was imperative. I used the official car and the Israeli security driver that were at my disposal. He drove as fast as he could, siren at full blast, careening through the darkening streets of Jerusalem to the Hilton. On the way, I switched my United States security badge for the Israeli one. I doubt if I have ever had such a hair-raising ride through Jerusalem's narrow streets. The driver was really enjoying his job, ignoring lights and seeing cars and pedestrians scramble out of the way. He was "licensed" to break the traffic regulations—and, for an Israeli male behind the wheel of a car, that is one of life's ultimate pleasures.

I rode the elevator up to Ezer's suite. I believe—like everyone else I'd met—Ezer was inordinately depressed, and even spoke about resigning from the Cabinet. Ezer was dog-tired, having had only two hours' sleep the previous night. "I don't have the spirit to carry on. I am beginning to have doubts whether some of my colleagues really want peace. I do fear for the worst, a negative vote, and then how would I continue to work with them?" he asked. It was obvious that the impasse had produced a real personal crisis for Ezer Weizman, the erstwhile hawk who had acquired the wings of a dove. Re'uma looked at him with a pale, worried face. I did my best to quiet him, urging him not to make any rash decisions. "Look, my late father always used to say that if you get worked up, you should not make a decision at that point, but sleep on it."

He calmed down and we talked. He then explained the Israeli side of the three crucial issues that were left unsettled: the exchange of Ambassadors, the Gaza liaison office, and the oil supply.

The doorbell rang. It was Bernard Kalb of WCBS-TV news for an off-the-record briefing. Kalb asked Ezer if things could change within the next 18 hours. Ezer said they could, adding that basically he was optimistic about the outcome. As the interview progressed, Ezer's mood picked up. Kalb left, and then Re'uma and I, seeing that Ezer had regained his usual good mood, expressed aloud our thanks that he had not made any rash resignation announcement as he had threatened shortly before.

Re'uma turned on the evening news, which was showing a replay of Carter's speech to the Knesset earlier in the day. Geula Cohen, an "anti-peace" Knesset member, was being hauled out for having interrupted Begin's speech so often. Ezer then informed me that Carter had told him how glad he was that the zealous lady politician had not gotten into full-blown heckling form and heckled *him* during *his* speech.

I informed Ezer of the memo to the President, spelling out the idea of enumerating the agreements on 95 percent of the issues and leaving the outstanding 5 percent to be resolved in the future. I added that Bob and I would communicate further with the President before midnight.

Just then the phone rang; it was Harold Brown, very upset at the turn of events, warning his Israeli counterpart that "if things should come apart, it would be a strategic calamity." Ezer, in a different mood than when I arrived, agreed that there was trouble, but expressed his hope that things would work out and a compromise be arrived at. He decided to go to sleep.

I drove back to the King David Hotel. Jerusalem's quiet darkness, with few people on the streets, contrasted starkly with the turbulent activity throbbing through the various diplomatic channels, official and unofficial, at that hour. Lights were burning late at the temporary White House at the King David Hotel, at the Prime Minister's Office in the Kirya, and at the Foreign Ministry compound.

The Midnight Oil

I found Bob in his room and I told him that we should write another memorandum for the President on the various problem points. He had met with the President earlier and given him our memo. Carter evinced a marked interest in its contents and said he would think it over.

Bob and I sat discussing the problems and alternatives. I had talked with a wide spectrum of Israeli friends and leaders, and then tried to formulate some creative ideas on the unresolved problems. Bob then wrote the following:

THE KING DAVID HOTEL

March 12, 1979
11:30 p.m.

TO: THE PRESIDENT
FROM: BOB LIPSHUTZ

This memo reflects a lengthy meeting which Leon Charney had with his Israeli sources.

Suggestions of how to resolve the three remaining issues:

(1) Gaza liaison personnel—this could be by *exchanging military* liaison personnel (i.e. Egyptians in Gaza and Haifa; Israelis in Cairo and Alexandria).

(2) Oil—Egypt agrees to sell X barrels per year at world market prices, provided it does not jeopardize (conflict with)

Egyptian national interests...backed up by the agreed United
States guarantee.

(3) Exchange of Ambassadors—if Israel agrees to the above
two items, Egypt probably would go along with Israel's position on this last item...or something close to it.

Before we formulated proposal 2, I explained the background to Bob. At the time of the 1975 withdrawal agreement
with Egypt, Israel had agreed to hand back some Sinai oil
fields, but the oil-supply issue proved a sticking point. The
1975 deal was settled only after the United States committed
itself to guarantee the oil supply for five years, in case of an
unforeseen difficulty. In the 1975 instance the Egyptians
refused to tie themselves down to a written agreement on oil
supplies. So my idea was to sweeten the pot for Israel by
proposing that the United States will guarantee double the
amount of oil in the five-year period.

Bob gave the memo to Phil Wise, the Appointments Secretary, to be delivered to the President first thing in the morning.

I left to get some sleep. As I emerged from the elevator, I met
Bill Quandt. He was depressed, of course, like virtually every
official in Israel. The clock on the hotel wall indicated it was
just after midnight, and Quandt, assistant to the President's
National Security Advisor, mournfully declared, "It's all over!
It's a human tragedy!" I muttered something about "living
and learning," and departed to the deserted streets of Jerusalem, enjoying the brisk mountain air. Despite all the talk in
the United States media of the danger in the Middle East,
especially in Jerusalem, I felt safe walking the city streets.

Comes the Dawn...

I breakfasted with Bob in the hotel coffee shop. While we
were eating, an Israeli TV crew photographed us, with the
Prime Minister's staff at the next table. (Yona and Kadishai
were very cordial; Kadishai even extended an invitation to

spend the Passover Seder night with his family, if I were still in the country.) We appeared that night on Israel TV news, much to my mother's delight.

Upstairs the Prime Minister and the President were breakfasting together. The entire world was waiting for the outcome. Later I learned that at the same time Brown and Ezer were discussing an arms agreement between the two countries. The departure—and the baggage call—was delayed, which was a positive sign.

During the famous breakfast meeting, Carter assured Begin that the United States would guarantee an adequate supply of oil at market prices, and that Sadat would agree to exchange Ambassadors as soon as Israel began withdrawing from Western Sinai. The issue of Egyptian access to Gaza was later dropped by Carter after the leaders conferred with Vance, Brzezinski, and Dayan.

Before the motorcade departed, Ezer called to bid the President farewell and express his optimism for the resolution of the remaining issues.

I drove to the airport with Bruce Williams. None of us yet knew quite what had happened. I spotted Israeli V.I.P.s who I knew, waiting around on the tarmac for the farewell ceremony. I stopped to chat with Yitzhak Rabin, who expressed his belief that if Begin did not close the agreement then, his future in power might come under question. Rabin had not been on very good terms with Carter when he was Prime Minister. He told me, however, that he had complimented the President on his speech when they had met at the State Dinner at the Knesset. Rabin said it was the finest pro-Israel statement ever delivered by a foreign leader. I next encountered Shimon Peres, who asked me how *his* Knesset speech had gone over. I told him it had been fine. The Labor Party Chairman appeared to need others to reassure him of how well he was doing. He then asked me why the President had not asked to meet with him personally. I found it peculiar that he asked *me* such a question, but I said something about there not having been enough time in such a packed schedule.

I had heard from Wolf Blitzer and Andy Meisels earlier in

the day that the Dayan people were spreading the story that Moshe Dayan "has saved the day with his formula." Well, I certainly could not swear to that, but I felt that where the praise went was somewhat immaterial as long as peace was achieved.

I managed to exchange a few words with Wolf before the plane left, and he told me many American newsmen were absolutely convinced the talks had ended in failure.

Peace in the Air

The farewell ceremony took longer than usual. The Israeli military guard of honor went through its paces; the military band played *Hatikva* and the *Star-Spangled Banner* rather nicely; a formation of Israeli-made Kfir fighter planes zipped overhead in a farewell salute to the President of the United States. Carter seemed very moved when a contingent of children of American diplomats cheered him from the stands.

Before Bob boarded the plane, he told me that in the morning he had had a few words privately with the President, who had told him that our suggestion contained a good oil compromise.

After returning to my Tel Aviv hotel, I called Ezer and told him that I felt in my bones that the Cairo meeting would end successfully. At 6:00 p.m. Bruce Williams called me to say he had just heard the news—Sadat had accepted the proposals. I phoned Ezer, announcing, "We've made it."

Ezer was sure that the treaty would sail through the Cabinet and the Knesset. Both Barlev and Rabin returned my calls, airing their happiness at the outcome.

Next morning I had breakfast with Ezer. When he arrived, he grabbed me and hugged me, saying, "Thanks, Leon, thanks very much!" He confessed his worry as to how peace would work out; it would not be easy for Israelis and Egyptians to learn to live together in peace. Then he phoned Re'uma and said, "You know, that Jewish lawyer from New York really has a grasp of Begin's psychology. He knows how to write just what Begin can take." We sat back down and he launched into a lecture on how important it was that the back-door channel continue to function. On no account, however, should either Bob or I go public about our roles. "Who knows," he conjectured, "how much we might need you again in the near future?"

Bob, meanwhile, was flying home on Air Force One. While in the air, he dictated a memorandum to himself, a kind of diary. Here are excerpts:

THE WHITE HOUSE
WASHINGTON

March 13, 1979
MEMORANDUM TO THE FILE

FROM: BOB LIPSHUTZ

This memorandum is being dictated as we return on Air Force One from Israel and Egypt on March 13, 1979.

Approximately one hour ago, President Carter announced at the Cairo airport, with President Sadat of Egypt standing at his side, that President Sadat had accepted in full all of the proposals for settlement of the various problems involved in the peace treaty between Israel and Egypt. President Carter announced that he had just talked with Prime Minister Begin, which I witnessed at the Cairo airport, advising him of this decision by President Sadat. And Begin stated that he would submit the final matters to his Cabinet. We heard shortly after takeoff from Cairo that Begin had called a meeting of the Israeli Cabinet for 10:00 a.m. tomorrow, Israel time, to discuss and decide upon these last outstanding matters. Clearly the final decision is in the hands of the Israelis...

On board Air Force One the atmosphere is one of exhilaration, tempered somewhat by the realization that there are still many weeks and months of difficult implementation lying ahead, assuming that the Israeli Cabinet will agree to the final details and that the Knesset will ratify these actions. The President himself has walked through the plane, thanking everyone who has been involved in the process for their help...especially Secretary Vance...Vance commented very forcibly that this was a successful team effort and that everybody on the plane particularly, as well as others, had made a significant contribution to the success of this long effort. One of the obviously important items which must be worked upon is the selection of the United States representative for the future negotiations between the parties, which are going to be extremely tedious, time-consuming, and complex. Secretary Vance mentioned that it is extremely difficult to find someone like Sol Linowitz, who was excellent in the Panama Canal Treaty negotiations, to handle such a project.

In reviewing many of the details of the agreements which have been worked out, it is obvious that the various specific recommendations which I passed on to the President as a result of my communications with Leon Charney...have been both accurate and helpful. It is important that first I write an appropriate letter to Leon and further that something from the President be sent to him as an expression of appreciation. This does not mean that the relationship is ended; to the contrary, it will probably continue for a very long period of time and hopefully be as helpful as it has in the past. It is obvious that Ezer Weizman and Harold Brown have an excellent relationship established and therefore it may be that many matters which we handled through these "back channels" can be handled in a direct manner in the future. I have not discussed this with Harold Brown, I do not know if he is interested in getting into the diplomatic or political aspect of relationships, but we should determine these things to make sure that we are coordinated and utilizing this entire relationship with Weizman in the most effective manner. Perhaps I should discuss this with the President first, and then with Harold Brown.

Having been so close to the day-to-day and hour-to-hour negotiations and other activities in connection with this matter, particularly over the past several days, it is difficult to comprehend the magnitude of the entire situation...

For me, personally, this of course is a tremendously meaningful experience. Perhaps incorrectly, I feel that one of the reasons that has made Jimmy Carter so tenacious in his efforts to bring about this peace in the Middle East...is his relationship

> with me personally.... And, it also makes the "slings and
> arrows" of the last two years, particularly from Jewish groups,
> lose their sting and dull their pain...

The President disclosed to me that the first people to con-
gratulate him after word got out of his successful Cairo-
Jerusalem-Cairo shuttle were the leaders of Saudi Arabia.
They called him while he was en route to a warm welcome at
Andrews Air Force Base, leading him to conclude that the
Saudi Royal Family had feared dire consequences if the mis-
sion had failed.

Enter Strauss

Soon after the President returned home, he got together with
Vice President Mondale to determine a suitable Middle East
envoy to carry on the peace process. They decided on Robert
Strauss. He had served as Special Trade Representative in the
Carter Cabinet. Carter and Mondale hoped that he could bring
to the West Bank and Palestinian issues the kind of success he
had achieved in various international trade negotiations.
Carter quoted Strauss' reaction when he was told of his new
assignment: "I've never even read the Bible—and I'm a Jew!"
But his Jewish connections were of the most tenuous nature. A
rough-and-tough self-made millionaire from Texas, he thought
he could apply the same approach to the infinitely more delicate situation of the Middle East. He was soon to learn how
wrong his assumptions were.

At first Carter kept his plan to appoint Strauss rather quiet.
He also failed to take into account the prickly reaction of
Secretary Vance. Vance, who was already embroiled in con-
stant guerrilla warfare with Dr. Brzezinski and his National
Security Council, warned Carter he would resign if, as it
appeared, his role was reduced to that of a figurehead. But
Vance quieted down after the President pointed out that it was
of no advantage to either of them to bear the brunt of this

difficult issue. Rather, they should let Strauss carry out the policy guidelines that both of them would set out. The word in the White House was that Strauss could better absorb domestic political flak from the Administrations's Middle East policy than the principals.

Bob Lipshutz asked me to come and meet the Texan, who wanted to talk to me. Strauss treated Bob with respect; later, I learned that the President had told the tough lobbyist, "There are two men in my Administration that you'd better not hassle—Bob Lipshutz and Charles Kirbo." That certainly was some kind of Presidential award!

Carter and Mondale both "took" to Strauss, seeing in him some kind of wizard. Strauss' original loyalty, however, was to "Scoop" Jackson. Nonetheless, the President was so deeply impressed with Strauss that when his re-election campaign began to take shape in October he picked Strauss to run it. In the election post-mortem there were those Monday-morning quarterbacks within Carter's inner circle who questioned that judgment.

In my estimation, Strauss, who had made a name for himself as a shrewd lawyer and a canny politician, first in Texas, then in Washington, D.C., was thrown into the labyrinthian complications of the Middle East without proper preparation. His loyalty to the President impelled him to tackle the job, but his unbroken record of success in business and politics did not prepare him for the shifting sands of Middle Eastern diplomacy. But Strauss' role in the peace saga was to unfurl only in the ensuing months.

12

Arms Make the Man

Ahead lay the formal signing ceremony at the White House, scheduled for the final week of the month. Beforehand the Knesset was to hold its cliff-hanging debate on the peace treaty, with the world awaiting the outcome of the vote on dismantling Sinai settlements.

Ezer was sent to the United States to finalize the financial details of the United States' aid package. The cost of withdrawal and redeployment of air bases had ballooned under the impact of Israeli inflation. Ezer's American mission was aimed largely at getting concrete numbers to help persuade the waverers in the Israeli camp. It was, however, regarded as a major test for Ezer's advocacy of putting Israel's trust in the United States and a personal test of Ezer's influence in Carter's Washington. The outcome could affect the future, not only of the peace process, but also of Ezer's career. Before we left Tel Aviv, Ezer told me, "My political career is at stake. The Cabinet has sent me to Washington to close this deal. I cannot come back a loser!"

I traveled on the same El Al flight with Ezer and his party. He slept most of the way to London. When I went downstairs from the first-class lounge I encountered Ilan. "Did you know that I've been ordered to buy you a present?" he asked me. "You don't know how highly Ezer speaks of your contribution. I'm really glad you are with us on this trip because, as you know only too well, Ezer *must* come home with tangible results." He quoted Ezer as saying, "The shopping bag not only has to be full, it has to be seen back home as being full."

After we ate, Ezer introduced me to Meir Rosenne, the Foreign Ministry's legal counsel who had been Dayan's aide at Camp David. Another traveling companion was Joseph Ma'ayan, Director-General of Ezer's Ministry, with whom I was on amicable terms.

There was one particularly touching moment on that journey. Ezer was informed by the Captain that he had had a message of good wishes from Egyptian Vice-President Mubarak, who was flying to Yugoslavia on a State mission. His plane had just passed by ours. Ezer was sincerely moved by the Egyptian's greetings, observing, "Thank the Lord, we now exchange messages from airplanes instead of rockets!"

From London's Heathrow Airport to New York's JFK, I sat with Ezer. Neither of us could sleep, so we talked through the night. We touched on everything, from books we liked to his plans for a home in Caesaria overlooking the sea and the ancient Roman aqueduct, to the state of health of his son, Shaul. We discussed my role as special counsel using the back-door channel, and as the hours sped by, and the others watched a movie, Ezer discoursed on Israeli personalities, from Begin to Peres to Rabin.

Whisked to Washington

As we neared New York, Ezer asked me to fly on with him to Washington aboard the special United States Air Force plane that had been put at his party's disposal. However, an Israeli security man warned me that there might be big problems over my luggage. I was not traveling with a diplomatic passport and thus was subject to clearance through United States Customs. But Ezer, tired and anxious to continue his journey and preoccupied with the "big picture," offhandedly ordered the man personally to handle the transfer of my luggage to the plane. As we moved into the Air Force plane Ezer kept saying, "I'm really depending on you to help me. This mission is really of great importance."

I settled back in a comfortable seat aboard the beautifully laid-out United States Air Force plane with its marvelously attentive crew and thought, "That is the life." (Only after my arrival in Washington did I learn that United States Customs officials back in JFK had created a huge rumpus after the security man had rushed my luggage along with that of Ezer's official party from the El Al craft onto the USAF plane without mandatory Customs clearance. I subsequently learned that United States Customs offices had formally informed El Al in New York that it would be fined $25,000 for violating official regulations. I was so horrified that Ezer's gesture might have such dire results that I called a friend at New York's City Hall and asked him to explain to the officials concerned what had happened. He must have talked with a magical tongue because the El Al office never heard anything more on the matter.)

I was seated in the rear of the Air Force plane when I heard Ezer call out, "Where's Leon? Where are you, Leon?" I went over to join him and Abrasha Tamir. He had finished his conferences with Arye Levy, head of the Israeli defense mission in New York, who had joined the group at JFK to fill in Ezer on the latest developments in America.

When the plane landed at Andrews Air Force Base, I was not quite prepared for what happened. Standing on the receiving line, waiting to welcome their guests from Israel, was a string of United States Generals. I froze in my tracks and whispered to the hugely amused Abrasha, "What the hell do I do?" He chuckled back, "Do as I do." So I followed Abrasha along that line, among Israeli Generals and Defense Ministry officials, shaking hands with one bemedaled United States

officer after another. All were very nice and trusted I'd enjoy
my stay in the United States. I replied that I loved being in
America, and I thanked them with feeling for their warm
hospitality.

When Ezer finished with the waiting press, we were piled
into a motorcade that plowed through the 5 o'clock rush-hour
traffic with sirens at full blast. I thought, "Now *that's* the way
to cope with traffic problems." On arriving at the Madison
Hotel, I found that only one of my suitcases had arrived. I was
too tired to care about the other, and collapsed into a deep
sleep.

Back Down to Earth

In the morning I went upstairs to Ezer's suite. He was getting ready to leave for his first meeting with Defense Secretary
Harold Brown. I asked him what he wished to accomplish and
wrote it down on some pieces of hotel stationery. He was
asking for about $4 billion more for military aid than was
currently granted. This would be repaid over a number of
years and would enable Israel to cope with the costs of new
airfields and redeployment.

I phoned Bob at the White House and arranged a meeting
for that morning. We had not met since I had bid him farewell
at Ben-Gurion Airport. I explained that for political reasons
Ezer needed a letter to take back with him. He told me, "Rest
assured. The President knows Ezer and you are in town. He
does understand Ezer's position." As I explained, Bob wrote
down on his White House memo pad: *Important for E.W. to
take back something in writing from President or Brown.* On
another page he wrote:

(1) Currently U.S. gives $1 billion a year military aid—per 1975
disengagement agreement.
(2) Plus $800 million in general aid.
(A) Israel (per E.W.) needs to increase the $1 billion to $1.5

billion (for the same period of time) primarily because of [Israeli] inflation. Plus $4 billion for over 3-to-5 year period for redeployment costs (Sinai to Negev). Technical teams are working on the details. Because of Israeli inflation it may be preferable—and cheaper—to use American contractors for redeployment.

That was about 11:30 a.m. By 4:45 p.m., Bob had received a White House memo with the following responses:

(1) 2 airfields: estimate cost $1.1 billion with coverage in full, even more.
(2) Plus $1.4 billion more for redeployment, etc. (E.W. wants $2.9 billion).
(3) Re: military aid, Brown wants it to stay at the level of the $1 billion.
A letter from Brown will be given. Delivery of new warplanes will be expedited. E.W. and H.B. discussing terms.

I returned to the hotel to find a most angry Ezer. Brown had been talking to him about $2.5 billion instead of $4 billion, apart from which he offered no change in current aid. Ezer was called to the phone, and Ilan drew me aside and said, "Ezer could be ruined politically."

I returned to Bob's office, and we spent some time drafting the compromise language. At the same time Ezer drove over to Foggy Bottom to see Cyrus Vance, after which Ezer informed me, "Things are getting a little better. Vance is a bit more responsive." I was able to advise Bob that:

"Vance understands better the Israeli political situation. Something is needed other than what Brown offered, plus the ongoing military and economic aid. As to redeployments, the

U.S. should send over a team to determine the costs. BUT E.W. would be satisfied more with a current estimate of $1.9 b. (rather than $1.4 b. or $2.5 b.), subject to confirmation from American experts as to cost. Israeli and American teams will agree on the definition of 'redeployment'."

When I returned to the Madison, I found Ezer still very angry. He refused to go out and eat, so we ordered from room service. Ezer stalked up and down the room blasting the Administration position. Ilan was upset at me for having told Ezer what was going on. I said, "I do my best to tell the truth however unpalatable it may be." I repeated that I had heard that many officials at various levels of the Administration favored withholding further aid as leverage on Israel on the West Bank issue. They were disinterested in the damage done to Ezer, even if he was Number One Israeli coordinator with the United States. Nor did they care about the concessions that Israel had made already to Egypt.

The next day was a Saturday, and I broke my personal rule of never working on that day. I went to the White House and toiled for hours with the tireless Bob on a memorandum for the President. I read it to Ezer over the phone before we had it transmitted on the White House teletype to the President, who was spending the weekend at Camp David working on energy legislation with some of his aides. The memorandum read as follows:

THE WHITE HOUSE
WASHINGTON

March 17, 1979

TO: THE PRESIDENT
FROM: BOB LIPSHUTZ

This memo reflects the discussions conducted over the past

24 hours with Leon Charney, who traveled back with Ezer
Weizman, and is staying at the same hotel, and is in constant
communication with him. Taking into account the Israeli political background, this trip indicated that the principal responsibility assigned to Weizman by the Cabinet is to try and
improve, and perhaps make more definite, the financial arrangements which have been discussed. Weizman was advised to try
and handle this matter with "his American friends," and Ezer
himself feels that he would be vulnerable politically were he to
return with only the same things as already outlined. It is
Leon's and my judgment that—as in other elements of negotiations—perceptions and cosmetics can be effective even if there
is little or even no firm change at this time in substance.

Bob then proceeded to outline the need to raise the allocation
from $1.4 billion to $1.9 billion, to recapitulate the issue of the
costs of the air bases and the Sinai redeployment, and ended
by recommending the expedited delivery of 55 F-16s to the
Israeli Air Force.

I thought Ezer might want to know that the memo had been
dispatched, so I called him at the Madison. My call came
through just as he was holding a press conference with Israeli
correspondents. One of his aides yelled out my name. I had
always kept my word to avoid headlines and to never leak a
word to any reporter, even to a close friend like Wolf Blitzer.
Wolf later gave me a verbatim report of the ensuing question-
and-answer session concerning me between Ezer and the
Israeli reporters:

Q. *Who's Leon Charney?*
A. *He's my lawyer. I have known him for a long time and
I can assure you he's O.K.*
Q. *Why does he wear a security clearance badge? Is he a
member of the delegation?*
A. *He's not a member of the delegation. He is someone
with good connections at the White House, and he is
most helpful to me.*

Q. *Why is he at the Madison?*

A. *(in an exasperated tone) First of all, it's at his own expense. He has first-class connections. He has Bob Lipshutz' ear, and the fact is that he's got the President's ear.... Moreover, Leon Charney is not only a good friend of mine but also of Yitzhak Rabin, of Chaim Barlev, and of Prime Minister Menachem Begin. They all know I'm resorting to his help.*

Q. *Is what he's doing for Israel? Or is it for his own benefit?*

A. *He's doing it for the love of Israel. Believe me, he doesn't need it, he's got enough money, he could buy all of us.... Ah, the mysterious Mr. Charney rides again. He's a good friend and I'm strongly defending him. Believe me, he's got more than enough from his law practice.*

Later I learned that the source that instigated the newsmen's interrogation of Ezer was the Israeli Embassy. Some diplomatic "professionals" had deeply resented Ezer's usurping their professional prerogatives with his own back-door channel to the White House. On more than one occasion I arranged on fairly short notice, through Bob, for Ezer to meet with Carter. In the history of the United States foreign relations there were few precedents of a Defense Minister of even the friendliest of powers being received so frequently by the President. It was certainly unusual in the course of relations between Washington and Jerusalem. Obviously my proximity to Ezer aroused a measure of jealousy among even some members of his circle, who regarded him with a certain possessiveness and perhaps resented the intrusion of an outsider. They too tried their best to break our relationship, but to no avail. Our chemistry persisted.

That night Ezer invited me to accompany him to a big party at the Israeli Embassy attended by Harold Brown, lots of Army brass, and the Egyptian Military Attaché at his country's Embassy in Washington. "We're making history, my friend," Ezer bubbled to the smiling Egyptian.

Ezer was very busy on Sunday with TV appearances and meetings, including a working luncheon with Brown and Vance. I had decided to take it easy. I had lunch with some Israelis and went off to a movie.

I got back to the hotel to find that all hell had broken loose. I took the elevator to the top floor, where I met a very pale Ilan. He looked as if he were going to be sick. It appeared that Brown's letter to Ezer, of which Bob had apprised me, contained no improvement on the aid situation. It was highly unsatisfactory to the Israelis and especially to Ezer. Ilan kept murmuring, "Ezer will be ruined! Ezer will be ruined!" He told me that Ezer had been pacing his suite, bellowing, "Get me Charney!"

Ilan called Ezer out of a meeting; he rushed over to me, furious. "Where have you been?" he asked, and was quite nonplussed when I explained, "I've been to a movie." He called me into the adjoining room so we could speak privately. He sounded almost desperate and very angry. "Your friend Carter and his people are fixing me truly and properly, you know. I won't go down quietly, I tell you." I replied, "I think that you have been much too good to them." So I picked up the phone and tried to locate Bob or Hamilton Jordan. But unsuccessfully. As we had an afternoon date for drinks at Bob's house in Arlington, I urged Ezer to come as planned and talk things over there. He was resisting the idea when the phone rang. It was Alfred Atherton, one of the top State Department Middle East negotiators. He wanted to arrange a meeting with Ezer about the Egyptians. I could see that Ezer was about to burst, and I kept whispering to him, "Don't create a crisis atmosphere. Cool it." Thankfully he heeded my counsel.

I had won my point with Ezer and he agreed to go to Bob's house. We took Ilan along, in addition to the usual security men. Usually it's a pleasant 15-minute drive to Arlington, but we took longer because Ezer wanted to talk. He was particularly hurt by rejection of his request to reinstate the $500 million aid package. He felt the Carter people were hitting at him personally, and at what he represented in the United

States-Israeli equation. He had put all his cards on the Carter ace, and look what they were doing to him!

I entered Bob's home with some trepidation; Ezer had been building up pressure and muttering to himself, "I'm really going to let him have it." But somehow I had the feeling that he knew what he was doing. We were welcomed by a smiling Bob and his gracious wife, Betty, and Ezer almost immediately let loose. He stalked up and down their living room shouting imprecations about Carter and Camp David and threatening to blow the whole thing up. Bob and Betty were aghast, the Southern gentleman and lady had seldom heard anyone talk like that before. Then abruptly the storm subsided and Ezer said, "I'm leaving." He walked out, taking Ilan with him.

That was the most unpleasant ten minutes of my life. It was certainly effectively nerve-shattering to our hosts and to me.

I suspected, however, that the outburst was premeditated. I had gotten to know Ezer pretty well, and behind the public image of the dashing fighter pilot and impetuous politician existed a very solid and punctilious person, with one of the fastest minds I have ever encountered in my years as a lawyer.

After Ezer walked out, leaving us all wrecked in the wake of the storm, Bob looked at me, and in his whimsical manner asked, "What do we do?" I suggested, "Call the President. Maybe he should invite Ezer to Camp David or at least establish some kind of contact with him." Bob grimaced; he really was reluctant to disturb the President at Camp David. However, he did put through a call, but was told the President would call him back. We waited. When the call came through I walked into the kitchen to let him talk freely.

When he joined me, Bob was sweating and visibly upset. He told me that he had never spoken to the President like that before, but he felt that it was his duty to do so. He had advised the President of Ezer's frame of mind and mentioned the devastating effect of Brown's letter. The President told Bob that he had just talked to Brown by phone and they had discussed Ezer's strong reaction during his luncheon that day with the Secretaries of Defense and State. He asked Bob to contact Ezer and tell him the President would call him the next day.

I tried to phone Ezer but the line was busy. I subsequently learned that he was conversing at that very moment with Brown. I could see Bob was still upset. He smiled wanly and said, "You know, it was a fruitful call to the President."

As I was leaving, Betty asked me if Ezer's outburst at Carter had represented his true feelings. I indignantly assured her it did not, but I could hardly explain the ins and outs of Ezer's complicated character, nor my suspicions of the reasons behind his outburst. More, much more, was at stake than all our personal feelings.

Back at the hotel, I found Ezer had quieted down, while I was still unnerved and feeling sorry for Bob. But I did advise Ezer to stand firm and act tough with the Administration. Ezer suggested we dine out alone, and we found a small restaurant. We picked a booth that would sit only the two of us, so the Secret Service men had to eat a few booths away. We talked for hours about his political ambitions, my personal life, and my plans for the future. Over coffee he remarked, "I have lived 100 years in the past two weeks." He also said that he and I would remain the best of friends for a lifetime.

The mood lifted and lightened, we joked and the long day ended in good humor.

Diplomatically Speaking

The next day, Monday, I arranged to have lunch with Bob at the White House mess. He told me over the phone that "some high-level people are working on the problem." I gathered they probably were Vice President Mondale and Hamilton Jordan.

I walked briskly to the White House. The guards knew me fairly well by now and I quickly ascended the stairs to Bob's office. He was more nervous then usual, and appeared quite tense during lunch. He was expecting a call from the President at Camp David and it had not yet come. He had telephoned Stu

Eizenstat, the president's Domestic Policy Advisor, to tell him about the situation with Ezer, and Stu promised to raise the matter. When we got back to Bob's office, I called Ezer at the Madison. He was fairly elated. He had just received a new letter from Brown with a commitment to improved terms. Of course it would be nice to get an additional letter raising the level of the grant, he added. Bob was very excited when I told him and asked to see the letter. I promised to bring a copy to him later that afternoon.

When I reached the Madison penthouse suite, I found Ezer finishing a luncheon with Israeli Ambassador Ephraim Evron and the Embassy's economic counseler, a bureaucrat called Eitan Raff. Ezer remarked to the Ambassador that I had been of great help in this matter with the President; Evron smirked at a complimentary mention of Bob's role. I remembered Wolf Blitzer telling me that the Embassy belittled Bob's influence. Staffers hinted to Israeli correspondents that he had no clout with the President.

Reading the Brown letter made me relieved and elated. When Evron expressed his concern about the terms of the loan, Ezer reported having met privately with Brown and having settled the matter "like gentlemen." Unlike some Israelis, Ezer did not complain about Begin's decision to ask for a loan for the withdrawal costs rather than for an outright grant. Evron and Raff began nitpicking at the terms of the loan, zeroing in on the interest rates. When I remarked that the long-term repayment of the loan would certainly make it almost a grant, Raff looked at me in sheer disbelief. I thought Raff was off base, and I said, "Eitan, you and I have met before on the Israel-British Bank scandal. We disagreed then, and events in that case have so far not upheld your economic counsel, to put it mildly."

Ezer then interposed, "I strongly suggest there be no leaks to the media. It took an enormous amount of energy and lobbying to achieve this breakthrough. Don't allow petty politics to get in the way of something that is truly for the benefit of the State of Israel." Ezer was alluding to the fact that every word or secret exchanged during that mission had appeared the following day in the Israeli press, although Ezer was 5,000 miles from home.

Tensions between Ezer and the Embassy surfaced on that occasion. Some Embassy personnel were resentful that Ezer's success had been achieved without their help and that they had no part in it. Evron had a reputation among Israelis as a master of intrigue, but even he could not claim credit for Ezer having obtained for Israel all the F-16 warplanes that had been intended for Iran before the fall of the Shah. The previous envoy, Simha Dinitz, had been similarly resentful about an "outsider" trespassing on his preserve. He also appeared annoyed that Ezer seemed to have direct access to the President without going through channels or following protocol.

At one point, Evron implied to Ezer in my presence that "Charney is getting in the way of everything." Ezer snapped back, "Charney has been most useful in achieving many benefits for the State of Israel. I prefer not to continue this kind of conversation." He spoke reprovingly to the envoy, reminding him that they had known each other since their childhood days in Haifa, and that he should trust the judgment of the Minister of Defense.

A Farewell to Arms

Bob Lipshutz was happy with Ezer's concluding press conference, in which he generously praised President Carter and Carter's "untiring friendship for Israel." I still felt bad about Ezer's treatment of Bob, so when we were once again aboard the United States Air Force plane en route to New York, I persuaded him to call Bob from the plane. He put a call through to the Lipshutz home and apologized handsomely to both Bob and Betty for his unseemly behavior. His charm worked even on the long-distance connection from thousands of feet in the air.

Everybody was happy. Josef Ma'ayan, Director General of the Ministry of Defense, pointed out that Ezer had obtained the biggest aid package ever secured by Israel to date—not only the loan and the planes, but the joint memorandum of agreement between Israel and the United States. We disembarked at JFK, Ezer and his party boarded the El Al flight for Israel, and I drove into town.

Ezer returned home to a warm Israeli reception, though he found the Embassy had planted various poisoned barbs. In little more than a week he was back in the United States with Re'uma and Shaul for the official signing ceremony of the peace treaty on the White House lawn.

For me, that moment of peace, of brotherhood, of leaders joined together, of high hopes and full hearts, was well worth the enormous effort, strain and sacrifice—both material and personal. I felt all my youth, all my training had been for this.

One of my law school professors, Jerome Prince, had a favorite aphorism: The role of a lawyer is that of the creative artist. I've always felt the law is a constant creative process, not a defined, scientific category. So I have always seen my job of attorney not merely as that of advocate, but also as that of counselor and advisor to help clients avoid costly and sometimes painful advocacy proceedings.

What better use could I ever put my talents to? I had helped my people avoid war.

New York, New York

After the signing, most of the Israelis, including Ezer's party, headed to New York for a few days of rest and festivity. I was always delighted to act as unofficial host when Israeli friends visited "my town."

The night of the signing I returned to New York to party. What a night! The following evening I chatted by phone with Bob. We reminisced a bit, and he expressed his hope that relations between Carter and Begin might improve. He spoke of the need even to develop concrete ideas resolving the West Bank issue. He ended the conversation by saying, "D'you know what? I have a feeling that Begin would like to leave that issue for another leader to tackle in five years' time."

I found Ezer in his Regency Hotel suite preparing for his

flight back home the next day. Ilan walked in and interrupted our short conversation about the West Bank with the observation that "Hussein is such a coward." Ezer, for his part, contended that Israel would display good faith by lessening military controls on the West Bank and Gaza. On the whole, it was his intention to work for a lessening of Israeli presence in those areas. Ezer then asked me to come into the next room to talk in private. He stressed how important it was for us to be in constant contact by phone, and that I should continue "the good work." Then a call came through from the Begin suite. Would the Minister please call on the Prime Minister in a half hour?

By the time Ezer got back, Re'uma had returned from a shopping trip. Ezer told us that Begin was "absolutely euphoric," and that Begin believed the relationship between Israel and the United States had never been better. The Prime Minister had been in such an optimistic mood that he spoke of his new vision of a confederation between Israel and Jordan. Ezer was almost in a state of shock on hearing Begin come out with such a—for him—novel idea, and managed to say that it sounded a bit too visionary.

The next morning Ezer and I had a farewell breakfast in his suite. He advised me to maintain a low profile "because people are gunning for you because of what you have accomplished." He trusted that a team as good as ours would continue to work as well as before. He was in a mellow mood, pondering how much work was left to finish now that the treaty had been signed. "You know, three to four years as Defense Minister are enough. I would like next to be Finance Minister. It's a great challenge, although admittedly I know little right now about the intricacies of economics or the inflationary spiral. But I do know that I could learn, and I could bring in the right people with the right kind of expertise. I know how to make decisions and that's the name of the game." Our conversation was interrupted by the arrival of friends, and we bade farewell for the time being. "Until the next crisis," he said, bubbling with laughter. Something about the way he said it and his manner confirmed my suspicion that his outburst at the Lipshutz home had been premeditated.

The Door Swings Wide

As the months passed the President's great effort toward peace in the Middle East appeared to be breaking down. Some of his political adversaries, such as John Connolly, who was then a Republican Presidential candidate, even warned that if the Camp David agreement should falter, "it might raise a big question mark over Carter's capacity to govern."

I admired the President and had a warm personal feeling for him. I wondered about the contrast between the deep loyalties he could arouse and his seeming inability to convert that talent for friendship to political clout among members of Congress.

Bob and I kept the back door open as details of the peace process were worked out. But as summer sauntered in, we found that the back door could be used also as an exit to freedom.

The door to another year: At a birthday party for Leon Charney in Israel

...in conversation with Ezer Weizman

...being greeted by Yitzhak Modai

...with his mother, about to cut the cake, as Ezer Weizman takes a turn at the microphone

...Yitzhak Rabin and wife, Leah, offer birthday greetings.

13

The Shcharansky Episode

It was late spring of 1979 when Ezer received at his office Avital Shcharansky. She had come to enlist his help in rescuing her husband, Anatoly Shcharansky, from his incarceration in a Soviet prison. After hearing her plea, Ezer suggested that I might be able to help. I had had much experience, particularly in the 1970's, with trying to obtain exit visas for Russian Jews. This and my White House connections made Ezer think I might be able to help the woman. I was in Israel on business at the time, so Ezer phoned me at my hotel and asked me to the Ministry to meet Mrs. Shcharansky. I agreed immediately to come and listen to her story. The newspapers had been full of the "refusenik's" case and of his wife's brave campaign on his behalf.

Both Ezer and I found the encounter with Mrs. Shcharansky to be a haunting experience. Her husband had come to symbolize the struggle of Soviet Jewry for its basic human right to assert its ancient heritage. Anatoly Shcharansky and thousands of other Soviet Jewish activists suffering for their

161

faith were demonstrably living proof that prison bars cannot contain an overwhelming ideal.

The renaissance of the Jewish national movement in Soviet Russia is one of that series of revivals that has miraculously appeared in cycles after near-annihilation and oppression throughout the millennia of Jewish history. The re-emergence of Soviet Jewry as a vital force in recent years has been a source of marvel. Apparently, the subterranean reservoir of spiritual energy began to flow to the surface in the wake of the birth of the State of Israel. The historical turning point was undoubtedly symbolized by a marvelous photograph of Golda Meir as Israel's first Ambassador to the U.S.S.R., standing almost engulfed by a silent crowd of Jews outside the Great Synagogue of Moscow. It is said that Stalin, at that point, resolved to crush what he regarded as a dangerous outpouring of sentiment alien to the Soviet system. In the post-Stalin era there have been mysterious fluctuations in the official attitude toward the Soviet Jewish minority. From time to time the gates of the Iron Curtain open to release some Jews, only to shut again without any cause. Some observers put it down to the vagaries of the Soviet bureaucracy. Others see it as a reflection of United States-Soviet relations, and indeed, many more Jews were let out of Russia during the Carter Administration than in prior years or subsequent years.

The shocking story of young Shcharansky's incarceration by the K.G.B. for the sin of seeking to join his people in Israel is well known. The major reason for the case's notoriety is the heinous nature of the charges of treason that were originally leveled against him. The K.G.B. tried to blacken the entire Jewish dissident movement with the stain of spying for "American imperialism." It thereby hoped that Jews would revert once more to a state of being a cowed, voiceless, and hopeless minority that would lose its collective will to survive as an entity.

Anatoly Shcharansky's tremendously impressive courage in facing up to the Soviet system had affected me when I read about it. But hearing the story from the lips of his young wife brought home to me in an entirely different way the magnificence of the human spirit in resisting tyranny. When Ezer introduced her to me, he explained that I was his personal lawyer, an American Jew who had the ear of President Carter. He was most enthusiastic about her case and expressed the hope—in her presence—that my connection would be of help to her. I assured her that I would do all in my power to help, but said that I did not wish to raise hopes in her heart. Again, when she called on me at my hotel, accompanied by a white-bearded rabbinical advisor, I promised her I would do what I could, but I stressed that I did not wish to arouse unrealistic expectations. We concluded that we would keep in touch, and if I had any news I would call her. After she left, I prayed that I might be able to contribute toward relieving the agony of this devoted young wife and her loved one who languished in a Soviet prison so far, far away from her.

Fulfilling a Promise

The anguished eyes of Avital Shcharansky stayed with me for a long time, and on my return home I began to seek ways to fulfill my promise to try to help. An opportunity soon presented itself through my friend, Phyllis Schmertz. She immediately offered to use her contacts with the Soviet Consulate in New York. For Russian diplomats, many of whom no doubt worked for the K.G.B., socializing with smart society women like Phyllis no doubt is a major charm of being posted to New York. She told me on occasion how fascinating it was for her to study the reactions of Russian envoys to the sophisticated Manhattan entertainment spots. She had befriended, in particular, Soviet Consul-General Y.L. Mishkov, who always behaved in a most civilized manner. Once he even asked her to show the sights of the city to V.M. Plechko, at the time one of Gromyko's three deputies. Plechko's reaction to the 21 Club rather amused her. She was not sure whether his avid response indicated disdain or envy of what he whimsically called "capitalist consumerism." Her instincts told her that he was not impervious to the charms of the place.

Phyllis once even made an attempt at private diplomacy by endeavoring, at my prompting, to get the Russian envoy to dine together with her and my dear friend, General Uri Ben-Ari, when he was Israeli Consul-General in New York. However, the Soviet Consul-General advised her that such an encounter, as private as it might be, could not be, considering current circumstances. He did not elaborate.

I urged Phyllis to arrange a meeting with Mishkov, who certainly could lead us to a solid contact with the Soviet Embassy in Washington, if not to Ambassador Dobrynin himself. (I had met Dobrynin on several occasions.) My opportunity came at a huge party held at the Metropolitan Museum of Art. It was quite a setting for a party, almost like a scene from a movie, with the wondrous exhibits of the museum providing a remarkable backdrop. The introduction to Mishkov was made on the huge staircase, cleverly lit up for the festive occasion. The Soviet Consul-General was a smooth well-tailored character, unlike most of the Soviet officials I had met during my mission to Moscow in the 1970's. I explained that I wished to speak to a high-ranking Soviet representative at the Embassy about the Shcharansky case. As impassive as only a Soviet official can be, Mishkov responded with utmost politeness and promised Phyllis and me that he would let us know soon.

We were informed a week later that an appointment had been arranged at the Soviet Embassy in Washington. We were ushered without ceremony into a small, unadorned room and then showed into a large lobby. There were no paintings on the walls, only portraits of Soviet leaders, all looking like replicas of "Big Brother." Eventually, I was called inside to one of the offices, leaving Phyllis outside to cool her heels. As I remember, the official I met was the Number 3 man in the Embassy hierarchy. He heard out my appeal for Shcharansky's release in a courteous manner. To judge by one or two of his remarks he had some knowledge of my connections with the White House. We discussed other matters too, and he promised to convey to Moscow my request regarding Shcharansky's release and left with a promise that I would hear from them in the near future. (Regrettably nothing materialized from this meeting.)

I took a cab to the White House to see Bob. I told him of my meeting with Mrs. Shcharansky and asked his help. Once more he revealed his deep humanitarian traits. What I had hoped was to enlist the power of the President himself in Shcharansky's behalf.

It was decided that I should deliver my message "in person" via the "scrambler" to Camp David where the President was staying. The secure line was in the Situation Room in the basement. It was a most impressive place, with a remarkable array of electronic equipment. There was an aura of the 21st century about that room, a sure inspiration for science-fiction movies. I delivered my message for the President to the appropriate quarters and returned upstairs. Bob also introduced me to Marshall Bremen, the Russian-affairs expert of the National Security Council, who kindly gave me more than an hour of his time to brief me on the situation in the Soviet Union.

Not even President Carter could pry Shcharansky from the Soviet grip. Other voices had joined mine in asking the President to try to get Shcharansky freed, and during the Vienna summit conference in June, the President urged Brezhnev to release Shcharansky and other dissidents. Brezhnev replied that "Shcharansky had been tried and convicted in a Soviet court of law." He added that he was bound to support his country's laws, leaving little hope for any action, even at the request of the President of the United States. Secretary of State Vance also brought up the human rights issue, including the Shcharansky case, during a meeting with Gromyko, but he, too, had no success.

Toward autumn relations between the two countries grew colder, as the Soviet presence in Cuba in early September caused a mini-crisis. This had died down only somewhat when the Russians invaded Afghanistan at Christmas time. Carter was forced to retaliate with economic sanctions.

Thus, although the Shcharansky matter had the attention

of the highest authority in this country, it remained unresolved. It is particularly unfortunate that President Carter's efforts on behalf of Shcharansky were not widely known. It is possible that if Jews had been more cognizant of Carter's acts of mercy, they might not have allowed the misdeeds of his brother, Billy, to blind them to his support for such important causes.

14

Conversations with Kreisky

Throughout this time, I was frequently in contact with Mrs. Shcharansky and did my utmost to cheer her, advising her that the matter was really being dealt with at the highest level. As part of my efforts I resolved to try to meet with Austrian Chancellor Bruno Kreisky, who was known for his excellent connections in the Kremlin. He had done much to help Soviet Jews and had provided them with a halfway stop in Vienna on their departure from the Soviet Union for Israel or the United States. So I phoned the Austrian Embassy in Tel Aviv and asked for the Cultural and Press Attaché, Barbara Taufer. I had become friendly with Barbara during my frequent visits to Israel and would often meet her in the company of our many mutual friends. She combined beauty and intelligence and was well connected. From conversing with her, I knew that she had access into Kreisky's Chancellery and knew Karl Kahana, whom I had met the previous summer in Jerusalem.

I explained to Barbara that I would like to arrange an appointment with Chancellor Kreisky at his convenience, and I could fly to Austria at a moment's notice. She was extremely helpful and efficient and returned my call in a matter of days. She advised me that an appointment had been arranged with her country's leader. She was going home on holiday and would meet me in Vienna.

I informed Bob of my travel plans and told him to inform the President about the purpose of my meeting with Kreisky. Bob soon called back and said he had done this. Carter had asked him to convey his best wishes for the success of my mission. Bob also reported that my scheme enjoyed the President's unreserved approval. As a personal footnote, the President had asked him to give me the following message: "A blessing on your head. Go with my blessing." This was a line from a song in the musical *Fiddler on the Roof*, one of the President's favorite shows.

I arranged my flight to Vienna. I did so with mixed feelings because of the associations that ancient city has for any Jew today. In its heyday as the capital of the Austro-Hungarian Empire, and even after World War I, it had been a cosmopolitan cultural center serving as home for some of the greatest Jewish names in science and the arts. Freud, Mahler, Schnitzler, and Werfel were only a few of the celebrated Jews associated with that city. Then came the *Anschluss* in 1938; the Austrians gave Hitler and his troops a delirious welcome and treated their Jewish fellow-citizens more cruelly than their brethren in Berlin had done some five years earlier.

It was now Fall of 1979. I was arriving in a city that was largely empty of its once-flourishing Jewish community but, paradoxically, was led by a Government headed by a politician of Jewish birth. I was arriving on a mission of mercy for one of the outstanding spokesmen for the Soviet Jewish National Movement and was going to see a man with strong Kremlin connections who symbolized to the world the assimilated Jew.

Viennese Music

Barbara met me at the airport and drove me to the hotel. That was a foretaste of the warm hospitality extended to me during my stay in Vienna. Later that evening Barbara picked me up to take me to a glittering charity ball and variety show to benefit UNESCO. This was held at the Amder-Wien Theater, one of the oldest and most exquisite theaters in the city. Barbara told me that some of Mozart's operas had had their first performances there.

At the bottom of the huge staircase I was introduced to a very charming woman, a close friend of Barbara's. She was Margit Schmidt, whose official title was Secretary to the Chancellor. In effect she was his *Chef de Cabinet* or, in White House terms, his Chief of Staff. In all, a most powerful lady. I soon found myself seated between the Chancellor's aide and the Austrian Cultural and Press Attaché in Tel Aviv—in the Presidential box. Later, Barbara and Margit had a good laugh on learning that some members of the audience had mistaken me for Chancellor Kreisky. The performers included Joan Collins, Bianca Jagger, and Yossi Yadin, the Israeli actor then playing Tevya in Vienna in the German language version of *Fiddler on the Roof*—the musical from which President Carter had selected a blessing to send me. The evening was great fun and ended with a huge backstage party.

Lunch with Kahana

My meeting with the Chancellor was set for early the next night. This gave me time to meet Karl Kahana for lunch.

Kahana was highly critical of Israel's policies and dwelt on the need for the Israeli leadership to emulate the Chancellor's meeting with Yasir Arafat. He spoke of Arafat as having adopted a policy of moderation because of Kreisky's influence. Kahana did not like what had become of Israeli society, nor did he at all approve of its underlying Zionist ideology. By implication he questioned the essential necessity of even having a Jewish State, arguing, "Jews are accepted throughout the world; look at Kissinger, look at Kreisky, look at Mendes-France."

It was apparent that the millionaire liked flexing his political muscle on his home territory. I was given to understand that he enjoyed considerable influence with the Chancellor.

He stressed Kreisky's admiration for Jimmy Carter, quoting him as praising the President for being "very human and very sincere." He spoke ominously of the prospects for another war between Israel and Syria, which could well suck the Russians in and thus spark off World War III. He tempered this apocalyptic forecast by speaking of the "inevitable establishment" of a Palestinian state, not necessarily headed by Arafat. Kahana launched into a personal assessment of Israeli politicians. He disliked Begin, downplayed Weizman, and predicted with absolute confidence that "Moshe Dayan will become Israel's next Prime Minister by establishing a dialogue with the Palestinians."

The Chancellor Speaks

Promptly at 6:30 p.m. on September 6, Barbara brought me to the antechamber of the Chancellor's office, where Margit greeted us. I thought it remarkable that the Austrians had managed to maintain the original facades of their historical buildings while converting the interiors to contemporary usage. Kreisky's office was housed in the imposing *Ballhausplatz*, one of the many baroque palaces abounding in the Austrian capital. Barbara had explained to me that the palace had been constructed by the Empress Maria-Theresa, and a previous occupant had been Metternich. The two men probably would have enjoyed each other's company.

Kreisky's Chancellery was beautifully appointed. The doors and walls were painted in gold-and-white lacquer, and hung with excellent paintings and thick, luxurious drapes. His working room was furnished with leather sofas and chairs. The place reflected a person who enjoyed the good things in life and liked his environment to be as comfortable as possible.

A huge telephone setup dominated his desktop. I learned subsequently that it afforded him direct and immediate connections to each of his Ministers. It was said that he enjoyed keeping them on their toes. They would never know exactly when he might call, demanding immediate action on a certain matter.

The Chancellor was extremely affable to me; he treated me as an equal from the moment we met. He was in an extremely relaxed mood, and like all good talkers was happy to find a good listener. He spoke openly and frankly with me, touching on a wide range of subjects. For me, it was truly a fascinating experience to listen to a world statesman of his stature speak his mind.

He was aware of the purpose of my visit to Vienna, having been briefed by Barbara and Margit. He revealed a real measure of compassion when the issue of Shcharansky and other incarcerated Soviet Jews came up. He said to me, "Do tell Mrs. Shcharansky that I have tried my best for her." It appeared that she had already turned to him, and two years earlier he had written a letter to the Soviet authorities about her husband's case. The Chancellor then produced the letter so that I could tell Mrs. Shcharansky that I had seen that he had, indeed, carried out his promise to intervene on her behalf.

Then and there he picked up his phone and asked to be directly connected with the Kremlin. "There's someone I'll try to talk to, whom I haven't bothered on such matters for quite a while," he remarked. But the person he had planned to speak to was not available. He then spoke for a time of his friendship with Kosygin who, he advised me, admired Henry Kissinger for the way Kissinger had managed to bludgeon Golda Meir into stopping the fighting in 1973.

Cautioning me that the human rights issue carried much less weight in Moscow than in Carter's Washington, the Austrian Chancellor pondered aloud on what might be the best reason for the Russians to let Shcharansky out. Talking about his active lobbying for the PLO and Yasir Arafat, Kreisky declared triumphantly, "Now *that* might be a first-class political reason for the Russians, tying in an Arafat visit with the release of Shcharansky. It might even help to improve Arafat's image with the Israeli press...." Before I had time to properly digest the impact of his idea, Kreisky returned to the issue of helping Soviet Jews, and mentioned in particular the sad plight of "refusenik" Ida Nudel, which he had tried to alleviate and of the Stern family, which he had helped emigrate to Israel.

Talking of Israeli politicians, he sneered at Begin, "That *shtetl* lawyer, he'll never change." (He then added, "That's Sadat's trouble, he can't read people properly....") Weizman? "I've heard good things about him, although I've never met him personally. I see him as the hope of Israel." While expressing his general approval of Moshe Dayan ("He's on the right track"), Kreisky was generally critical of the Israeli approach to the West Bank. "It's no use Jews talking to Jews about how best to solve the West Bank issue. They must talk to Arabs, and arrange a meeting where everything is put on the table for negotiation." Kreisky spoke angrily about Israeli Labor leader Shimon Peres, accusing him of having "betrayed me by supporting Begin against me." He was incensed that Peres had not extended him backing in the Socialist International when he had headed its Middle East subcommittee. He decried Peres as "not being sufficiently courageous on the Palestinian issue."

Kreisky continued in his relaxed mood and had some interesting things to say of the Russians: "You know the Soviet leaders do not like to be in a position they cannot control. Well, they're not in control of things in the Middle East. They do respect the Israelis, and especially their military capabilities. But don't think they're all that fond of the Arabs. They don't care that much for Arafat either, because he is bourgeois and does not toe the Communist line."

Kreisky wished that the Americans, in particular, would appreciate Austria's Middle East policy as a necessary function of its struggle for survival. "The Middle East will be the starting point of the next cold war, and that will hurt us here. You know, if the Russians decide they have to protect Syria, they won't stop there but will move in elsewhere. That means they could march back again into Austria as well. People should realize that the price of oil is not really affected by the events in the Middle East. Not at all. That's another reason why it is so urgent to bring peace to the Middle East, for then the threat of oil being used as a weapon will disappear."

He leaned back in his chair and returned to one of his favorite subjects, Yasir Arafat. "I planned my meeting very carefully with him, and that included the timing as well." He boasted, "I have created a world leader out of Arafat. After all, if Kreisky can put himself out to receive Arafat, why shouldn't the others?"

He spoke of Arafat admiringly, "You know, he could easily have become an oil millionaire like all the others in Saudi Arabia." I never got around to asking the Austrian Social Democratic leader about the speculation concerning Arafat's extensive personal fortune in numbered Swiss bank accounts. I suppose he would not have told me if I had asked. It would have marred the magnanimous image he was projecting of the man who, in Israel and throughout the United States, was regarded as a mass murderer and an arch-terrorist.

"Arafat would recognize Israel, of that I am convinced. But the question is what kind of Israel would he have to deal with?" the Chancellor continued, always putting the onus on the Israelis, never on Arafat and his supporters, to make the right moves. He was deadly serious when affirming, "Believe me, Arafat is a true moderate. After all, the Palestinians are bankers, lawyers, and qualified men throughout the Arab world. They have no interest in destroying Israel. The United States should know that an independent Palestine would serve as a buffer state and not interfere with Israel." He wished to assure me that Arafat was in control of the Palestinian mainstream, adding, "The Palestinian radicals were angry with me because I received Sadat. After all, how could I not welcome him even if he did sign the Camp David agreement? It would only have served the Israelis." Talking of other Middle Eastern leaders, the Chancellor dwelt on his good relations with Syrian President Assad, and then on Saudi Arabia and Kuwait, which, he claimed, needed Palestinians to build up their countries.

"Hussein? Hussein is finished," he declared with a grimace.

"Not that I don't like him personally, but I'm convinced that the days of the Hashemite dynasty are numbered.... After all, Bedouins can't build a country. He's in a minority in his country, so it's unrealistic for him to think he can succeed. Now, if the Palestinians should join with Jordan, there would be the greatest power in the Middle East!" That sentence was delivered with a marveling tone in his voice.

Pursuing another tack, Kreisky wanted Washington to know that the Arabs would accept "a really attractive autonomous arrangement" on the West Bank if it included their own flag, their own passport, and other symbols of autonomy.

We talked of the mediation efforts in the Middle East of Romanian President Ceausescu, with Kreisky declaring the Romanian Communist leader to be "not serious," adding, "He can't be a true mediator because he lacks the necessary vision for it." Talking of Middle East mediators, the Chancellor wanted it to be known in Washington that he had a low opinion of Presidential envoy Robert Strauss. "Surely your President can't be serious about sending such an amateur to such a complicated area," he said. He then offered his unsolicited advice to the President, "Ignore the pro-Israeli lobby, and you'll be elected anyway."

There was a lull in our conversation as refreshments were served. I ventured to ask him *the* question that I had wanted to put all evening. It came out rather bluntly, "Are you Jewish?" The speedy reply: "I'm of Jewish extraction but I'm first and foremost an Austrian." He spoke of his interest in Judaism from its historical and cultural aspects. He felt that the ideology of assimilation, which had been fostered by his mentors in the Austrian Social Democratic movement, had proved workable. In another connection, he spoke of how the ultra-Orthodox—I think they were disciples of one of the ultra-Hassidic sects—had thanked him for encouraging Russian Jews to go to Israel.

In the course of conversation, he asked about my background, and I told him about my yeshiva training and religious upbringing. When I wondered about the phenomenon of a Chancellor of Austria being of Jewish extraction, he smiled benevolently and proceeded to give me a short lecture on "how to secure one's political base first and foremost."

The reasons for his political success had been full employment, a low inflation rate (about 3.9% per annum), and always tending to his Party people. Apart from which the National Bank of Austria was full of dollars, so the population was satisfied with the Government and the Chancellor. Before we parted, he returned compulsively to the issue of Arafat and the PLO, as if straining to get important points across to both Washington and Jerusalem. "The Americans are wrong in keeping their meetings with the PLO at a low level. They are meaningless, and if a move is not made now, it may be found that time has run out." On the other hand, he stressed, "Arafat has human feelings toward the Israeli people. He can be negotiated with, and should be properly recognized."

An Assessment

As I emerged into the outer office, I saw one of the secretaries gazing at me wonderingly. I looked at my watch. It was 9 p.m. My meeting with the leader of Austria, scheduled to last 45 minutes, had taken two-and-a-half hours. I hurried to the Cafe Imperial, where Barbara had been waiting for me with friends for a pre-dinner drink. She was all agog at the length of time the meeting with the Chancellor had lasted. "What did you talk about?" she kept asking again and again, but I fobbed her off with vague phrases. Her excitement was shared by the others at the table, who included the well-known Austrian Jewish author Friedrich Torberg and his companion, Marietta, another good friend of the Chancellor's.

Late that night I called Bob at the White House and gave him a digest of my fascinating conversation with the Chancellor. I also passed on to Washington Kreisky's view that Robert Strauss should not be let loose on the Middle East at the moment. I advised Bob that I was proceeding to Israel, where I would be seeing my friends and where I intended to pass on the information that Kreisky had conveyed to me on the Arab attitude toward the autonomy scheme. I thought that that was one of the most immediately productive elements of our long conversation.

Later it dawned on me that Kreisky, having been apprised of my connections with the United States President and the Israeli Defense Minister, might have decided to utilize me as a vehicle to expound his theories to both sides. My personal impression of Chancellor Kreisky was of a man possessing fine humanitarian qualities. He sincerely and genuinely believed that what he was advocating was for the benefit, not only of Austria, but of world peace. However, on the Palestinian issue, he was biased, unrealistic, and had a closed mind. He really did not understand the true situation, perhaps because of his background and his geographic location. One cannot comprehend the complex facts of Middle East problems without firsthand knowledge. Kreisky's inviting world leaders to his Chancellery and studying large maps with them did not make him an expert on this issue. Unfortunately, at times, it made him look rather foolish, and he suffered great embarrassment.

I found him a fascinating and complex character, a man of intelligence and a political leader with a clear desire to leave his imprint on the world. He sought to use Austria's neutral position to bring East and West together. I had the impression that he was bored, and sought to play a role on the world stage.

Obviously, I disagreed with his views on the Middle East. But one should not forget that he is a man who at times has had insight into world affairs. Moreover, no one, especially a Jew, should forget the tremendous opportunity he offered to emigrating Soviet Jews through the transit facilities he put at their disposal in Austria. Who knows how many of these people might still be languishing behind the Iron Curtain if not for the efforts of the Austrian leader. Though no longer part of the Jewish community, he still practices the ancestral tenets of our faith.

Auf Wiedersehen

I did not know it as my plane took off from Vienna for Tel Aviv Friday morning but the back-door channel would bring me back to Austria within three months...on an entirely different mission. But for now, I was anxious to impart my conversation with Kreisky to Ezer.

After we were airborne, I was pleased to find Friedrich Torberg on the same flight. He proved to be a delightful traveling companion. He was en route to Jerusalem as the guest of Mayor Teddy Kollek's Jerusalem Foundation. He was thrilled at the prospect of staying at the *Mishkenot Sha'ananim* residential quarters. Facing onto the Citadel of David and the Old City Wall of Jerusalem, the Jerusalem Foundation has provided writers and artists with congenial accommodations for their stays in the Holy City.

I hired a car at Ben-Gurion Airport and drove immediately to Ezer's office in the Tel Aviv Kirya. Although it was a Friday afternoon, he was working late. I recapitulated as concisely as I could my conversation with Kreisky, arguing that these were rather powerful words from the Chancellor of Austria and should be reviewed. There and then Ezer picked up the phone and called Begin at home. He said, "Mr. Prime Minister, Leon Charney, who you know, has just come from an interesting conversation with Kreisky." Begin cut their telephone call short. He was totally uninterested in anything that Kreisky had to say. The Austrian's low opinion of the Israeli Prime Minister was fully known to the latter. Yet, as Ezer noted, "So they dislike each other, but Kreisky's the head of an important country, and our Prime Minister should listen to what he has to say." Ezer was boiling mad and lamented, "You see what we have to deal with." He was peeved at Begin's attitude in this and other instances, feeling that a Prime Minister should not permit himself to indulge his personal feelings about the heads of other nations. A political leader must undergo a certain transformation on achieving power, he went on, and personal feelings in such matters are luxuries that a head of government cannot afford. Kreisky was not precisely Ezer's model for anything, but he occupied a fairly influential position in the world and should be dealt with accordingly. Ezer felt that the Austrian's connections in the Soviet bloc and the Arab world might be useful at some juncture, and he should not be dismissed so lightly. In the cold world of *realpolitik*, sentiment regrettably did not play much of a part, as the masters of statesmanship have preached over the years, whether they be Metternich, Talleyrand, or Kissinger.

15

Negotiating the Channel

The subject of leadership and statesmanship occupied Ezer's mind during our journey across the Atlantic the following week. I mentioned to Ezer having spoken earlier in the year to the genial Finance Minister, Simha Ehrlich, who had complained bitterly to a group seated with him in the Knesset cafeteria that "the Likud appears to lack the culture of government."

Ezer was proud of the key role he had played in the Likud's successful election campaign that had brought it to power in 1977 after decades in the political wilderness. He and others in his family had long felt the need to move away from the outdated socialist concepts that had dominated the Labor regime. But he was disappointed in the way that the fundamentalists in Begin's circle sought to pull the ship of state away from the course of peace, as if the years of siege and imminent war were preferable.

179

All around us passengers slept; at such a time a man speaks from the depth of his heart. Ezer spoke of his political future and made no secret of his desire to become Prime Minister. After all, politics are about power and politicians are men seeking power. At home he was in a paradoxical situation, finding himself forced to cope with young demonstrators of the "Peace Now" movement. Many of these were Army reservists serving in the elite combat units—in short, his kind of people. The demonstrators felt that the Government was not moving as fast as it could to clinch the peace process. Ezer felt their overzealousness might be misinterpreted in other countries as a sign of internal wavering and could weaken Israel's bargaining position.

Begin's fundamentalist colleagues, in seeking to undermine Ezer's position as heir-apparent (which he most decidedly was as long as he stayed in office), would point to him as a "Peace Now" patron. They implied that he was somehow associated with the slogans chanted by the demonstrators, such as, "Peace is better than a Greater Israel." For, if anyone was identified with the cause of peace in the Begin Cabinet, it was Ezer Weizman.

Even if Ezer was critical of the way the Prime Minister was allowing things to proceed, he remained loyal to him. This was especially true when it came to foreign critics of Menachem Begin. Ezer was quick to remind them that Begin was the democratically elected leader of the State of Israel. I wonder how much the Prime Minister and his circle appreciated the measure of that loyalty? Whenever an official in the United States Administration would fume about the need to replace Begin, Ezer would reprove the person in the strongest terms, telling him or her that such talk could be misconstrued as seeking to intervene in the internal political affairs of another country. He was less than happy at the way that both President Sadat and President Carter appeared to cultivate the Israeli opposition leaders and went out of their way to receive Labor Party Chairman Shimon Peres. He saw those gestures as aimed at undermining the legitimate government of the country.

During our flight to the United States, Ezer reiterated how much he liked Jimmy Carter, yet he had misgivings. He had heard reports that Carter's people were trying to pressure Israel in order to achieve some headline-catching foreign policy goals, even at Israel's expense, to bolster the President's sagging ratings in the popularity polls. Ezer had told his Egyptian friends that attacks on Begin would be only counterproductive; as for the Americans, he once told the top men at the Unites States Embassy in Tel Aviv if the United States thought it could get places by twisting Israel's arm, then the Americans better think again. The message he flashed to Washington via official channels was that the Carter Administration should not seek an easy victory at Israel's expense.

It was fun riding once more in an official motorcade from JFK to Ezer's Park Avenue hotel. The next morning, Ezer informed me that he planned to visit my office. "You hang around my work place so much, I want to see where you spend your working days," was how he put it. His decision set in motion a high-powered security operation, and soon a gaggle of security men descended on my building in downtown New York. My neighbors were probably mystified by the sudden activity that beset our office building, and not a little discomfited by the security men "confiscating" one of the elevators for the duration of the Israeli Minister's social call.

It was a beautiful Fall day, and Ezer, stealing two hours from official duties, enjoyed himself like a young schoolboy playing truant. He has been described as "humanity bursting through protocol." That lack of stuffiness and pomposity probably is what makes him so attractive to the general public. He admired the panoramic view from my office window. The seasonal colors gave a special quality to Battery Park. Watching the seacraft plying the waters of the Hudson River proved very relaxing for both of us, as we followed the boats circling around the Statue of Liberty and Ellis Island or heading for the shores of New Jersey or Staten Island.

The break was good for Ezer. I recall another time when he lowered the tension level by going off on a social excursion.

During one particularly trying period of negotiations with the Administration in Washington, Ezer decided he needed a mental break and asked to meet Herman Wouk, the author whose writings both of us admired. It turned out that the writer was delighted to host the Israeli Defense Minister at his lovely home in Georgetown. Wouk sat in his robe like a *rebbe*, and he and Ezer discussed military tactics. I recall I even displayed my cantorial talents at Ezer's urging, much to our host's pleasure. Wouk spoke with pride of the fact that his son had gone to live in Israel and was at the time serving in the Israeli Navy. He laughed when Ezer expressed the pious hope that no *Caine Mutiny* situation would occur in the Israeli Navy. Later that year, I bought Ezer a present on the birth of his grandson—a copy of Wouk's *The Winds of War*.

Sharks in the Potomac?

The next day, I flew with Ezer to Washington. His mind was on his forthcoming meeting with Defense Secretary Harold Brown, and on the matters to be discussed—especially whether the United States would permit Israel Aviation Industries (I.A.I.) to sell warplanes to Taiwan. At Ezer's request I met the Israel Aviation Industries people, including Gabi Gador, and their representative in Washington, Marvin Klemow. We met at the Madison Hotel, and Klemow explained to me some of the problems encountered in obtaining official American permission to promote the sale of Israeli planes to places like Taiwan. United States permission was essential because major components of the planes were made in this country. I soon learned the intricacies of the international arms trade, and how the powerful Washington lobbyists of the big military-industry complex shaped United States Government attitudes toward such arms sales to prevent competition.

I rode in Ezer's motorcade from the airport to Washington, and managed to alight near the White House, while the others proceeded on to the hotel. I went straight to Bob's office and told him Ezer's wish to see the President in person. I had

hinted at this by phone before leaving Israel. Then an unforeseen hitch arose. The President could receive Ezer only at the
same time as the Israeli Minister was scheduled to meet at the
Pentagon with Harold Brown. It took a while, but a suitable
arrangement was worked out.

An undercurrent of tenseness still pervaded Ezer's relations
with the Israeli Embassy people. His informal access to the
President did not endear him to the Embassy diplomats, nor
did it make them like either Bob or myself. After all, it only
highlighted the limitations of their operation, for the Embassy
had to observe the rules and regulations of protocol strictly,
especially where meetings with leaders of the Administration
were concerned. They had to go through official channels. But
Ezer demonstrated he had his own way of cutting through
bureaucratic red tape. The same applied to the President,
which made those involved less than popular with the Embassy
bureaucrats *and* the Foreign Service. I had encountered a
similar frostiness in the American Embassy in Tel Aviv. I was
the outsider and trespasser, so to speak.

A Chill in the Air

The slightest autumn chill was starting to tinge the Washington weather during that trip. It was the week just before the
White House celebration of the first anniversary of the Camp
David accord, and relations between Jerusalem and Washington were not at their best. Weizman aired the tension in a
highly public manner that set the American capital buzzing.
A loud row erupted between him and Harold Saunders during
a reception given for Ezer by a visibly shaken Israeli Ambassador Evron. All the guests, including the working press, witnessed the bitter exchange sparked by Saunders' reproving
remark to Weizman that "Lebanon might turn out to be
Israel's Vietnam unless you cease your pre-emptive strikes."
Weizman was stung by the rebuke, especially as Saunders had
blamed him personally for the tough Israeli policy. Ezer
retorted in a rising voice, "You should talk. America is losing

its credibility after failing to respond decisively to what has been done to you in Iran—not to mention Cuban provocations in Latin America, Angola, and elsewhere." Evron tried to stop the much-too-public confrontation but was rebuffed by Weizman. I just stood off to the side fascinated by what was happening. It was like being a spectator at a drama. Ezer told Saunders in a harsh tone, "Look here, Washington is the last place to offer us advice on how to deal with our security.... I can tell you this, and listen carefully, the present lull in reprisals into Lebanon will end the moment any PLO terrorist act is perpetrated."

16

A Shift to the PLO?

Shortly after Carter had appointed Robert Strauss his chief representative in the Middle East negotiations in the Spring of 1979, he tried to pass the day-to-day responsibility of Middle East affairs to Strauss, with Harold Saunders as his expert advisor. Notwithstanding Strauss' appointment, most insiders in Washington continued to regard the dominant influence of the Administration's Middle East policy-making as being Saunders, the soft-spoken but assertive Assistant Secretary of State. They also held that Strauss, a novice in the region's problems, was totally influenced by Saunders and that this was reflected in his public and private statements. As far back as 1975 it was Saunders who had testified before the House Foreign Affairs Subcommittee on the Middle East, presenting a pro-Palestinian formulation of American policy toward the region. Saunders had caused an uproar in Israel after meeting with West Bank Arabs at the United States Consulate in East Jerusalem, where he reportedly promised

185

them an independent state plus control of East Jerusalem. Here he was seen as cleaving to the Brookings Institution report's recommendations, which through Dr. Brzezinski were thought to have colored much of the thinking of the Administration in its earlier stages. Various Israeli diplomats reacted differently to Saunders. Reportedly, Simha Dinitz, then Israeli Ambassador, had told Dr. Kissinger that he regarded Saunders as anti-Israel. However, his successor, Ephriam Evron, developed a good working relationship with the Assistant Secretary of State, and found him knowledgeable of Israel's security needs.

Strauss the Mediator

I had a few meetings with Robert Strauss during his spell as United States mediator. The first was in Bob Lipshutz's office in the Spring of 1979, just after the Strauss appointment. Bob filled Strauss in on the workings of the "back-door channel" and Strauss expressed eagerness for our help and counsel. I had met him peripherally during my days as counsel to Senator Hartke and we had mutual acquaintances in New York.

During his first meeting with Bob and me, Strauss was very cordial and told us something of his life and his humble beginnings. He regaled us with anecdotes from his days as an FBI agent, an unusual occupation for a Jew in those early years. However, it was already apparent from that meeting that he preferred to use us as a sounding board for his own ideas rather than heed any advice that either Bob or I might offer.

I warned Strauss of the many difficulties he could expect. Moreover, I advised him, he should know that in Menachem Begin he would be encountering an extremely formidable personality who would be totally different from any American politician he had dealt with. Strauss treated the matter rather airily, and at one point declared, "So what's the difference between a Texas Democrat and Begin?" To which I rejoined, "The difference is 5,000 years deep."

Varying Mediation Methods

Strauss was a direct, straight-shooting Texan. These are traits not easily understood by many Middle-Eastern minds. Throughout all the months the back-door channel was in operation, I used to seek a compromise between the Israeli and American positions and convey them via Bob to the President. The attitude of "all or nothing at all" that seemed to grip some of Begin's closest comrades was abhorrent to my approach to life. I tried to propose interim *ad hoc* arrangements that could be codified and written down as points of agreement. I tried to tell people like Bob and Strauss, "Problems that have already lasted for 2,000 years cannot be solved overnight. If you try to aim at 'quickie' solutions, they're going to backfire and you're in danger of having the whole structure collapse on top of you." My attitude was to adopt a process of elimination and to formalize ideas, thereby creating the parameters of what would hopefully be eventual agreement. Abrasha Tamir and I would sit for hours tossing about various ideas, playing intellectual ping-pong. We were pragmatic, very much against perfectionism. I knew from Washington what the American position was; I learned from Abrasha—who was on the Israeli military team negotiating with the Egyptians—of the Egyptian position and of the Arab point of view. In this matter he was scrupulously honest in his intellectual perceptions, managing to separate them from his natural feelings as an Israeli.

As much as I enjoyed talking to Abrasha, I did my best to talk to lots of other people at various levels of the Israeli political spectrum: people in the Prime Minister's circle, Modai in the Likud, Ezer naturally, and also top Labor people—particularly Chaim Barlev and often Yitzhak Rabin. I also endeavored to get a sense of what the Israelis could take in concessions by discussing things with knowledgeable newspaper editors I knew and respected, like Hanna Semer, Dov Yudkovsky, Ari Rath, Gershom Schocken, and Moshe Zak.

I followed a technique I have always followed in my approach to my profession—not to rush matters, adopting a piece-by-piece approach. In this case, I concurred with Abrasha that a gradualist approach to the negotiations was the only way that people on both sides could become accustomed to the actual existence of peace, so they could adjust to its very idea after all those years of war. I thought it advisable to put off the tough, knotty issues like Jerusalem until the climate had become more amenable to peace. Yet the question that was begging was how Begin's Likud people could really and truthfully say they favored the autonomy scheme and still continue their settlement expansion policy. Another trouble, as Abrasha put it, was that too many people on the Israeli side were trying to give advice. As an illustration he quoted the story about the Captain of the famous illegal immigration ship, *Exodus*, who nearly gave up after he found himself saddled with 200 competing Captains. That brought me to comment, "Abrasha, you say that because you are a military man, used to working with a clear hierarchy of command. Politics and diplomacy don't work that simply."

During trips to Israel that spring and early summer I encountered echoes of Strauss' method of work. There was talk from Government circles and the Labor opposition about the Texas tactics that Strauss was employing. Back in Washington in late June I met Strauss in his office, together with Bob. He said the President had told him he had a mandate to do as he pleased "and to feel his way around." I asked him, "What is your long-term aim?" He responded vaguely, "I want to keep the kind of level of momentum going to the point that will keep people happy."

He concurred with us that he should adopt a low-key approach and do his best to create as much cordiality with Begin as possible. He informed us that his Arab contacts were quite pleased with Washington's hard line toward Begin; it made them feel stronger. I told him I thought he had an unequaled opportunity to forge a new link. Strauss replied that *now* he realized how little he knew about the Middle East. He stressed the President's insistence on pushing the peace process. I observed that, according to my sources, neither Egypt nor Israel were at that point overwhelmingly interested in rushing things, each for its own reason.

In mid-August Bob, Ed Sanders (the Presidential liaison with the Jewish community), and I had a final meeting with Strauss. It ended in clear disagreement. Strauss claimed to be striving to comprehend Begin's approach and the Israeli viewpoint. Just because the Israelis would not cease their settlement expansion, he had to seek an alternative solution. He was looking to the United Nations to produce some kind of compromise. Strauss also asserted that because of the Israeli Government's economic difficulties, Begin would endeavor to switch the people's attention away from domestic issues to the overall Middle East. He showed me a letter from Begin wherein the Israeli leader stated his position on maintaining the settlement drive in Judea and Samaria.

Reflections from Strauss

Talking of the various Israeli Ministers, he dismissed Dr. Yosef Burg, the Interior Minister, whom Begin had put in charge of the autonomy talks, as "lacking any real power." As for Justice Minister Shmuel Tamir, Strauss thought him a canny politician—perhaps he reminded him of someone back in Texas. Talking of Agriculture Minister Ariel Sharon, the General who was the settlement czar, Strauss called him an impetuous man, possessing an extremely volatile temperament. "But that does not stop me from finding him charming," he added.

Referring to his meetings with the Saudis and the Jordanians, Strauss declared that the former wanted a decisive say in the future of Jerusalem. Here he added, "Nobody really cares what happens to the Palestinians." Reflecting on the Administration's position, Strauss said that everything must be done to bring the Saudis into the peace process. But at this juncture he revealed that from his recent visit to Amman he had learned that Jordan did not want to include them. He then went on to outline his intention of adopting a highly critical position toward Israel on his next trip to the Middle East. I felt that Strauss thought that Israeli intransigence was a main obstacle.

At this point, I told him it might be preferable that he not go to the Middle East, because he would manage only to rupture the delicate web of trust that had been built up between the two capitals despite the tensions threatening to disrupt the entire process. Later that day I called Tel Aviv and told Ezer of Strauss's feelings and of the general tenor of his approach. He, in turn, conveyed my information to Yehiel Kadishai for Begin's ears.

Actually, I remember once asking Strauss for his help. The Israeli Airline, El Al, had been suffering from steeply rising costs of fuel. Ezer had suggested to the airline president, Mordechai Ben-Ari, that I might be able to help get a fuel price closer to that paid by other airlines at New York's JFK Airport. As far as I remember, The El Al fuel bill was then a crippling $18 million a year; other airlines paid much less. Ben-Ari approached me, and the gist of his appeal was that I should seek to use my political connections with the Department of Energy. I emphasized to him that I would do what I could for the sake of Ezer and for the State of Israel, and certainly not for any remuneration. At the same time I suggested that in return he might do something for me. "What do you want?" he asked in a prickly tone. "I think that perhaps you might improve the quality of the food and the cabin service," I said with a smile. "It's a deal," he rejoined with a laugh, shaking my hand.

I pointed out to Strauss that such a favor might be something that could be used in the negotiating process. In the end, I think it was Bob Lipshutz who in his quiet way recommended through channels that something be done for El Al to improve United States-Israeli ties.

Fiasco at the United Nations

Carter was forced to take back the reins of the Middle East negotiations from Strauss that summer. The United States Ambassador to the United Nations, Andrew Young, who was serving as President of the United Nations Security Council, met in his official residence with the United Nations representative of the PLO. Young informed the Israeli Ambassador to the United Nations of the fact, and the issue exploded across the nation's front pages and TV screens. Israel's supporters in America argued that the Carter Administration was undermining the Ford Administration's commitment never to negotiate with the terrorist organization. Throughout the Jewish community the feeling began to grow that Young, Carter's long-time ally from Atlanta, was betraying the Administration's goal and moving toward recognition of the PLO. At the State Department, diplomats claimed that Young had stepped beyond the parameters of official policy and should have kept Washington properly informed. Young's next step was to resign, which in turn prompted a furor among black leaders, some of whom unjustly blamed the Jewish community for causing the removal from office of one of their most prominent leaders. The noisy ramifications of this incident reflected once more the emotionally charged nature of anything to do with the Arab-Israeli dispute.

A Shift Back to Peace

Whenever I visited Israel, I used to spend long hours with Abrasha Tamir in his office near that of Ezer, questioning him at length on the nature of the problems involved in the autonomy scheme for the West Bank. This is the section on the west bank of the Jordan River that was won by the Israelis in the 1967 Six Day War.

The problem was how best to get things moving and to frame proposals that would work and be acceptable to the parties concerned. The underlying view was to reach an agreement on what it was possible to agree on. As the months elapsed I saw Dayan and Ezer, the Ministers most committed to peace, becoming increasingly isolated in the Cabinet, as Begin gradually succumbed to the extremists' influence. The result, of course, was that both these outstanding men were maneuvered out of the Government.

As early as mid-May 1979 I was conveying ideas on an autonomy scheme via the back-door channel. Three months later I authored a step-by-step proposal to keep the autonomy process in motion. Thus Bob recorded the following for May 18, 1979:

Three Elements of West Bank Autonomy:
People—Likud proposal
Land—Labor proposal
Water—?

—Essential prerequisite is "time."
—Assuming Jordan does not come in now, Egypt could enter into a "fig leaf," an approach as a stand-by solution... i.e., requiring the consent (for implementation) of Jordan and the Palestinians (along with Israel and Egypt).
—Elections in Israel will be in Spring of 1981.

Re: U.S., E.W. continues to urge U.S. not to take initiative or aggressive role at this time.

Then again, on June 19, 1979:

—E.W. wants to get off the (autonomy negotiating) Committee. He is unhappy with the way things are going along.
—Uncertain about Washington's position. E.W. will try to be helpful to Bob Strauss.

On August 8, 1979, my notes contain:

—Spoke with Ed Sanders.

—Lunch tomorrow with Dick Veits (he is leaving for Tanzania as Ambassador in September). I'm convinced that I have ideas that will work. Please inform President and Bob Strauss. Need a couple of more days. Returning Wed. or Thurs. E.W. concurs. I've seen Barlev also. Believe Pres. Carter and RJL will concur.

Stick to Camp David letter. Note also side letter. Optimistic, although was pessimistic when arrived in Israel. Begin invited E.W. to visit him at his home tomorrow.

On August 9, 1979, I noted:

Had lunch with Veits. Made arrangements to use red phone. May return Tuesday. Told him of the "plan."

Also I told E.W. that the President had volunteered the remark about "I doubt that we could have worked out the peace treaty without this channel of communication."

On August 12th, 1979, Bob wrote down:

—Bob Strauss coming earlier than planned...leaving at noon Thursday...back in Wash. noon Tuesday...(Begin and Sadat both asked him to come earlier.)

—Am working on a whole presentation.

—Begin specifically said that he wanted Strauss to see E.W.

—Leon arriving N.Y. Tuesday a.m.

On August 20, 1979:

E.W. will be here within the next two to three weeks.
"...it is time for some creative quiet diplomatic initiative..."
E.W. to Leon C.

I then submitted my eight-page proposal with a preamble to the President. As it turned out Bob Lipshutz and his wife, Betty, were spending the weekend at Camp David with the Carters. So, after I talked by phone with Bob, he ordered the telex operators in the White House communication center to transmit the proposal to him. Once the material had moved over the line, he handed it to the President for his weekend reading, with a handwritten covering letter.

CAMP DAVID
August 24, 1979

To: The President
From: Bob Lipshutz
Re: Middle East Autonomy negotiations

Attached is an outline of a proposal for handling this matter which has been transmitted to me by Leon Charney.*
Leon recently returned from a trip to Israel. His ideas, as they have in the past, represent the thinking of...ideas which presumably would be supported by both Israel and Egypt.

---

* See Appendix.

Autonomy Proposal in Summary

Briefly this memorandum proposes the following:

In order to keep the momentum of the autonomy process, the parties that have said authority as of today, namely, Egypt, Israel, and the United States, break up the five-year transitional autonomy period into two different periods.

1. Three-year temporary transitional autonomy period.
2. Subsequent two-year period to conduct intensive negotiations for all aspects of a viable autonomy plan.

All of this may be accomplished under the Camp David framework. However, the real result would be that we defer the hard and unresolvable issues to the future and at the same time resolve those issues which are capable of solution immediately. This avoids a breakdown in the autonomy process. This could defer the Palestinian question to the two-year period. This allows for time and space so that the parties involved can acclimate themselves to living in peace rather than in a state of war.

Leon H. Charney
August 22, 1979

17

Carter and the Jews

It was a mindless demonstration of ignorance and bad manners. It happened at a testimonial dinner in the course of my response to good friends and well-wishers, such as Bob Lipshutz and former Mayor Beame. The dinner, given in my honor, was held at the Waldorf-Astoria Hotel in mid-June of 1980, sponsored by the Youth Towns of Israel. This group is aligned with the Herut Party in Israel. At that time its Honorary Chairman was Prime Minister Menachem Begin. In my address, I dwelt at length on President Carter's tremendous help to Israel and his assistance to Jews in distress elsewhere. Ezer Weizman had left Israel's Defense Ministry the previous month. I quoted him, telling of his deep appreciation of Carter's active concern for Israel's security needs. Suddenly a section of the audience started shouting and hooting "Down with Carter" and "Carter is anti-Israel." Someone even walked out of the room in protest.

Knowing Menachem Begin as well as I do, I am sure that he would have strongly disapproved of the misguided conduct of his followers and would have firmly rebuked them. After all, despite disagreements, the three principal Israeli participants in the peace negotiations—Prime Minister Begin, Defense Minister Weizman, and the late Foreign Minister, Moshe Dayan—had all praised publicly, and at length, the signal role played by President Carter in achieving peace for Israel.

In those days Bob Lipshutz and I belonged to a minority of the American Jewish community who recognized Carter's true worth to Israel and to the Jews. But time has passed, and I sense that a re-evaluation of the Carter presidency has begun.

I think it would help in that re-evaluation to pause here and review precisely what is fact and what is myth, media myopia, or malice about Carter's record on support of the Jews and Israel.

There were fears and often prejudices in the Jewish community even before Jimmy Carter entered the White House. It is to be regretted that these apprehensions were fed in May 1976 by a scurrilous story spread by a former Carter speech writer. He accused Carter of having said, " 'Scoop' Jackson has all the Jews; I won't get over 4 percent of the Jewish vote anyway, so forget it." This nasty charge was swiftly refuted by Stuart Eizenstat, one of Carter's numerous Jewish aides. Jewish leaders in Atlanta quickly pointed out how well-liked the former Governor of Georgia had been in their community—the largest in the South. Some of their most prominent sons and daughters had been involved in the Carter campaign and later would join his staff in Washington, D.C.

Most of the fears of American Jews were based on misconceptions as to how Carter's Southern Baptist religion would affect his Presidency. At the time, an early Carter supporter, Morris B. Abram, former president of Brandeis University, resolved that, as a native of Georgia and a Jew, he should explain to the American Jewish community that they need not fear having a Southern Baptist in the White House. He wrote, *inter alia*, in *The New York Times*, "I understand the suspicions that many Northern liberals have of Southern Baptists.

They are like the suspicions of the Southern Protestant toward the Catholic...as will all generalizations, this one falls apart under scrutiny...I do not claim that Jimmy Carter knows all the nuances of American pluralism. But on his record, and knowing him, I believe he wants to learn. Nothing that has happened in the months of his Presidential campaign has changed my mind."

Carter was sensitive to the problem raised by his religion. On June 6, 1976, he tackled the issue in reply to a question put at a meeting in a New Jersey synagogue. He said that his religion should not concern the U.S. Jewish community, and pointed to the fact that the late Harry Truman, also a Southern Baptist, was President when the United States took the lead in recognizing the newly born State of Israel.

There were many prominent Jews who were persuaded that Carter's strong sense of religion might prove beneficial for Israel. They felt that he, like Truman, would support the Jewish State because of convictions stemming from the Bible, rather than because of political expediency. Carter was quoted as declaring that "as a Christian [he believed that] the establishment of Israel was the carrying out of the Almighty's purpose and the fulfillment of Biblical prophecy." Eizenstat went on record in stating, "Carter's religious beliefs are that Israel was ordained as a Jewish state in the Bible."

According to the Gospel

Quite early in his presidency, Jimmy Carter conducted a Bible study class during which the role of the Jewish people in the Crucifixion of Christ was discussed. A number of reports appeared in the press on his comments, which aroused wide attention from Jews and Christians alike. The President then chose to reply at length to a letter from one of Washington's distinguished Protestant churchmen, the Reverend John F. Steinbruck, Pastor of the Luther Place Memorial Church— and Reverend Steinbruck responded in turn.

The President's letter from the White House, sent on May 12, 1977, contained the first such exposition of views on the subject from an incumbent Chief Executive. The President expressed his gratitude at the opportunity afforded him to "clarify any misunderstandings" arising from incomplete accounts of his convictions. He wrote, "The Christian religion, according to my understanding, holds that Jesus of Nazareth, who was a Jew, gave his life to redeem the sins of humanity. The Gospels declare that His death was foreordained, and without that death and the Resurrection which followed it, Christians would not be saved in Christ. Yet the Crucifixion required human instruments. Among these were Judas, who was a Christian disciple, Caiaphas, a Jewish priest appointed by the Roman authorities, and Pilate, a gentile, who actually condemned Jesus to death."

Carter continued that "in accordance with the Gospels, I know that Jesus forgave the human instruments of His death, but I am also aware that the Jewish people were for many centuries falsely charged with collective responsibility for the death of Jesus and were persecuted terribly for that unjust accusation, which has been exploited as a basis and rationalization of anti-Semitism."

He went on to write, "I know and am personally gratified by the fact that the highest authorities of the major Christian churches—Protestant, Roman Catholic, and Greek Orthodox—have totally and decisively rejected the charge that the Jewish people as a whole were then or are now responsible for the death of Christ. My own denomination, the Southern Baptist Convention, adopted an official resolution on June 7, 1972, declaring anti-Semitism as un-Christian and...[declaring that it was] opposed to any and all forms of it. Further, the Baptist Churches have resolved that 'we covenant to work positively to replace all anti-Semitic bias in the Christian attitude and practices with love for Jews, who along with all other men, are equally beloved of God.' " Carter then concluded with the personal observation, "To that, I can only say 'Amen' with all my heart!"

Reverend Steinbruck, in reply, wrote that "...there is no

question that the authority of your office as President of the United States, combined with our respect for you as a committed Christian, will make this response an historic repudiation of the 'Christ-killer' canard that has so long and so unjustly been the burden of the Jewish people, our older sisters and brothers. Furthermore, your action will create a new basis for the embrace and reconciliation of the whole family of Abraham after 1900 years of estrangement."

The Reverend further related that he had been involved in discussions with Christian leaders and heads of the American Jewish Committee. He noted, "They share with me the profound appreciation of this moment in which you have made a compassionate, just, and constructive contribution to destroy the poisonous roots of anti-Semitism and prejudice. Both my Jewish and Christian friends perceive the sensitive healing action you have taken."

Subsequently this correspondence produced a comment in a letter to Bob Lipshutz from Rabbi Marc Tanenbaum, then National Director of Interreligious Affairs for the American Jewish Committee, wherein the President's rejection of the "Christ-killer" charge and its derivative anti-Semitism was regarded as an historic development. Rabbi Tanenbaum wrote, "To my knowledge, this is the first time in the history of the American Presidency that a President has made such an explicit declaration on the classic religious roots of anti-Jewish prejudice...and will be so acknowledged in both religious and secular history books of the future." He thanked the Counsel to the President for his role in having made possible the issuance of the Presidential statement.

An Equitable Attitude

Bob, who has been associated with Jimmy Carter for many years, told me that, unlike many politicians, Carter has always had an equitable attitude toward Jews. Bob remarked that while he thought some former national leaders might prefer not to have dealings with too many Jews, most people at the top make a point of having some Jews around for the impression it makes. "But for Jimmy Carter, as far as having Jews around him that kind of reason did not exist." I think a good illustration might be found in the anecdote told at the time by another Jewish aide of Carter's, Gerry Rafshoon, the Presidential media counselor. He was illustrating the fact that Carter never paid attention to the religious identity of his aides. When Rafshoon told Carter that he was getting a divorce, the then Governor of Georgia retorted, "That's not a Christian thing to do." "But Governor, I'm not a Christian," Rafshoon answered. Although they had worked together for years, Carter apparently did not know that Rafshoon was Jewish!

It was Rafshoon who had remarked to me jocularly, on Air Force One in late October 1980, "We can make almost a *minyan* from the number of Jews on board." His reference to the mandatory ten adult male Jews required for communal worship was illustrative of the fact that Carter included quite a number of Jews on his staff. Indeed, his inner circle from the early years of his campaigning in Georgia included such prominent members of the Atlanta Jewish community as Bob Lipshutz, Stuart Eizenstat, and Gerry Rafshoon. They were among his instinctive choices for the senior White House staff, including Anne Wexler, one of his closest aides who had, previously, been very active in Connecticut Democratic politics. One of his senior Ministers, Defense Secretary Harold Brown, is of Jewish origin. Carter chose for his Secretary of Commerce, World Jewish Congress President Philip Klutznick, and for his Secretary of Transportation, Neil Goldschmidt. In addition, there were a number of Jewish staffers in the White House.

Bob Lipshutz also related that, when it came to appointing judges to Federal courts, Carter appointed more women and members of minority communities than had Presidents before him. "Because it was not necessary for him to consider 'I have to have Jews and Catholics,' the results were that more Jews were appointed to the Federal bench than hitherto.... There was only one case [where], because of problems in a certain state, we had to take specific action to bring a Jew onto a bench," Bob reported. (What Bob did not mention was the fact that when he left the White House, he turned down Carter's offer to nominate him to either the U.S. Circuit Court of Appeals in the District of Columbia or to an expected vacancy on the Fifth Circuit Court of Appeals in Atlanta. Bob chose to return to his private law practice, but the offer certainly indicates the President's high appraisal of his legal qualifications.)

As Carter's attorney, Bob Lipshutz, before, during, and after his White House days, has attested to the former President's consistent and immediate response to Jewish needs. In addition, there was his tremendous assistance to Israel. The Carter presidency's record, in this context, includes aid to Israel for the resettlement of Soviet Jews and the first serious effort to deport Nazi war criminals who had managed to filter into the United States. Moreover, President Carter went out of his way to alleviate the lot of Iranian Jewish students at American colleges during the crisis with the Khomeini regime, when restrictions were imposed on Iranian nationals living in this country. At Carter's initiative Iranian Jewish students were allowed to stay here without having to claim political asylum, which might have caused hardships on their families back in Iran. Bob disclosed to me that the President gave a verbal order in this connection to top officials of the Justice and Immigration departments.

Bob also recounted that, when the Khomeini regime's terror mounted and a number of prominent Iranian Jews were sentenced to be executed for "serving the Zionist Satan," Carter personally interceded on their behalf. Ed Sanders, then the Presidential liaison assistant for the Jewish community, raised the urgent issue with the President. Relations between Washington and Teheran were so bad that Carter could not approach the Iranian authorities directly. But he telephoned the Pope and President Giscard d'Estaing to ask them to intercede with the Ayatollah to end the persecution of the Jewish community of Iran and, above all, to end the summary executions of Jewish leaders. I, and others, believe that had that kind of humanitarianism been more widely known, Carter's re-election campaign might have been successful. His natural humility made him underplay his good deeds.

The Fight for Soviet Jewry

President Carter insisted on morality in international relations. He devoted much of his attention to protecting human rights throughout the world. He saw the struggle of Soviet Jewry within this context, and argued forcefully with the Russians on this matter.

He tried his best to intercede for Soviet Jewish activists languishing in Russian jails. In some cases he succeeded—for instance, with Eduard Kuznetsov and Mark Dymshitz, who were part of a spy-swap deal. And the President endeavored to plead personally with the late Soviet leader, Leonid Brezhnev, for Anatoly Shcharansky. He even gave his blessing to my efforts to ask Austrian Chancellor Bruno Kreisky to appeal to the Kremlin. Unfortunately, none of these intercessions produced concrete results.

Not widely known is the extent to which the President went out of his way to succor the hundreds of Soviet Jews stuck in a transit camp in Italy, waiting for their immigration papers to be processed for entry into the United States. On hearing of their desolate situation, he gave orders to Attorney General Griffin Bell to expedite official procedures. It should not be forgotten that over half the Soviet Jews who managed to leave the U.S.S.R. under his Presidency were allowed into this country. In addition, the Carter Administration inaugurated a program to provide $20 million in assistance to them.

Many of my fellow American Jews choose to forget the concrete outcome of many Carter policies. During his administration there was considerable improvement in Jewish emigration figures from the U.S.S.R. In 1976, the number was 14,261; in 1977, 16,736; in 1978, 28,864; and in 1979, 51,320. In 1980, after the Afghanistan invasion and the ensuing rise of world tension, the number dropped back to 21,471. Yet, as Carter himself remarked in an interview in my presence, although more than 50,000 Soviet Jews got out during one year of his Administration, only a meagre 2,400 managed to leave during one year of Ronald Reagan's Administration.

Holocaust

Further, Jimmy Carter was the first President to recognize that the trauma of the Holocaust—which will be a stain on all mankind for eternity—had never been properly remembered in this country. It was on his initiative that the President's Commission on the Holocaust was established in 1978, beginning the effort which is now culiminating in the designing and building of a suitable American memorial to the victims.

'No' to the Boycott

Another aspect of the Carter Administration is largely ignored—namely, its firm opposition to the Arab boycott of Jewish businessmen. The Nixon and Ford Administrations had refused to confront the Arabs on the boycott because of fears of further economic reprisals. Stu Eizenstat was actively involved in drafting appropriate legislation to put the U.S. on record against the boycott, and he skillfully brought it to enactment with the fullest backing of the President.

The boycott first became front-page news in the United States in 1974 when Kuwaiti pressure succeeded in barring three prominent European banking houses with Jewish directors from Eurobond underwriting syndicates. Further disclosures soon emerged—the Army Corps of Engineers was not recruiting Jews to work in Saudi Arabia, American banks had refused to open branches in Israel, and some American firms were "laundering" their letterheads to omit Jewish names.

Three major national Jewish organizations—the American Jewish Congress, the American Jewish Committee, and B'nai B'rith's Anti-Defamation League—responded swiftly and effectively. They also garnered powerful support in Congress through the years. But it can be argued that if Jimmy Carter had not been President, the legislation opposing the boycott would not have been enacted in the form it was. It is of significant interest to note that, so far, *the* major violator of this piece of legislation has been Bechtel, a California-based multinational corporation that has provided some of the senior members of the Reagan Administration.

Incidentally, Carter was not only following his concept of fairness, he was also honoring an election commitment. He promised during the 1976 campaign: "As President, I will not permit international bribery. This includes yielding to boycotts against our own domestic corporations because they have Jewish citizens in executive positions. I will seek legislation to make it illegal for companies to yield to any boycott of this nature...."

Koch and Carter

New York's Mayor Ed Koch rekindled old charges of Carter's supposed lack of support for Jews when he alleged in his book that Carter planned to "sell out" Israel if he had been re-elected in 1980. Koch's revelation of a luncheon meeting with former Secretary of State Cyrus Vance, during which he quotes Vance as concurring with Koch's "sellout of Israel" theory, has not been well-received by Vance's friends and admirers. We have no reason to doubt the veracity of the Mayor, but the Vance followers are puzzled at this apparent departure from Vance's typical style. Although the current Mayor of New York may not be aware of the fact, it seems that he is using his own inimitable style and manner in an attempt to regain the New York Jewish community support that he lost during his campaign for Governor of the State of New York. His memories and recapitulation of his relationship with Carter are quite severe. Although they may seem true to the Mayor, obviously they are his own subjective perceptions. His Honor, as a citizen and a Jew, has every right to speak his mind on any subject, including his feelings about the Jews and Carter. However, I am sure he is wrong about the facts, and in view of his high profile, it would seem prudent for the Mayor to be a bit more cautious before making inflammatory remarks—which could well have the effect of polarizing the American Jewish community. As a lawyer, I defend Koch's Constitutional right to speak on any subject. But as a citizen of New York, I would be happier if he used his public relations flair and know-how to fill the city's potholes, improve its sanitation and its public transport.

As a Jew, what does concern me is Koch's lack of sensitivity to the true record of Jimmy Carter regarding Israel and the Jewish people. I am certain that Jimmy Carter does not possess even a scintilla of anti-Semitism in his bones, nor has he ever been anti-Israel.

Many people in Israel whom I have met, whose sons died in the defense of their country, will tell you in no uncertain terms that Jimmy Carter was the best American President ever, as far as Israel was concerned.

I would like to point out to Mayor Koch and like-minded people that the greatest tribute to President Carter is that since the Camp David peace treaty was signed, the sands of Sinai have ceased to be reddened with the blood of young men. For the people of Israel, peace has meant the saving of thousands of young lives, and for that, I am convinced, President Jimmy Carter will surely be remembered in the annals of Jewish history.

Koch, in a way, is following in the footsteps of a Republican Senator who, in seeking to sway Jewish votes to his party, told the May 1978 annual dinner of the American Israel Public Affairs Committee (AIPAC) that "the Carter Administration is following the pattern of tyrants and demagogues in blaming its problems on the Jews." On that occasion, Bob Lipshutz, who represented the President, took the rostrum to counter these charges. The Republican's assertion that "the President's National Security Adviser advocates that this nation disengage from its historic alliance with Israel" was denounced by Bob as a falsehood and a grave disservice to the United States, to the State of Israel, and to the cause of peace. That the Republican Senator was dead wrong, the history of

the Carter years proved. Six months after this speech, the
Camp David summit took place, and the peace treaty signing
ceremony was held the following March on the South Lawn of
of the White House.

I think it worthwhile to quote an article written for B'nai
B'rith's *The National Jewish Monthly* by Senator Frank Lautenberg, a former UJA chairman, explaining, during the
Democratic 1980 election campaign, why he was supporting
Jimmy Carter. He wrote, "On those issues of interest and
importance to me as an American and as a Jew, Jimmy Carter's record is a strong one.... Nowhere in the multitude of
tasks President Carter has undertaken is his personal commitment to peace and human rights more evident than in an
area of vital concern to all of us: peace and security for the
State of Israel." Mentioning the "great personal and political
risk" taken by Carter in convening the Camp David summit,
Lautenberg noted how the President's "personal involvement
and courage brought about one of the most substantial foreign
policy achievements of any recent administration." Lautenberg also noted that Carter "has provided more military and
economic aid to Israel than any President before him." Lautenberg pointed out that, under Carter, Israel received more
than $10 billion in aid, more than twice the amount that went
to Egypt, which received the most aid of any Arab nation. A
record 30 to 35 percent of all American bilateral aid went to
Israel, despite budgetary pressures to make cuts.

Thus, under President Carter, Israel received about half of
all the aid it ever received from America. Moreover, Carter
approved the sale to Israel of some of the most advanced
military equipment used by American forces: F-15 and F-16
aircraft, AIM 9L missiles, and M-60 A3 tanks, making Israel
that much more militarily secure against a potential aggressor.

Against the unsubstantiated charges of Ed Koch one should
balance the praise meted out by Israel's top leaders to the 39th
President of the United States. Prime Minister Menachem
Begin lauded Carter's outstanding support for the Jewish
State. The late Moshe Dayan declared, "President Carter has
done more and gone further than any former President in

order to bring peace between us and the Arabs, not only involving himself at Camp David, but also becoming a real partner." Ezer Weizman also felt very strongly about Jimmy Carter's historic contribution toward the strengthening of the Jewish State. On three occasions while visiting the United States, he aired his views at the risk of being accused of getting involved in American politics. Weizman's aide, General Avraham Tamir, who also served as Israel's National Security Advisor to six Defense Ministers, and who was one of the inner-circle advisors at Camp David, stated that, if not for Carter's intense persistence, the peace agreements would not have come into being. More recently, while working in Washington on his upcoming book, *The Strategic Aims of Israel*, General Tamir told me, "I am convinced that, were Jimmy Carter to have been re-elected for another four-year term, he would have found a solution to the Palestinian problem and achieved a comprehensive peace settlement for the Middle East."

Right or Reputation?

In my opinion the Carter Administration's most serious mistake, responsible for alienating many Jewish voters, was the American vote at the U.N. Security Council in the spring of 1980 calling for the dismantling of settlements and the return of parts of Jerusalem to the Arabs. Although Ambassador McHenry's vote remains indefensible, this should not blur the overwhelmingly positive nature of the overall Carter record on Israel. Indeed, in Carter's memoirs he explained his bewilderment at the turn of events, and I see no reason to doubt the veracity of his version. It would appear that he was double-crossed somewhere down the line in the State Department and in the United States delegation to the United Nations. But the damage had been done, and it cost Carter the pivotal New York and Connecticut Democratic primaries against Senator Kennedy. That in turn affected the outcome of the Presidential campaign, because Carter overextended his energy combating Kennedy before the real contest with Ronald Reagan.

Then there was the rumor spread by Republican and Democratic opponents that Carter planned, if re-elected, to recognize the PLO in his second term. The facts speak otherwise. Carter's PLO stand is perhaps the strongest defense of his support of the Jews. At the height of the election campaign, Carter turned down an opportunity to recognize the PLO in exchange for assistance in freeing the hostages in Iran. I personally can attest to this: The offer was made to the White House when Bob Lipshutz—as the President's unofficial envoy—and I flew to Vienna to sound out Austrian Chancellor Kreisky at the height of the hostage crisis. Despite the tremendous political advantage that might have accrued to him, Carter never revealed the "Viennese connection," nor his refusal to legitimize the PLO and reward their terrorist actions under the most tempting of circumstances. Nor did he reveal, publicly, the close ties of the Khomeini regime with the PLO and possibly with the Soviets, because it might have endangered the hostages' lives. Moreover, he never disclosed that an unofficial approach had been made to Israel as to the feasibility of staging an Entebbe-style rescue mission. Nor did he tell the public that the Israelis had concluded that such a mission could not succeed. Once more, in order to protect the hostages' safety from the PLO's Iranian allies, he never revealed these facts to Israel's enemies.

Thus Jimmy Carter rejected an enticing proposal which might have ended the hostage crisis earlier but would have tainted the honor of the American people. Furthermore, he sacrificed his personal political interests by stubbornly rejecting actions that might well have jeopardized the hostages' lives. The historic fact remains that Carter ended the Teheran hostage crisis with clear results—not one American hostage lost his or her life, and the nation's most vital interests were protected.

Another Mayor's View

If Ed Koch's tenure at Gracie Mansion has had strong show-business overtones, the term of former Mayor Abraham Beame will go down in New York's history as a rescue mission from the Administration of John Lindsay. Beame recollected that, after Carter took office, he was invited down to Sea Island, Georgia—along with Governor Carey of New York—where they had a serious discussion of New York's problems with members of the Cabinet. The former Mayor remembers seeing Rosalynn Carter and Joan Mondale in the kitchen preparing lunch with their own hands. He spoke of Carter as "a very considerate man, who was regrettably not as outgoing as he might have been." Beame thought this was at the root of Carter's subsequent difficulties with Congress. The first Jewish Mayor of New York found it difficult to grasp why any member of the Jewish community should entertain suspicions toward a President who had so many Jews around him.

The Carter View

Despite the torrent of media, and to some extent public, denigration that has tended to dwarf our 39th President's image and positive record, I have always regarded Carter as a great man and a great President. I refuse to condone the label of *provincialism* which the East Coast establishment and the media have pinned on him. For me he remains one of the brightest, most sincere, and most responsive men who has ever been leader of our country. He was swept into the White House by the national demand for a different kind of President, after the stewardship of Richard Nixon. I sincerely believe that Carter will become a folk hero and a legend in due time. Compare what people said about Harry Truman when he was in office to what they say today. Today, Truman is regarded as one of the strongest leaders of recent decades.

I am aware that people like Bob Lipshutz and myself are at odds in our evaluation of Carter with many if not most of our fellow American Jews. But I am convinced that they too will eventually swing round to our viewpoint. After all, we have the facts on our side.

Carter explained how he saw his Administration's relationship with Israel in a letter the President addressed to the late Senator Hubert Humphrey on May 12, 1977, after meeting with the Senator's subcommittee of the Senate Foreign Relations Committee, which was considering putting into law an arms-transfer policy. Carter wrote that Israel had not been placed in the category of NATO nations in his Administration's proposals "simply because we believe it goes without saying that the United States will do everything necessary to ensure Israel's security.... I recognize the special responsibilities the United States has toward Israel in this regard, and the particular consideration that therefore must be given to our military arms and co-production arrangements with Israel.... I have inserted explicit language which acknowledges our special security relationship with Israel.... [I do not wish to] jeopardize the delicate role we have in the Middle East as a firm friend of Israel and yet the honest broker between Israel and the Arabs.... I believe this role is essential in achieving peace in the Middle East."

In his speech to the B'nai B'rith convention in Washington in September 1980, the President declared: "We will stay the course in our commitment to justice and peace and to the security and well-being of Israel.... Ever since President Truman recognized Israel's independence on the very day it was proclaimed, our two nations have had a special relationship, based on a common heritage and a common commitment to ethical and democratic values. It is in the strategic and moral interest of the United States.... I cannot assure you we will always agree with every position taken by the Government of Israel. But whatever differences arise, they will never affect our commitment to a secure Israel. There will be no so-called 'reassessment' of support for Israel in a Carter Administration...."

This brings to mind my conversation in May 1983 with the former President, when we touched on what he termed "the not-all-that-supportive position of the American Jewish community" after Camp David. As he saw it, this was because "we had to address some controversial issues, like withdrawal from Sinai and Palestinian rights...otherwise we could not have completed the peace treaty." He proceeded to say, "I hope and pray that the results will bear up. We did what was right and what was compatible with Israel's rights...we don't want it to be undone...."

All in the Family: The Good Guy...

Carter selected a Vice President whose views on Israel were similar to his own. Mondale, Democratic candidate in the 1984 Presidential campaign, has a record of actively supporting the cause of Jews throughout the world.

I recall that I had a telephone call at my office from Mondale one day, telling me how disturbed he was that Jimmy Carter was not getting a fair break from Jewish constituents, and we thought collectively of ways that we could improve the situation. In the infrastructure of the White House I personally always considered Mondale one of the best friends of Israel and the Jews. I know that Ezer shared my thoughts on the matter, for more than once we had in-depth discussions concerning many members of the Administration, and Mondale always came out high on the list. Moreover, Mondale was always accessible to Bob Lipshutz and me on every Jewish problem. It was my understanding that when Carter got into trouble with the Jewish vote on the U.N. resolution, Mondale, along with Hamilton Jordan, advised him to reverse his decision.

...And the Bad Boy

In Mayor Beame's view—and not only his—the antics of Carter's brother, Billy, are responsible for much of the electoral damage among the Jewish community. And not only among Jews. "He was never able to sufficiently disassociate himself from Billy, his remarks, and his behavior," Beame contended. It boiled down to what one perceptive columnist wrote at the time: "People think Billy says what Jimmy really thinks...."

One fiasco involved Billy's forced registration with the U.S. Justice Department as a foreign agent of the Libyan Government. This followed an 18-month investigation confirming that Billy had received $220,000 from dictator Muammar al-Kaddafi's regime. It badly hurt Jimmy Carter's image. The involvement soon became known as "Billygate," and was blown up out of all proportion by the media.

The White House also came in for sharp media criticism after it was confirmed that on November 29, 1979, Carter's National Security Adviser, Zbigniew Brzezinski, had asked Billy Carter to arrange a meeting with Ali el-Houderi, Libya's chief representative at the United Nations. The meeting was to sound out the possibility of Libyan assistance in securing the release of the hostages. When Billy was criticized for his links with one of the prime centers of international terrorism, he blamed "the Jewish control of the media." In June 1980 the President did his best to repair the damage by telling a nationally televised press conference that it was "a possible instance of bad judgment in his Administration's handling of the affair." He stressed that, "I can't condone what Billy has done."

In December of that year, after he had lost the election and was preparing to leave office, Carter addressed the State of Israel Bond Organization dinner honoring AFL-CIO President Lane Kirkland, also in Washington. He declared, "We Americans care about Israel. We care about its people, but our support...is not just a case of a big nation looking out for a smaller one.... It is, and should be, recognized as a partnership.... Administrations change. Policies are altered. People disagree. Governments have differences. But the values the United States and Israel hold in common must and will endure.... The process we have undertaken, the lesson that has been learned, can be the beginning of a full and lasting peace.... That goal...can be won through negotiations—not through terrorism or a continued state of belligerency...."

He concluded, "I came to the Presidency determined that the security of Israel would never be threatened by another war. I leave office having helped in forging the only recognized and formal peace that Israel has ever known...my commitment to Israel...will remain with me forever."

In February 1983, former President Carter returned to the Middle East. During his visit to Egypt he journeyed up the Nile to view the ancient sites. While touring the Valley of the Kings at Karnak, he suddenly heard the sound of song. It came from a group of Israeli youth singing in Hebrew, "*Heveinu Shalom Aleichem* (We have brought peace with us)." He reportedly told one of the party traveling with him that it was the finest present he had been given for a long time.

As for me, the day after Jimmy Carter lost the Presidential election I decided to go out and console myself by buying Number One Times Square!

We remained in touch after the 1980 Presidential election. Indeed, he appeared to be quite moved when I phoned him on the morning after the results to commiserate and express the unceasing support of one private citizen. During Carter's final days in the White House, I had flown to Carter's hometown of Plains, Georgia. Bob Lipshutz had asked me to find a buyer for the Carter family peanut-farming business. Having found a prospective purchaser in Europe, I ventured into the Deep South to survey the property, talk to the Carters' warehouseman, and even taste the fare served up at the only diner in Plains. (Very plain indeed!) The deal, however, fell through.

In 1982 I had a long conversation with the former leader of the Free World, at his office in the Richard Russell Federal Building in the heart of Atlanta. The aura of statesmanship was still there. (As a former President, Carter was, and still is, briefed regularly by National Security Council officials.)

When talking of the latest news from war-torn Lebanon (midway through the Israeli invasion), Carter intimated his profound unhappiness over the firm encouragement that General Sharon had reputedly obtained from the United States. Carter was still deeply upset by the assassination of President Anwar Sadat, and feared for the fate of the Camp David peace process—the monumental achievement of his Administration. Two of the principal peacemakers were out of the picture—Carter in retirement, Sadat in his untimely grave. We considered Ezer Weizman's likely role, in the coming days, in shoring up the peace process.

It was still a most vital issue, one that Bob and I could have handled well through our back-door channel.

18

A Change in the Communication Line

I was in Israel on September 29 when Bob Lipshutz
informed President Carter that he was resigning. He later told
me it was a combination of political and personal factors that
brought him home. Mostly it was the keen desire of his wife,
Betty, to return to Atlanta. I also think he was too kind and
gentle a soul for the Washington rough-and-tumble. Even
after he was no longer White House Counsel, Bob still
remained Jimmy Carter's private attorney and good friend.
He traveled frequently to Washington, nearly always staying
overnight at the White House. And he insisted that we keep
the back-door channel going. After all, he argued, the President had found our channel distinctly helpful, and Bob still
had the President's ear.

In his letter of resignation, Bob wrote to Carter, "...your
dedicated effort to bring peace in the Middle East between
Arabs and Jews deserves the gratitude of not only Americans,
Egyptians, and Israelis, but also of decent people throughout
the world. I am proud to have been a participant in this noble
and rewarding effort."

The President, in his reply, expressed his confidence that "I can count on you to continue my human rights policy in this country and abroad and our mutual search for a comprehensive peace in the Middle East. Your contributions to these two goals are too valuable for me to lose."

It was only a short time before I again had to use the backdoor channel, but in a newly found way.

Into Lebanon

It must have been the end of autumn, on a Friday at midnight, that Ezer rang me at my apartment from Tel Aviv. He sounded very tired, apparently having been on duty all night at the Ministry. There had been another terrorist incident that demanded an appropriate answer. Ezer wanted me to call the President and inform him that Israel would have no choice but to strike at terrorist bases in Lebanon. He asked me to reassure the President that this was a limited reprisal intended as a deterrent and nothing more. Ezer stressed the absolute urgency of getting that message to the President.

As soon as he hung up I decided to call Bob at his home in Atlanta, despite the late hour. But there was no answer. I tried again the next morning. Still no answer. After another try later that day, I decided to call the President. He had told me to call him directly on any matter that warranted his immediate attention. I dialed the White House number and asked for the President.

I was connected immediately to Camp David and to Phil Wise, Carter's Appointments Secretary. "Ah, it's you, Leon. What's the problem?" he asked. I told him I had to speak to the President as soon as possible. "Is it that important?" he inquired. I said that it wasn't an emergency but that I thought the President would like to hear what I had to tell him. Almost apologetically, Wise answered, "I'm sure the President will want to talk to you, but he's tied up in conference right now. We'll get back to you."

The next evening the phone rang and a brisk voice (it must have been a Marine) demanded, "Sir, are you Mr. Charney, sir?" When I replied in the affirmative, he went on, "The President of the United States would like to talk to you. Will you hang on, please." The next moment I heard the familiar drawl saying, "Pardon me, Leon, I hope I'm not interrupting your dinner." I don't know whether I was standing at attention or not, but I certainly wasn't seated. I quickly answered, "Don't worry about my dinner, Mr. President. There are more important things than dinner." Then I passed on Ezer's message. The President expressed his gratitude at Ezer's consideration. He then proceeded to think aloud about what could be done to expedite the autonomy scheme. I mentioned a few ideas that might be of use. The gist of my concept—that a step-by-step approach might be useful, that what could not be agreed upon immediately be overlooked for the time being— appeared to arouse his interest.

He thanked me for my help to his Administration in furthering the peace process. The President chose to stress the importance of our relationship in his quest for peace in the Middle East. He declared, "You know how much I appreciate your counsel and insights. I know I can count on you in the future as well. Please stay in personal touch with me at all times. I want you to know that you always have a direct line of communication to me." (Indeed, events would have me in touch with him shortly.)

There was something wonderful about hearing the President's words. They implied trust. I felt overwhelmed to be trusted by the President of the United States. Such an honor certainly never occurred to me when I started out on my career in law.

PART TWO
THE OPENING OF DOORS

19

My law career started, I think, because of my tendency to become involved. During the early 1960's, in my second year in law school, a man sitting near me in a movie fell seriously ill. His wife screamed that her husband was having a heart attack. I rushed out and found a physician, but he was hesitant to come to the man's aid for fear of a malpractice suit. The poor man—I never learned his name—succumbed, probably because of the lack of medical attention. I was so upset by the situation that over the next year I began to dig through law books trying to find legal precedents. I then wrote an article for *The Brooklyn Barrister* law journal, entitled "Is There a Doctor in the House?" It was something of a landmark; it was the first time the journal had ever published an undergraduate's paper. I followed this up with another article in the same law publication entitled "The Good Samaritan—A Possible Solution." It set forth a legally acceptable way of enabling doctors to tender emergency aid without fear of lawsuits. The article was read into the proceedings of the New York State Legislature in Albany, where it was incorporated into New York State law, and subsequently adopted by many other

With Mrs. John (Kathy) Ritt (left) and Mrs. Lee (Anna) Strasberg (right).

At the U.S. Senate with Mrs. Vance (Martha) Hartke and Red Buttons, 1975.

LC with Kris Kristofferson and fan, 1976.

states. My contribution to the law journal put me in the lime-light, although at the time I was only 25 years old.

In 1965, out of a job, newly wed, and with the grand total of $200 in my bank account, I opened my own law office in a tiny room off downtown Broadway. My first earnings came from the field of labor law. A friend, having trouble with a union contract, asked me if I was an expert in labor law. "Of course," I said, and then spent the entire weekend poring over three large volumes on the subject. I was lucky. I won my friend's case, and subsequently he recommended me to five other people with similar problems.

If I'd planned to become a special counsel I might have started my law career differently. But as it is I spent the initial phase of my legal career defending comedians against people they had offended. Increasingly, I became engaged in entertainment law and with show business personalities. In 1965, my client, a songwriter, parked his car legally, outside his apartment building, on a Sunday night. Early the next morning, he came downstairs to find that during the night Transit Authority workers had painted a brand new yellow line in front of his car. Because of the yellow line, he was illegally parked at a bus stop; and there was a parking ticket on his windshield. The songwriter, justifiably upset, asked me to fight the case in court. My law books came up with the answer. I filed a demurrer, meaning that the charges as stated were true, but as a matter of law they were insufficient to constitute a crime or offense. The judge had no choice but to dismiss the charge. One of the court clerks told me that it had been 20 years since such a tactic had been used in the court. The fuss I kicked up drew attention. One reporter wrote, "It has been said that the law is never dead, though it often sleeps. Leon Charney likes nothing better than to jolt it awake."

A year later, in 1966, I was instrumental in establishing a legal precedent in entertainment law—in the sphere of Common Law Copyright. A little-known comedian, Lee Tully, asked me to represent him in a case against two British comedians who had stolen and used part of his material on CBS-TV's "Ed Sullivan Show." I brought an action against the comedians, Ed Sullivan, and CBS for the violation of Common Law Copyright, claiming that, like everyone else, a comedian has property rights under Common Law on any material he or she creates. The case was ultimately settled between the litigants. But what was most important was that the court did not uphold the defendants' plea that Tully's claim should be dismissed. This came to be regarded as a landmark case in entertainment law: performers' rights to the material they create is now upheld by the court. As a result of this case, my office phone was busy—other comedians in the same dilemma were seeking my legal services. Academy Award winner Red Buttons and singer John Raitt, star of such Broadway blockbusters as *Carousel* and *Oklahoma!* soon became my clients, as well as many other well-known persons in show business.

Joe Franklin interviewing Joe Louis, Leon Charney and Abe Margolies.

Joe, Sammy, and Frank

One of the most charismatic figures I was ever close to was Joe Louis. As the Heavyweight Boxing Champion of the World he would literally stop traffic and be swamped by crowds of people showering him with adulation. Through Joe I met Sammy Davis, Jr. early in 1969, and since Sammy had converted to Judaism in the mid-1950's I suggested that he visit Israel, tour the Holy Places, and perform for the troops. After arduous negotiations the visit was arranged. When we stepped off the plane, he hugged me, declaring, "Baby, it's great to be in my Motherland!" To which I replied: "Sammy, get it right. It's your converted Fatherland." He was mobbed the moment he disembarked at the Lod Airport, and we had trouble extricating him from the crowds of youngsters who surrounded him everywhere. It was very touching to see how

"Baby, it's great to be in my Motherland."—Sammy Davis at the Wailing Wall.

the young wounded soldiers reacted to him when he visited an army hospital. Davis insisted on a visit to the Western Wall. He had vowed when he converted to Judaism to pray at the Holy Site.

In 1976, the celebrated columnist Earl Wilson authored a book called *Sinatra, An Unauthorized Biography*. The singer sued the columnist through his brilliant attorney, Micky Rudin. I had known Wilson for a number of years. He would call me from time to time for interviews for his columns. When Sinatra decided to sue him Wilson's devoted assistant, Tim Boxer, recommended me as counsel.

The suit took over a year and was one of the most publicized stories of 1977. It was finally settled under terms that by mutual consent remain undisclosed until this day. In the only authorized statement released to the public, Sinatra recognized that Wilson did not intend to injure him and that Wilson was not guilty of any sensationalism in trying to sell his book. I was glad to use my legal talents to help defend Wilson because I found him to be one of the most honest and truthful persons I have ever had dealings with.

Subway to the Senate

My introduction to Senator Hartke came about a few years earlier. In the beginning of 1970 I was still representing entertainment celebrities. One of my clients was a guest on the popular TV show "The Smothers Brothers." Some material relating to President Nixon and the Vietnam War had apparently been found offensive by network executives, and the entertainer had been asked to delete it from his act. We decided to fight this censorship, and the resultant publicity brought me in contact with Senator Vance Hartke. He was head of the subcommittee on communications, which supervised the licensing of the networks. He took an interest in the case and cabled me, "I believe everyone has the right to be heard on TV." He asked to meet me to discuss the case. Hartke came to New York with Jacques Leroy, his long-time Chief of Staff. We dined at the restaurant of a good friend of mine, Abe Margolies, who is also a Broadway producer.

Hartke and I became friendly and met frequently when he flew into New York. Three months later he asked me to become his special counsel in a consultative capacity. I agreed, on condition that I could waive being on the payroll. I felt then as I feel today, that I would never wish to serve in Government full-time in a paid capacity. I preferred to preserve my independence of action and thought.

I found Hartke a fascinating personality—far-seeing, courageous, and intellectually brilliant. An iconoclast who lacked the trick of cultivating the Washington press corps, he was never credited for much of his sterling work in the Senate. He was, somewhat, a political anomaly, a third-term Democratic Senator from Indiana, which is traditionally a Republican stronghold.

In the next six years I flew to Washington twice weekly from my New York law office to serve as the Senator's special counsel and legal advisor. Working with Hartke was an education. He was the second-ranking member of the all-powerful Senate Finance Committee. Through him I acquired an excellent grounding in the intricacies of international trade and finance and valuable insights about the national budget. Also, at Hartke's side, I was introduced to the heady world of the United States Senate. It was quite something, sitting on the balcony of his plush third-floor office in the Old Senate Office Building, enjoying a lavish luncheon with a foreign Ambassador or a major power broker.

Then there were those rides in the Senate "subway" from the Old Building to the Senate floor, where one savored, if vicariously, the aura of power emanating from the assembly of some of the most powerful men in the world.

The Happy Warrior

I am obliged to Hartke for having afforded me the privilege of getting to know the late Vice President, Hubert Humphrey. The moment you entered Humphrey's presence you sensed

that you were in the company of a truly great man. He was a
close friend of Hartke's and served as chairman of the Indiana
Senator's short-lived 1976 campaign for the Democratic nomination for President. I had been a long-time admirer of
Humphrey, revering his humanitarian approach to the world
and, particularly, his constant friendship for the Jewish people and the State of Israel. One recollection of the late Vice
President remains vivid in my memory. We were riding to
National Airport. By then Humphrey was displaying signs of
failing health. Cancer had taken its toll on his body, though
definitely not his spirit. During that ride to the airport, the
former Vice President spoke with serenity of how much at
peace with himself he was at this late phase of his life. He
regretted only that he would be unable to complete so many
tasks he had set for himself. We reminisced about how
Humphrey had almost won the Presidency. He concurred
rather sadly that things might have developed differently for
America if he had won.

The Senator and the Party Secretary

   Through my connection with Hartke I became a frequent
visitor to Indiana, which I crisscrossed campaigning for him.
I made many friends there, finding the residents of the Hoosier State much to my liking, with their down-to-earth approach
and attachment to basic American values.
   The same year I became the Senator's special counsel, 1970,
Hartke went to the Soviet Union, heading an official delegation of seven Senators and their staffs. When he returned
home Hartke regaled us all with stories of that visit. The
purpose of the mission was to improve U.S.-Soviet relations on
all levels, and Hartke, a fervent believer in détente from the
first, hoped that the week-long visit might contribute to that
end. The Senator kept asking his Intourist guides to set up a
meeting with the Party Secretary Leonid Brezhnev, but tour
organizers dodged the issue. However, the group did meet
other Soviet officials, especially those who dealt with com-
mercial relations.

At one dinner party Hartke was sitting next to V.M. Patolichev, who was then Minister of Trade. Patolichev was an
influential Party figure and had been a member of the Central
Committee of the Soviet Communist Party since 1940. During
their dinner conversation, Hartke and other members of the
delegation told Patolichev how disappointed and upset they
were. They had come to pay their respects to the Soviet
Government and enhance Soviet-American relations, yet
their request to meet Brezhnev had been ignored. On the spot,
the Minister asked Hartke, "What's on your schedule at 11
a.m. tomorrow? Why don't you reserve 11 a.m. for a meeting
with the Secretary?"

Early next morning the top Intourist guide rushed up to
Hartke in the dining room where he and his wife were breakfasting and complained in a mortified tone, "You have
insulted me. Now they think I don't know how to run our tour.
Your itinerary has been taken over by the Ministry of Trade."

Promptly at 11 a.m. Hartke and the other seven Senators
and their staffs were led into the meeting room of the Politburo
in the heart of the Kremlin. It was an austere room, dominated
by a huge portrait of Lenin. The U.S. Embassy had provided
an interpreter. Brezhnev greeted them jovially and his good
mood lasted throughout the meeting. On one side of the long
table sat the seven U.S. Senators and their interpreter; on the
other, Brezhnev, Soviet Foreign Minister Gromyko, Patolichev, and some assistants. The Soviet leader opened by
declaring with a smile, "Shouldn't we have something to
drink? But I think it's a bit too early for Scotch." Trays were
brought in bearing glasses and bottles of some unidentified
soft drink. They discussed international affairs and U.S.-
Soviet relations at length. When the issue of Jewish emigration from the U.S.S.R. was raised by one of the Americans,
Hartke remembered Brezhnev replying, "If the Jews have a
legitimate reason for leaving, there'll be no trouble about letting them go. But if the Soviet Union has paid for their education, then they will have to reimburse us." Brezhnev displayed
no signs of knowing English and spoke to the American vis-
itors through the interpreter. Gromyko, who was known to be

fluent in English, preferred to speak in Russian on this occasion, and would often loudly correct the interpreter's translations. Hartke also told us that at one point there ensued an animated argument in Russian between Brezhnev and Gromyko. The former, who was all smiles, gave his permission to the interpreter to translate his subsequent comment to his guests: "Do you see what I have to put up with? I have put up with this man for more than 25 years. And nobody wins in this kind of discussion." This produced general hilarity.

The courtesy visit, which the U.S. Embassy projected would last ten minutes, actually took five-and-a-quarter hours. The Americans were famished, as no food had been offered. Hartke related that they were all standing exchanging farewell pleasantries and getting ready to leave, when he found himself alone next to Brezhnev (aside from the interpreter). He said, "Mr. Secretary, as one politician to another, I want to present to you a very serious problem." Brezhnev looked at the American questioningly, and asked "What is that?". Hartke said, "I have to go to the toilet." That reply produced a roar of laughter from Brezhnev, who took Hartke by the arm and via the interpreter said, "Let's get rid of all these people and I'll take you to a famous toilet." So the senior senator from Indiana found himself using the Politburo urinal together with the leader of the Soviet bloc. As they left, Brezhnev attempted to explain the place's fame. "Do you remember the Great Purges of the 1930s?" Hartke nodded his head. Brezhnev went on, "It was a time when Stalin's primacy was still being challenged and the vote at the Politburo was very close. At one point, Stalin leaned over to one of his chief adversaries and asked, 'Why don't we talk things over by ourselves?' Stalin ushered his rival into this toilet, then took out a gun and shot him on the spot." Brezhnev indicated the spot on the floor. "So," the Soviet leader continued, "Stalin walked back into the Politburo meeting with a satisfied look on his face, gazed around at his comrades, and asked, 'Is there any further discussion?' "

As Hartke said, his immediate reaction was that it was remarkable for the Soviet leader to have told him that story.

He had responded by saying to Brezhnev, "That's a most serious indictment of your political system, Mr. Secretary." At which the Russian leader declared, "Senator, you must remember, our society is really only 50 years old. As I recall from what I know of American history, Andrew Jackson killed 15 people in duels before he became President. The kind of conduct I've told you about is no longer the rule in the Soviet Union." Brezhnev appeared to have taken a liking to Senator Hartke, which he publicly demonstrated when he said farewell to the Senate delegation. This rare personal relationship between the top Soviet leader and the Senator from Indiana was confirmed by the subsequent deferential attitude toward Hartke by the Soviet Embassy in Washington and its Ambassador, Anatoly Dobrynin. Hartke used this direct connection to the Kremlin's inner sanctum to help victims of the Soviet system, and particularly members of its Jewish minority.

On his return from Russia, Hartke and the delegation were invited to report to President Nixon, who had learned of their meeting with Brezhnev.

A famous instance of the Senator's influence with Brezhnev was Hartke's success in persuading the Russians to allow Cardinal Mindszenty to leave years-long self-imposed incarceration in Budapest and travel to Vienna. I was scheduled to go with Hartke and his wife, Martha, to Vienna to call on the Cardinal after he reached there in 1970. At the last minute I was forced to cancel my trip. But in the planning stages, the Cardinal's aide was shocked when he heard that Hartke planned to bring both Martha and myself into the prelate's presence. "He has never received a woman nor a Jew," the aide told the Senator. Hartke hardened. "Well, tell the Cardinal that there is always a first time." The Senator prevailed and the audience was scheduled for all three of us.

On the Senatorial Trail

I found it fascinating to follow the Senator around the diplomatic circuit. Through him I met not only the American

political luminaries of the 1970's, but top foreign diplomats as
well. It was quite an experience to chat with East European
envoys and be introduced to the Kuwaiti Ambassador, the
Sultan of Oman, and other Arab dignitaries. Hartke introduced me to Dobrynin, who impressed me as a rather smooth
character, a really professional diplomat, among the best
posted to Washington. Hartke grew to respect him, speaking
of him as a highly intelligent man, dedicated to his country's
cause. He was persuaded that Dobrynin was devoted to reconciling the animosity between the two super powers. The Senator saw in him an instrument for cohesion rather than div-
isiveness in international life. He did not regard Dobrynin as
an influence in Soviet policy-making, but as a first-class
spokesman of the policy-makers.

Hartke was on good terms with the Embassies of both Israel
and Egypt. Ambassador Yitzhak Rabin would often lunch
with us on the Senator's balcony. In parallel fashion the Senator also developed friendly relationships with Egyptian personalities. At about that time the Israeli Embassy communi-
cated to Jerusalem information on Senator Hartke's special
relationship with Brezhnev, and the fact that his counsel was
a New York Jewish lawyer with a deep commitment to help
Jews everywhere.

An invitation from the Israeli government to visit the Jewish State soon reached the Senator. When he and his wife did
travel to Israel as official guests, in October 1972, they took
along his Chief of Staff, Jacques Leroy, and myself. It was a
very hectic five days. Apparently, the Israelis love to wear out
their official guests.

At one point the Senator was the recipient of a brilliant
dissertation on Israeli policy by then Foreign Minister Abba
Eban, but Eban did not let the U.S. Senator get a word in or
ask any questions. Somehow, Hartke and Eban did not get on.

While in Jerusalem, Hartke received an Honorary Fellow-
ship from the American College. On this occasion I stood as
"proxy" for the Prime Minister of the Netherlands Antilles, a
co-recipient. Actually, although I *did* have a slight knowledge

Somehow, Senator Hartke and Israeli Foreign Minister Abba Eban did not get on.

of the Netherlands Antilles, I had a more direct knowledge of its Prime Minister.

A client and good friend, Robert Parker, and his father, Raymond Parker, president of the Concord Hotel in upstate New York, owned a hotel on the half-French/half-Dutch Netherlands Antilles island of St. Maartens. During a visit to the island, in 1970, I had met Ranjy Isa, a prominent lawyer of Lebanese-Christian extraction, who later became Prime Minister of the Netherland Antilles. He had expressed interest in the region from which his family had originated and I suggested that he might play a role in bringing Israelis and Arabs together. As a start, would he accept an honorary degree from the American College in Jerusalem? Isa was unable to travel to Jerusalem for the occasion and had asked me to receive the honor in his behalf.

Once when I was visiting on St. Maartens, I ran into Senator Edward Brooks of Massachusetts. I knew him from my work with Senator Hartke. Brooks had a vacation home on the island. One night I offered to drive the Senator back to his villa after he'd lost his car keys at my hotel. With my unfamil-

During a visit to the Netherlands Antilles island of St. Maartens in 1970, I met Ranjy Isa, a prominent lawyer of Lebanese-Christian extraction who later became Prime Minister of the Netherlands Antilles.

iarity with the island, rudimentary roads, and no street lighting on a moonless night, I managed to take a wrong turn. Just then I heard a familiar sound above the noise of the engine, causing me instinctively to stop the car. It was the crash of waves breaking on the shore! We were about four yards from the sea! So I turned to my distinguished passenger and said, "It seems to me that one Chappaquiddick incident is enough for a Senator from Massachusetts. Let's walk." He laughed, and we got out and walked for about ten minutes until we came to a good-sized road. We managed to stop a car, and its friendly driver took us to the Senator's villa.

A Prophetic Ben-Gurion

Whenever we would speak of Israel, Hartke would dwell on his boundless admiration for David Ben-Gurion, whom he had met frequently on previous visits. He was awed by the simplicity and overpowering personality of the great man. That was something, because the Indiana Senator prided himself on being an iconoclast and taking leaders with a large amount of skepticism. One Sabbath, Ben-Gurion invited him and Martha to lunch at his home. Paula Ben-Gurion prepared the luncheon and served it herself, dressed in casual sweater and slacks. Hartke confided to me that Ben-Gurion looked to him like an ancient Hebrew prophet. The Prime Minister told him, "We must plant as many trees as possible. For when you plant trees, you plant something that grows. I want the desert to become green, I want Israel to grow, and I want the results to benefit all mankind." That was the real voice of Israel, Hartke told me.

A 'Cold' Golda

The Senator was less enamoured of Israel's fourth Prime Minister, Golda Meir. Before he left for the official visit to Israel, Hartke had talked to Egyptian friends, particularly Sa'id Mari, one of President Sadat's confidants. He also had asked Israeli diplomats in Washington whether their Government would be receptive if he should persuade his Egyptian friends to agree to a meeting between representatives of the two countries. The reply that the diplomats brought to him was that Israel was amenable to such a meeting at any place, at any time, so that some kind of a dialogue could begin. Hartke contacted Egyptian Ambassador Ghorbal and told him of the Israeli response. Cairo's reply, via its Washington Embassy, was enthusiastic: They would await some kind of message from Golda Meir.

Hartke's meeting with Golda was less than succcessful. After the usual pleasantries, Hartke told her that one of his aims on this visit to Jerusalem was to arrange the beginning of a dialogue between Israel and Egypt. To the Senator's chagrin and surprise, Golda reacted rather coldly. The Prime Minister puffed on a cigarette and declared, "We are not interested in meeting with the present Government of Egypt. We have inside information that Sadat is no longer in control and

Photo by Photo-Emka Ltd.

Senator Hartke's meeting with Golda was less than successful.

will fall in six months' time. Then we will be prepared to deal with his successor."

Hartke responded, "You know, Golda, I have all the respect in the world for you, but you are something of a stiff-necked woman...." I was a bit taken aback at the way the Senator addressed the Prime Minister. Coming from someone else, it might have been taken amiss. But I think that everyone, including the Prime Minister herself, appreciated that Hartke's voting record in the Senate was ample testimony to his long-standing friendship for Israel and his understanding of its needs. At one point, Hartke asked Golda where she got her endless reservoir of energy. She laughed and declared, "From my vices—cigarettes and black coffee." During the 90-minute meeting Golda had lived up to her reputation, finishing off a pack of cigarettes and five cups of strong black coffee.

It seems strange—in retrospect—that about one year before Sadat launched his offensive on the Suez front, the Prime

Minister of Israel was predicting his impending political demise.

Historians may well record that Israel's fourth Prime Minister refused to negotiate, while Menachem Begin will be remembered as the first Israeli Prime Minister to sign a peace treaty with Israel's leading Arab adversary.

Toward the end of the Senator's visit, he and his wife met some of the many Soviet Jews he had helped bring out of the U.S.S.R. This was at the *Mevasseret Zion* immigrant absorption center near Jerusalem. The Senator found it a very heartwarming experience.

Mission to Minsk

Hartke's reputation for aiding Soviet Jews had spread throughout Israel, and when I was visiting early in 1973 I was approached by the Israel Council for Soviet Jewry to help on behalf of Jews in Minsk. The K.G.B. had started mass investigations in the Byelorussian capital, involving about 100 Jews who were questioned regarding supposedly illegal activities. It soon became a *cause célèbre*. Those connected with the Jewish national movement in the U.S.S.R. feared this might herald an official crackdown on emigration to Israel. The investigation not only covered Byelorussia but other Jewish centers outside of Moscow, including the Ukraine and the Baltic republics. Some "witnesses" were even brought to Minsk from as far away as Kharbarovsk in the Soviet Far East. The news came to the outside world after a letter reached Jewish activists in Moscow signed by 98 Minsk Jews. They wrote about K.G.B. officials questioning dozens of people and making house searches. The K.G.B. was trying to collect evidence to establish its charges of an illegal Jewish organization.

The main burden of their charges became known as "The Jewish Officers' Plot," later referred to as (K.G.B.) "Case #97." The so-called plot centered on a number of retired Red Army officers, particularly three Soviet World War II heroes. These Jewish veterans were accused of "fomenting Zionist propaganda" and advocating immigration to Israel. The three heroes—Lieutenant Colonel Yefim Davidovich, wounded five times in battles against the Germans and awarded 15 orders and medals for bravery in action; Lieutenant Colonel Lev Ofsicher, a former pilot with 15 decorations; and Lieutenant Colonel Nahum Alshansky, with 13 decorations—were part of a group of Minsk Jews who had applied for emigraiton visas to Israel.

I alerted Senator Hartke who made suitable and urgent representations to the Russians. Shortly afterward, we heard the news that the Byelorussian authorities had closed their investigations of this "case." Washington pundits interpreted it as a goodwill gesture in advance of Brezhnev's visit to the United States the following month.

I was in Israel when the highly welcome news reached me by telegram sent by a newly arrived Israel immigrant from Minsk. It read as follows:

Message to Leon about his help in Russia.

20

The Yom Kippur War

I was officiating as cantor in the Yom Kippur services at the congregation of some friends in Paterson, New Jersey. It was the first week of October, 1973. Suddenly, prayers were interrupted by a highly agitated rabbi. "War has broken out in Israel. Israel is being attacked at this very moment," he cried. We suspended the course of service for the Day of Atonement to make a special prayer. I felt numb, totally outraged by the Arab assault on the most solemn of Jewish days of worship, and at the same time terribly worried about the safety of dear friends in Israel. I managed to get through the day, and after breaking the fast at the rabbi's home did my best to learn about the latest developments. I resolved, there and then, to go ahead with intended plans to fly to Israel on the following Tuesday. It seemed more imperative than ever to be there.

At my apartment the phone rang incessantly. One of the first calls was from Senator Harke: "What do you think, Leon?" He reminded me of his unsuccessful attempt to per-

suade Prime Minister Meir to arrange a meeting with the
Egyptians on his last visit to Jerusalem a year earlier. He
asked me to come up with ideas to present to the Senate that
might help stop the war. The Senate did not have the power to
negotiate between countries, but its members could use their
influence on the Executive branch. He disclosed having put
out feelers to his Egyptian contacts about his flying to Cairo to
visit his friend, Sa'id Mari, the head of the official party, the
Arab Socialist League, and one of Sadat's closest advisors. I
told him I would check out the idea with my Israeli contacts,
and counseled him not to do anything before I called him back.
I got through to the office of Israel's U.N. Ambassador, Joseph
Tekoah, with whom I was on good terms. He was tied up in a
meeting with Foreign Minister Abba Eban.

The next call was again from Vance Hartke. He had spoken
to Senator Jim Abourezk, a pro-Arab Senator of Lebanese
origin, and the two were pondering the notion of traveling
immediately to Egypt. "Jim and I thought we might do something to help out there, but we're not quite sure exactly what,"
Hartke told me. We spoke about 12 times that night, discussing how he might exert influence. Our last conversation was
at 2 a.m. All this time I felt emotionally drained. I sensed from
my contacts, and the news coming over the radio and TV, that
things were going badly for Israel.

Sunday morning I received a call from the Israeli Consulate;
they asked me to come over. Shortly afterward I was ushered
through the heavy security cordon around the Consulate's
offices on First Avenue up to Consul-General David Rivlin's
office. He was extremely upset by the news from Israel. With
him was Abba Eban, who had just completed taping an
appearance on TV's "Face the Nation." He told me of the
gravity of the situation and the need to mobilize Congress in
Israel's behalf. I called Hartke, and filled him in on developments. He seemed to be looking to me to provide the answers.

Later in the day, while at a friend's home, I received another
call from the Consulate. People there seemed frantic. Would I
please fly to Washington to meet their people at the Embassy?
It was a national emergency for Israel. My connection with a

senior Senator would be of importance. Naturally, I agreed to do all I could to help. I told them I'd be in Washington shortly and that I was in constant contact with the Senator, but I thought I could be of more use in New York at the moment.

When I next spoke to Hartke he suggested I might want to check in person on a rumor that the Russians were supplying the Syrians and Egyptians with massive arms and supplies, including SAM 16s. We agreed it was fortuitous that I had planned to go to Israel at this time.

On Monday morning I had a disturbing phone conversation with one of my oldest Israeli friends, Lieutenant Colonel Micha Paz, head of the Land Forces Supply Requisition department in the Israel Defense Ministry purchasing mission in New York. They were in urgent need of various military supplies that were being held up by high officials in Washington. Micha told me that when the news that war had broken out reached New York, the entire staff had convened to determine the necessary things for them to do. Meanwhile, he had, on his own initiative, activated personal connections throughout the American military establishment. Sensing that supplies were getting low back home, he called the head of the Foreign Military Assistance program of the U.S. Army Materiel Command, General Joseph Fix, at his home in Alexandria, Virginia. He also called his contacts at the U.S. Army Commodity Command/Tank Automotive Command in Detroit, and at the U.S. Army Armaments Command at Rock Island, Illinois.

Micha said, "I told my contacts that war had broken out, and 'you all can expect to get instructions to supply control items to Israel.' It was wonderful to see the marvelous responsiveness of these individual Americans and their demonstration of goodwill toward us in our hour of great need. They volunteered information willingly as to where various items of supplies would be available and where the most convenient airfields could be found for picking up ammunition and equipment."

As I learned later from Micha, in parallel fashion, Israel's Military Attaché in Washington, Brigadier-General Motta

Gur (later the I.D.F.'s Chief of Staff), began filing formal
applications with the Pentagon to obtain permission to fly out
equipment. According to Micha and his boss, Defense Ministry Purchasing Mission Chief Bondi Dror, the response in the
Pentagon and throughout the U.S. armed forces was marvelously encouraging. "We discerned that the Defense Department was responding in a positive manner to our ultra-urgent
requests," Micha said, "but we failed to grasp why the order to
move the equipment had not been given. Soon we perceived
that the delay was of a political nature. Our contacts in the
Pentagon told us, 'It's up to Munitions Control, and that
comes under the State Department. They and we are waiting
for the green light from the White House.' "

Micha also related that his pals in the U.S. Army were
hinting of a dispute between Defense Secretary James Schle-
singer and Secretary of State Henry Kissinger over granting
the approval to Israel's requests. They also spoke of President
Nixon's holding up the supplies on Kissinger's advice. Micha's
voice that Monday morning was despairing. "We're going
absolutely *meshugga* here. We're not quite clear on how things
are going on the battle fronts, but we feel terribly uneasy. I
think things are not going well. And the Americans are holding up urgent supplies that could save our boys' lives, all
because of Kissinger's machinations. Our aircraft could pick
up the equipment, but official permission hasn't been given
for them to land." When I asked him what I should do to help,
he advised me to talk it over with Bondi Dror. I had heard
about Dror, a near legendary fighter, from other friends in the
Israeli military. When I called Dror, he spoke in a cautious
tone, explaining that he did not wish in any way to hurt
official relations with the U.S. Government. But he urged me
to go to Washington, contact the Embassy people to see how
things were progressing, and do my best to use my influence
through the Senator to help Israel get its urgent armaments
requirements.

I called Hartke. We agreed that I would take the next shuttle
to Washington, have lunch with him in his office, and get back
to New York immediately so I could keep my scheduled plan of

flying to Israel the following night—Tuesday. I was already booked on the 8 p.m. flight from J.F.K. I had already alerted friends on *The New York Times* and *The New York Post* and friends on television networks that I might have a big story for them. I was going to go public with the supply-holdup story before boarding the plane if the logjam was not removed. But I decided to hold back until the very last moment, praying that such publicity would be unnecessary.

In Hartke's office in the Old Senate Office Building all was calm. People were dying in the sands of Sinai while I was drinking orange juice and eating tuna fish. It felt unreal. Hartke declared that he would do all he could to help. He had after all always supported pro-Israeli measures. "Of course, I will do anything for the sake of our friendship." However, he stressed that he was not in the least sure what position the Senate might take in a showdown over Israel's actual survival. Frank Flower, one of Hartke's main aides, displayed a clearly pro-Arab position at this juncture. The other aides were noncommittal.

With Senator Vance Hartke (left) and Ambassador Yitzhak Rabin.

I left very depressed and went to the Israeli Embassy, where I was asked to press Hartke to issue a pro-Israel statement. I called the Senator, and he shied away from the notion, taking the opportunity to remind me how unpleasantly the Israeli Embassy people had treated him and how little support he had obtained from Jews in Indiana. Then he asked me, "Leon, you're not offended, are you? You know I will issue a state- ment, but only out of friendship for you." On those grounds I refused. The Embassy people were disappointed when I informed them of Hartke's response. But I tried to see a silver lining in this cloud, holding that the senior senator from Indi- ana would be more valuable by keeping a low-key position. Anyhow, I told them, I was sure he would come around eventually.

I went to meet some Arab contacts of Frank Flower's. It was a pointless encounter. Later over dinner I advised Hartke to drop the idea of going to Egypt with Abourezk, especially as it was now clear that Egypt was in no mood for any compromise. I urged him instead to utilize his connection with Brezhnev.

On Tuesday morning I was in my office, getting frantic calls from my friends about the deteriorating situation on the Israeli battlefronts. An unexpected call came in from Flora Lewis of *The New York Times* who was in Paris. She wanted to know whether it was true that the U.S. was holding up urgent arms for Israel. She felt my reply was unsatisfactory, but I had sworn to hold on to the story until that evening.

It was the fourth day of the war. That's what was uppermost in my mind as I packed my things and made my way to J.F.K. At the airport, at 7:20 p.m., I called Micha. He sounded elated. At 7:00 his group had been informed that the White House had given the green light for the supplies. So I boarded my plane with a sense of relief that at least *that* obstacle in the path of Israel's survival had been removed. No press releases were necessary.

Later Micha was to tell me of Motta Gur's sterling role in that trying period, and how he, Dror, and Micha had taken turns doing night duty at the Washington Embassy, often sleeping on the floor, waiting for instructions to come from

Israel about armaments. The Americans started their airlift with Galaxies and C-141's after the Middle East Task Group was set up. But even before then, an El Al airliner was readied to rush top-priority material to Israel; the plane, with its familiar white markings, landed in a military airfield in Norfolk, Virginia, to pick up much-needed artillery and airplane ammunition. Micha also told me of help displayed by American Jews through the U.J.A. His office became a warehouse to stock underwear and towels bought in New York stores. Micha said the U.J.A. volunteers cleaned out the reserves at Bloomingdale's, Macy's, and Alexander's, and they had contacted manufacturers, who provided them with warm clothing at cost price. He was looking urgently for anti-fragmentation vests, the lack of which had resulted in many Army casualties. Through one of his contacts in the U.S. Army, he discovered a depot full of these items near Boston.

After the war, he told me how wonderfully the American military rank-and-file had behaved in the supply crisis. They had been so cooperative that he was able to have equipment packed on pallets ready to be flown the moment the White House gave the green light for the Army to help Israel help itself. Months later he was advised by Motta Gur that the military attaché's office had received an official complaint from U.S. General W.A. Sumner, of the Middle East Task Group, urging him "to reprimand that red-headed officer of yours. Tell him to stop calling our commodity centers directly, and instead to go through the proper channels."

To Israel, to War

I stayed overnight in Paris in a tense mood, constantly on the phone to the Senator in Washington. In the course of those transatlantic calls we discussed the kind of position he would adopt in the Senate. My advice was to contact Dobrynin on ways of using the Soviet desire for most-favored-nation treatment to reduce its involvement in arms supplies to the Arabs. As he was to tell me later, when he did meet Dobrynin, the Soviet envoy gave him grounds to believe that the Russians would welcome some kind of U.S. move in trade matters. If a nation did not comply with the "carrot" request, the "stick" would be to impose trade sanctions in direct ratio to the other nation's supply of weapons to belligerents. Hartke dabbled with presenting a bill related to the supply of arms and the most-favored-nation issue.

I was given priority on an Israel-bound plane because the Senator had officially appointed me his emissary to check on stories of Soviet weapons involvement and report back. The plane was packed with people and military materiel. I saw violinist Isaac Stern a few rows away. He had volunteered to play for the troops during the war, cancelling a prior concert engagement. The mood was rather heavy in that aircraft, everyone deep in thought. We landed in pitch blackness at Lod Airport. I bumped into an old pal from El Al, Jack Gelbwachs, the station manager, carrying a flashlight. Through the dark I could discern gigantic shapes of the Hercules cargo planes that had begun the airlift. They were unloading by flashlight, and I felt very proud of the U.S. presence. There were no cabs, so we traveled to town in Gelbwachs' 20-year-old Mercedes. Tel Aviv, that lively, brightly lit, Mediterranean city, was completely blacked out. Only a few cars groped their way through empty thoroughfares. The next day, I noticed there were hardly any men around, and those that were, were in uniform.

Before I left the U.S., I had decided that the best way for me to see how the war was going was to become a war correspondent. I had a rudimentary knowledge of journalism. I had arranged for Joe Franklin of New York's WOR-TV to appoint me as his program's correspondent. Next morning I went to the Israeli press center, swarming with journalists from all over the world. Arye Peytan, who was in charge of the foreign press, arranged my credentials as a war correspondent. Originally from South Africa, he was by now a veteran Israeli and a very nice man indeed. Naturally, when I heard that Prime Minister Golda Meir would be giving a press conference, I attended. She looked absolutely worn out. I had never seen her looking so haggard. The way Golda looked was living testimony to how Israel was then faring. Instinctively, I put my hand up when her aide asked for questions from the floor, and for some reason I was picked from among the throng of newsmen. I asked her, "Mrs. Prime Minister, have you been getting full help and cooperation from the United States in supplying equipment?" She replied, "It was a bit ragged at the beginning, but cooperation is proceeding as it should now."

Photo by Mark Berger

Taking a rest with a war photographer and Israeli troops on the way to Sassa, Syria, October 1973.

Photo by Mark Berger

At the Israeli Army's front line in Sassa, Syria, October 15, 1973.

The office of the Army Spokesman arranged a tour for a group of us, and our escort officers included such reservists as actor Chaim Topol, accountant Dan Bavly, and political scientist Ron Medzini. Traveling with us was my old friend, journalist Noah Klieger. Our first call was along the Syrian front, and there we had our first taste of shelling. I have never fallen to the ground so quickly, before or since. From the impression gained and the reports we were given, it appeared that the northern front situation was well in hand. The Israeli forces in that area seemed well organized and morale was high, at least as far as we could judge by the faces of the young soldiers in the gun emplacements, or the soldiers singing in the trucks carrying them to new destinations. We also saw vehicles conveying the casualties to temporary graveyards, a too common sight in that war.

On my return to blacked-out Tel Aviv I phoned Franklin at WOR-TV to report the situation. I mentioned the high rate of casualties, which was just starting to be reported to the Israeli public. They had not, as yet, been fully informed of the difficulties on the battlefront. The Government, for reasons of its own, had kept the nation in the dark far too long for its collective mental health. Rumor instead of news had taken over. I heard stories of Moshe Dayan's forces falling to pieces under the impact of the initial reverses; the Barlev Line collapsing under the Egyptian offensive. The usually optimistic mood of the people turned into one of deep depression. Jews were afraid for their survival once again.

The next day I joined a party of six correspondents heading southward. We flew part of the way, but most of the journey was by road. As we approached the front our vehicles raised clouds of desert dust. We saw prisoner compounds and many corpses. We passed by mounds of wrecked tanks. Testimony to

Photo by Matthew Naythons

Photo by Matthew Naythons

As we approached the front our vehicles raised clouds of desert dust.

the destructiveness of war was everywhere. I heard that my good friend Uri Ben-Ari was in the area, and as we moved nearer the line I began to ask where I could find him. I was told that he had crossed the Suez Canal. I managed to get across one of the bridges and eventually located him. Uri looked tired, unshaven, but magnificent. He radiated authority, and the men treated him with respectful affection. He was extremely surprised to see me. I suppose I seemed out of place amid the wreckage of war. Even while he was greeting me we had to duck into a shelter to avoid the ricochet of Egyptian sniper bullets. Uri said he had not slept in five days. He spoke reassuringly about the outcome of the war. He felt that Israel

Relieving the tension....

Photo by Matthew Naythons

had now turned the tables on the Egyptians after the enemy's initial successes, largely due to the element of surprise. "Thankfully, Chaim Barlev is in charge and he will save the situation."

I could see that Uri was on edge about something, and learned that it involved Ariel Sharon's controversial crossing of the Suez. The General-turned-politician had crossed the Canal with a fanfare of publicity. His supporters claimed that he had saved the course of the war by doing so. However, I was given the impression that his detractors and several generals on that front did not concur. This later developed into what in Israel became known as "the war of the generals," who employed memoirs and the media as their artillery and ammunition.

Photo by Matthew Naythons

With General Uri Ben Ari at the Israeli Base in Faid, Egypt, November 1973.

After the cease-fire, I returned to America. My Israeli friends were bitter about Dr. Kissinger. They accused him of preventing Israel's total victory at the very last moment by making a deal with the Soviets at Israel's expense and in Egypt's favor. It was apparent that Kissinger behaved consistently, since he had allegedly tried to weaken Israel's war efforts by holding up essential military supplies at the start of the war. No wonder Golda Meir reportedly called him "Dr. Metternich," after the cunning Austrian diplomat for whom the United States Secretary of State reputedly felt a close affinity. That Golda Meir was forced to leave office in the wake of mounting protests following the war's end was a great historical irony, especially as she had been the one to predict with confidence the political demise of Anwar Sadat by mid-1973.

Photo by Matthew Naythons

U.N. check-point 101, West Bank Canal, Egypt, November 1973.

21

Red Passports

From the Senator's office we continued our efforts on behalf of Jews trapped in the Soviet Union. A mounting pile of correspondence grew between Hartke and Dobrynin. The Soviets often regarded these people as pawns in international trade relations. Yet their reaction was quite unpredictable, and even top Kremlinologists could not establish a pattern as regards Soviet emigration policy. Early in 1973 Jacques Leroy and I decided that we would travel to Russia that September in an official capacity to evaluate the situation for ourselves. The Senator's office contacted the Soviet Embassy for visas and to finalize our travel arrangements inside the Soviet Union. We were granted red passports* by the State Department. But it would seem that the various departments of the Soviet

* These are official passports issued by the State Department to persons travelling on U.S. government business. They are akin to diplomatic passports.

bureaucratic apparatus were at loggerheads about letting us into the country. Numerous obstacles were put in the way of our departure. Hartke's Administrative Assistant, Dolores Davies, applied for the visas in May—months before our planned departure for Moscow in the last week of September. She was in contact with the Soviet Embassy people, and everything appeared to be in order. She had handed them our passports for the usual processing and insertion of Soviet entry visas. However, a week before we were set to go, she was told by an Embassy official, "Sorry, they are not ready." She got the same reply each day when she called. Her blood pressure rose when a similar response was forthcoming on the very day of our scheduled departure. We were flying to Paris that night to catch our connecting plane to Russia. Just after 5:00 p.m. she called the Soviet Embassy only to be told, "Sorry, we're closed." Asking for the duty officer, Dolores explained the problem and asked him to call her at home as soon as possible. At 5:45 p.m., he called back, saying, "I can't do anything for you. The passports are in the Embassy safe. Sorry." So the resourceful Dolores found the number of the Soviet Ambassador's residence. She dialed it and asked for His Excellency. A rather surprised Dobrynin came on the line. Introducing herself, Dolores said, "I'm really sorry to disturb you. But I have a very serious problem. Your people have been unconscionably unhelpful. Senator Hartke's top two aides plan to leave tonight on an official visit to the Soviet Union, and their passports with visas are locked up in your Embassy safe. Their plane is due to leave Dulles Airport at 8:00 p.m. and it is after 6:00 p.m."

As Dolores told us later, she was at her wits' end. The Senator was out of touch, traveling in Indiana. Thinking to herself, "What do I have to lose?" Dolores reminded the Soviet Ambassador of her boss's relationship with his chief, and said, "The headlines about this story in *The Washington Post* wouldn't help U.S.-Soviet relations, would they?" Then, as a last resort, she ventured, "Do you want the Senator to ask the President to call you on this matter?" That apparently was the most persuasive argument. Dobrynin told her to send someone within the next hour to the Embassy. One of his staff would be waiting with the passports. At 7:15 p.m. Dolores managed to track down another Senatorial aide, Bob Kobeck, and instructed him about the arrangements. Meanwhile she had been keeping us briefed on developments and we hurried to the airport. Time was running out. The Paris-bound plane's take-off was getting near. So we decided to use our regular passports for this lap of the journey, and began departure procedures. Dolores assured us by phone in the departure lounge at 7:50 p.m. that Bob was on the way with the passports. Meanwhile he had driven to Embassy Row as fast as traffic regulations would permit to find the red passports waiting. The time was 7:40 p.m. Bob proved his mettle as a driver and reached the airport in record time. Using his official Senate pass, he managed to board the plane with our passports at 7:55 p.m., just before it took off.

To Russia with Apprehension

That kind of bureaucratic obstacle course was just a foretaste of our Soviet visit. I confess to being rather unnerved by my first impressions at Moscow's Vnukovo Airport. The presence of uniformed men everywhere contributed to the pervading oppressive atmosphere of a totalitarian society. The scary

As Jacques Leroy observed, "Well, you really are tasting the diet of the average poor Russian."

feeling abated somewhat when we were greeted by some very nice people from the U.S. Embassy. As we had diplomatic passports, we were whisked through customs to a waiting Embassy limousine. Before we entered the car one of the aides whispered to me, "Be very, very careful what you say. It's bugged." Once inside the U.S. Embassy building, we were given to understand that the entire place was bugged except for one or two rooms where it was safe to speak openly.

I had a problem with the food during the entire six-day journey across the U.S.S.R. because of my observance of *kashrut* rules. I survived those six days by eating herring, black bread, and rice. As Jacques observed, "Well, you really are tasting the diet of the average poor Russian." Our itinerary was set by Intourist, which assigned us very polite and very winning women guides. They were extremely professional as guides, but there was always an undertone of watchfulness. We were told what was out of bounds.

In Moscow, as we were rushed from one tourist site to another and from one Government office to another, I managed to get a glimpse of the capital of the Soviet Empire, with its huge boulevards, but few cars. The general architecture was "Stalinist monumental," just as I had seen in photographs. The buildings were covered with slogans and huge pictures. Our guide explained that they showed the current winner of the "Worker of the Month" award. As I had been led to expect, there were always long lines of people outside the department stores. Indeed, I saw few smiles on people's faces in Moscow or in the other Soviet cities we visited.

Despite my frequent requests, I was not allowed to go to Jewish homes. There was always some excuse tied to our schedule or to an official appointment. But I did manage to get to Central Synagogue. It was an old building with more uniformed policemen outside than warranted. I had arrived in time for the morning service (*shacharit*) and found a congregation of 15 old men. I was overcome by strong emotion at seeing this remnant of the great Jewish community from which part of my family derived. I started to sing out some of my favorite cantorial tunes. All of a sudden the house of worship filled, as if by magic. Jacques Leroy, who had never visited a synagogue, was quite astonished by the number in attendance. We learned later that my arrival in an Embassy limousine had prompted a rumor that I was a Jewish Senator.

Before leaving home, I had spoken to Jerry Goodman of the National Conference on Soviet Jewry about the trip. It would seem that his contacts had alerted Soviet Jewish activists to our arrival. I also carried with me a list of "refuseniks" with whom I wished to establish contact, if only to provide them with moral encouragement. One aim of my visit was to bring spiritual succor to as many Jews in Russia as possible, to demonstrate by my presence that they had not been abandoned by their fellow Jews and that the outside world knew of their fate. The fact that Jacques and I were traveling on behalf of a powerful member of the United States Senate was another element I wished to make known, and that their cries for help had been heard in the Free World.

The Embassy people in Moscow were extremely helpful. But I also confess to an ulterior motive in my calls at the Embassy compound. It was to gain access to their marvelous commissary—delicious omelets, French toast, and decent coffee! Our Intourist guides took us on the usual round of show places: the Bolshoi Ballet (superb), the Moscow Opera (old-fashioned), and the Moscow Circus (marvelous). We joined the pilgrims at

Inside the American Embassy in Moscow, Leon Charney with Russians who took refuge.

Lenin's Tomb, a highly impressive sight indeed. The changing of the Guard is an extremely dramatic performance.

Jacques and I were informed that we would be meeting with
Andrei Verein, whose official title was Director, U.S.S.R. All
Union Office of Visas and Registration (O.V.I.R.), Ministry of
Internal Affairs, the top man in O.V.I.R. In short, he had the
final say on approving Soviet exit visas. It was obvious that
Verein also held a high rank in the K.G.B. Two American
diplomats holding the rank of Consul—Robert Fairchild Ober
and Steven E. Steiner, accompanied us. They had been trying
to arrange an appointment for two years! They told us that as
far as they knew we were the third or fourth Americans to
have met Verein. He had received only New York Congressman Mario Biaggi and John Lindsay, then Mayor of New
York.

Verein's office was as stark as all Soviet bureaucratic
departments; the only adornment was the standard portrait of
Lenin. Along with Verein were his deputy, Colonel L.N.
Ovchinnikov, and an interpreter, who was not identified. I
wondered who was whose watchdog, Verein or Ovchinnikov?
The latter did not speak at all during the course of our hour-
and-a-half meeting.

The Embassy had been pressing for a meeting with Verein
for two years concerning a list of 850 multinational citizens
who wished to emigrate to the United States. Many of these
people had relatives in the U.S. and some were even American
citizens. Vice President Nixon originally presented the list in
1959, and by the time of our meeting—14 years later—only 14
percent of the people involved had been granted exit visas.

Verein opened the meeting by stating how much the Soviet
Union welcomed the easing of tensions with the United
States. Jacques responded by expressing gratitude for the
meeting. He mentioned Senator Hartke's visit to the Soviet
Union at the head of the Senatorial delegation. He also mentioned that a photograph of Brezhnev and Hartke had resulted
in worldwide media coverage, and that he hoped the new,
more positive relationship between the Soviet Government
and Congress would continue. Jacques mentioned his interest

in Soviet history and launched into a brief explanation of the role of free immigration in the development of the United States.

Jacques proceeded to describe Senator Hartke's position in favor of extending the most-favored-nation status to the Soviet Union. The Senator was upset, Jacques related, that so many families still were not allowed to emigrate to the United States to join their loved ones. Talking in firm tones, Jacques proceeded to mention the deep disappointment of members of the United States Congress and of the American people in general that only a small minority of those on the U.S. Government Representation List had received permission to join their families in America. A copy of the list of 850 names was given to Verein. Ober pointed out that 20 of the persons who wanted to emigrate were married and had been separated from their spouses for as long as 15 years.

Verein promised to look into the matter. He said, "It's apparent that, until Secretary-General Brezhnev visited the United States, totally distorted information about Soviet emigration policy was in circulation among Americans. I'll give you a prime example—all those groundless reports, as if tens of thousands wished to emigrate from the Soviet Union. In fact, as Secretary-General Brezhnev has pointed out, 97 percent of those who file applications do receive exit permits." He also complained about "lots of publicity in the Western press about one Tyomkin. You may ask why he has not received permission. I'll tell you. He wants to emigrate, but his daughter and his wife—from whom he is divorced—do not wish to leave the U.S.S.R. And he only wants to go if his daughter accompanies him. So what can we do in that case? The trouble is that some people abroad make lots of noise about nothing. It's all rumor." (Verein was referring to the case of Professor Alexander Tyomkin [Temkin] whose daughter, Marina, was forcibly separated from him.)

The O.V.I.R. chief concluded his reply by declaring, "The Union of Soviet Socialist Republics is a country of 250 million people, and if two-and-a-half million Jews wish to leave, it is of little concern to other citizens. For that would have little consequence on the overall well-being of the Soviet Union. Moreover, I might add, a lot of Jews who left the country now wish to return."

Steiner and Ober entered the discussion to point out that none of the 850 persons on the Embassy list held crucial jobs or had any particularly sophisticated knowledge in technological or scientific matters. They were just ordinary citizens, and the granting of exit visas to them should be purely on humanitarian grounds. Verein scanned the list and took notes as the Consular officers spoke. When they had concluded, Verein asked, "So, this is purely an American list?" On their affirmative answer, he declared, "It will receive serious consideration."

I explained my official position with Senator Hartke and that I was his advisor on day-to-day problems, especially those concerning veterans' affairs and immigration. I told Verein of the intense interest in the United States regarding Soviet emigration to Israel and of the hundreds of letters we received regularly from American citizens who have relatives seeking to emigrate from the U.S.S.R. I spoke of my Jewish background and told him that I had extensive contacts in the American Jewish community. I proceeded, registering my appreciation for the recent award of exit permits to two Jewish families from Kishinev. Their names were on a list of 23 cases recently brought to Ambassador Dobrynin's attention by Senator Hartke. Here I went out of my way to lavish praise on Verein personally, on the Senator's behalf.

I brought up the fact that both the Senator and I were doing everything possible to support the granting of most-favored-nation treatment to the U.S.S.R. "But," I added, "you and other Soviet officials are surely aware that serious political and public relations problems have been encountered in the area. I would be most appreciative if I would be able to transmit some indications from an authoritative Soviet official, such as yourself, that progress would be forthcoming on the refusal cases of intended emigrants to Israel."

I do not know if I was breathing harder than usual at that point, but I felt very tense indeed. After all here we were, confronted by a senior K.G.B. official who held the key to life and death for millions of people throughout the Soviet Union. Moreover, if his *deputy* held the rank of *Colonel*, was Verein a General? After I told him that the United Nations Charter on Human Rights stated that every person should be able to emigrate to the country of his or her choice, Verein declared, "As you most probably know, a sophisticated understanding exists between our two countries at present, and this understanding will probably be even more furthered once the Congress of the United States sees fit to accord the U.S.S.R. the most-favored-nation treatment in trade."

I responded quickly, telling him that Senator Hartke had publicly addressed this question and had voiced a favorable stand on this issue. I could also assure him that I would also issue a statement to the U.S. press in my private capacity as an American citizen stating that most-favored-nation was a very important provision of the trade bill and should not be used as a sledgehammer to smash bilateral relationships between the two countries. What mattered, I told him, was to keep all channels of communication and exchange open and take into account the total perspective of the two countries' relations.

Verein started his answer by declaring, "I am indeed pleased to hear what you have to say, especially because you are a Jew. I wonder that you are not afraid of issuing such a statement because it would not be in conformance with the general policy of Jewish organizations in the United States. Perhaps you might become an outcast, a subject of rancor and animosity." I replied, "I feel that my responsibility toward my conscience is far greater than winning any popularity contest. I feel duty-bound to advocate what I believe to be in the best interests of both our countries. As for any personal consequences, well, I will be willing to take them." This brought Verein to say, "That is the sign of true strength of character. I hope that your wishes will be fulfilled."

As for his policy on emigration, the O.V.I.R. chief then proceeded to give his explanation for concern abroad over Soviet emigration policies. Repeating his claim that 97 percent of exit requests were actually granted, he then picked up a

Leon Charney with Verein, the mystery man (right) and Verein's interpretor, his military aide (left).

full bottle of drinking water and poured it into an empty container. Doing so, he declared, "You see, when water is poured from a bottle, it initially comes out very quickly." Then indicating the drops dripping from the bottle, he compared them to unresolved cases, saying, "As you can see for yourself, the last drops are always the slowest, but they always reach their destination, although they do appear to come very, very slowly." He indicated that all such cases "would be considered."

The atmosphere was so friendly, with Verein conveying his satisfaction with the meeting, that Jacques then proposed that a photograph be taken of Verein and me. The Embassy officials told us they doubted whether Verein would agree, since it was not customary for Soviet officials to have their pictures taken together with Senatorial aides. But, contrary to their predictions, Verein was eminently amenable to the idea, and even agreed to walk outside into the courtyard for the sake of a better photograph.

On our way out both Steiner and Ober told me that Verein's consent to be photographed with us indicated a measure of approval on his part and that a future relationship might develop from the meeting. They further explained that all gestures of Soviet officials should be suitably scrutinized and evaluated. They felt that a diplomatic door had been opened, which no other Jewish representative from the United States had hitherto managed to do. It was also their considered opinion that Verein's mention of his wish for "a sophisticated understanding" was a portentous sign in the relations between the U.S. and Russia. Moreover, if I made my "as a private citizen" comment to the press, the door would open even wider.

Next Stop, Minsk

We proceeded with our planned itinerary. We traveled in the comfortable, old-fashioned train compartment put at the disposition of foreign V.I.P.s. Kiev turned out to be an entirely rebuilt city, in a lovely landscape, and we were taken round to the usual sights. But it was only after much insistence that our guide drove us to Babi Yar. All that remained of that terrible place of slaughter was a wooded ravine and a monument, but no mention of Jews at the site of such great martyrdom. I also overcame the guide's resistance and persuaded her to take us to meet the remaining Jewish community of Kiev. The synagogue was very small but quite clean, and it was one of the few congregations outside of Moscow with a rabbi. The congregation included some young men who spoke poor English, and I conversed in Yiddish with the ones who dared come up to me. It was apparent that they were fearful of speaking to me, whispering, "Help us to get out." It was one more memorable night in that oppressive country. I had a feeling that I was being watched constantly.

Next stop was Minsk—one of the goals of my visit to Russia. A big, ugly city of Stalinist buildings. The Minsk Jews had been informed in advance of my coming. I met them in the synagogue, which was housed in a shanty. I was met outside by what looked like a reception committee: a small group that included the three war heroes Davidovitch, Alshansky, and

Above: LC with the three Russian war heroes who were being harassed for requesting exit visas: Davidovitch, Ovsicher, and Alshansky. Picture was taken in the courtyard of Minsk synagogue September 1973. At right: wearing their medals.

Ovsicher, who greeted me warmly and thanked me for the help extended to the Jews of Minsk by Senator Hartke and myself. They had come to meet me before I entered the synagogue in order to warn me not to talk too loud as we were being closely watched. They told me that some members of the congregation were K.G.B. agents. They spoke in Yiddish and explained their plight, declaring that the claim of the Soviet Government that they knew security secrets was a big hoax. "Only pressure from the United States can save us." They were impressive men of proud mien and had come to the service wearing all the medals they had won for defending the Soviet Union from the German invaders. Davidovitch grasped my arm, and told me of how he had recently suffered another heart attack after his re-arrest by the K.G.B. He declared with deep emotion, "Either Israel or death," words I can never forget.

I promised to do all I could for him on my return. Davidovitch, speaking on behalf of the others, said, "In the past we always regarded ourselves as Russians first, and only lately have we returned to our Jewish identity." They said they were not observant but had come to the synagogue as a demonstration of Jewish solidarity. So we entered the synagogue, which had a predominantly elderly congregation, to participate in the first evening service of the Jewish New Year, Rosh Hashanah.

Jacques was very understanding and helpful, although he did sigh, on one occasion, "I know you are asking for trouble by insisting on meeting with these out-of-bounds people. I sense that whoever is keeping surveillance over us is more watchful of you than of me. But I realize that you must do what you have to do, and I will do what I can to help you." The next morning we went to call on the local O.V.I.R. chief, who was most courteous. But no discussion was possible. It was as if we were talking on two separate telephone lines, each of us making our set speech. It was a dialogue of the deaf. I spoke of our position at the United States Senate and of the Americans' concern for human rights, and about the Jackson amendment and M.F.N., and about furthering U.S.-Soviet relations. He spoke of the problems in Minsk with "those people because they possess secrets about state security."

Rosh Hashanah in Leningrad

Our final stop was Leningrad, a truly magnificent city, with the European flavor that Peter the Great intended it to have when he built it as his capital. We were provided with truly beautiful girls as our guides, one of whom discussed the virtues of Frank Sinatra and Elvis Presley to illustrate her knowledge of American culture. When I asked to visit the synagogue because it was Rosh Hashanah and I wished to attend services, she said, "It's not an important place, but if you insist that much, I'll take you there." I found a most impressive house of worship with a fairly sizeable community (mainly elderly men). For some reason they thought I was a Senator, again probably because of the U.S. Embassy limousine that had brought me there.

Before leaving Moscow our Embassy contacts had advised me not to engage in cantorial singing because it might prove to be what they called "disruptive." I still do not know precisely how I got into the situation, but suddenly I found myself standing on the *Bimah*, the high platform, and singing *Mussaf* prayers, backed by a choir of six old Jews. What I did during the service was to transpose all the liturgical melodies to well-known Israeli songs—*"Erev shel Shoshanim," "Hava Nagila," "Anu Banu Artza,"* and so forth. When it came time for the *Kedushah* prayer, I substituted for the traditional melody that of *Hatikva*, the Zionist song that had become the national anthem of Israel, singing of everlasting Jewish hopes and prayers for Jerusalem and Zion. A wave of emotion engulfed the assembled worshippers. They sang as if in one

Suddenly I found myself standing on the Bimah, the high platform, singing Mussaf prayers, backed by a choir of six old Russian Jews.

voice. I saw tears in many eyes. I confess to having had a tremendous sense of exhilaration and, yes, fear. It was one of the most poignant experiences of my life. The question remained, if the U.S. Embassy car bearing the Stars and Stripes had not been parked outside, what might the K.G.B. have done to me? I sadly missed Herman Malamod, good friend and collaborator in cantorial liturgy, who has sung with me in various congregations. Herman is well known as a New York Metropolitan Opera tenor. Afterward, the congregation crowded around me whispering, "Let our people go," and, "Help us get visas."

When we reached Leningrad, Jacques said, "Leon, I do understand you, but enough is enough. You've stretched the rope too much. The K.G.B. might act against us for what you have been doing." He did not accompany me to the Leningrad Synagogue but instead went to view the art at the Hermitage Museum. But I *had* to go to the Synagogue, not only because it was Rosh Hashanah but because I wanted to show that people in the outside world did care for the Jews in Leningrad. I wanted them to know that they had caring brethren with connections in high places in America—that their voices were being heard.

That last night in the Leningrad hotel we were extremely tense. Jacques was convinced we were going to be arrested by the K.G.B. at any moment. He was even sure that they might try to arrest us on the Paris-bound Aeroflot plane, so we planned what we might do if either of us was detained. We did not feel free until we left that Russian plane at the Paris airport. We could have kissed the tarmac.

That visit to Russia and my encounter with the O.V.I.R. chief brought me to certain conclusions. First, because of a series of bad harvests the Soviets were urgently interested in most-favored-nation status, and that could be used to get more Jews out of the Soviet Union. Second, the Jackson amendment, which I had hitherto supported enthusiastically and brought Hartke to co-sponsor, no longer served our purposes. I came to understand that we could get more Jews out of Russia by playing ball with the Soviets while employing various measures at the same time.

...And Home Again

We managed to get more individual cases tended to through Dobrynin, like that of 22-year-old Jan Krilsky, who had been incarcerated in a mental home for four years for seeking to emigrate to Israel. His father, a 72-year-old immigrant in Tel Aviv, appealed to us. We contacted the Soviet Embassy and the younger Krilsky was allowed to leave for Israel.

I decided to formulate my second thoughts about the effectiveness of the Jackson amendment. The draft bill I submitted to the Senator was a continuation of the Jackson amendment, but it focused on how to maintain an open-door policy. In my view, the concept was correct but the *modus operandi* was not. If trade stopped, that meant interrupting communication, and in order to get Jews out of Russia we needed to keep those channels open. The detailed proposal involved the establishment of "an international trade pact for peace; through a world foodstuffs bank" from which member countries could draw what they required under certain conditions. Since trade, energy, and peace were tied together in one package, one commodity could be bartered for another. The bill included the proposal of a kind of economic U.N., to impose penalties relating to the harassment of human beings. Senator Hartke took to the idea with alacrity and unveiled it in a speech to the United Automobile Workers union at the Midwest Trade Conference in Indianapolis, early in 1974.

Meanwhile, we continued our efforts to dramatize the fate of Soviet Jews, and in late February 1974 Senator Hartke hosted an informal meeting at the Senate attended by Boris Ainbinder, a spokesman of Moscow Jewish activists, recently out of Russia. The meeting drew seven of the most prominent members of the U.S. Senate, who heard first-hand testimony about the fate of Soviet Jews.

I still kept an eye on the Minsk community, especially the

three war heroes. Both Hartke and I were very upset to receive a heartrending note from Colonel Davidovitch: Our efforts had been in vain; he was still suffering from harassment. He wrote, "I have been placed outside the law. My apartment has been turned into a K.G.B. tape-recording studio. The house is under 24-hour surveillance. A gravely ill war veteran is followed step-by-step by K.G.B. agents. Let me go to Israel: Israel or death! I have no other way. I have lived long enough. I shall know how to die with dignity."

I had made the Davidovitch case an international cause after Flora Lewis wrote a long article in *The New York Times* describing the struggle of the three war heroes and including a photograph of the bemedaled Davidovitch. In early June after hearing that the three Colonels were on a hunger strike, Hartke sent a telegram to President Nixon seeking his personal influence to obtain visas from the Soviet authorities. He received a reply from a Presidential aide, on White House stationery, assuring him that "your matter will be called to the prompt attention of the President and the appropriate members of the staff." We were also gratified that we had contributed our part to help get the ballet star Valery Panov out of Russia, and that subsequent pressure from the Senator on Dobrynin had added to the international campaign that eventually forced the Soviet authorities to allow Panov's wife, Galina, to leave with him.

Leon Charney with Russian dissident from Minsk.

Meanwhile, I was getting flak from friends in official Jewish organizations over the modified trade bill that I had drafted for the Senator. He aroused some negative reaction after closely questioning Secretary of State Kissinger at a Senate Finance Committee hearing (on March 7, 1974) regarding the Jackson amendment on most-favored-nation status. Kissinger indicated that he would be inclined to recommend that the President veto the bill in its present form. Hartke urged that it be suitably modified, to preserve détente and promote individual emigration rights. As Hartke put it in his colorful language, "I do not want the public to be afraid that we would all have to build bomb shelters again if Congress does not grant most-favored-nation treatment to the Soviet Union." Later that day, over a candlelit dinner table at the White House, Kissinger confessed admiringly to Martha Hartke that "your husband, the Senator, really grilled me

Photo by Arie Kanfer

Colonel Naul Alshansky greeting L.H. Charney along with another Jew from Minsk at the refugees' temporary home in a Tel Aviv immigrant center, August 1975.

today. He made me feel quite uncomfortable." When we heard this, Hartke and I had a big laugh, since I had prepared his cross examination.

Finally two of the Minsk Colonels were allowed to emigrate. I was a happy man on the day in early August 1975 when I met Colonel Alshansky once more—this time in Israel. He was living temporarily at an immigrant absorption center near Tel Aviv and readying himself for his new life. We spent the day talking of my visit to Minsk two years earlier, and discussing the dreadful way the Soviet authorities had been treating Davidovitch. Alshansky was relieved to hear that we had formed a public committee in the United States to help his friend. Its members included former boxing champion Joe Louis, noted director Lee Strasberg, comedian Red Buttons, and Judge Louis Kaplan.

Regrettably, the Soviet authorities remained totally impervious to any kind of plea or pressure when it came to Davidovitch, whose victimization took on particularly nasty forms of personal terror. Deprived of his veteran's pension and deprived of his reserve rank, the war hero was told time and again, "Your application for an exit visa is denied; it is not in the State's interest to let you leave." He was exemplary in his courage, and on May 9, 1975, he appeared in full military uniform at a memorial service commemorating the slaughter of the Jews of Minsk during the war. He told of the sufferings of those Jews under the Nazi occupation, and the subsequent suppression by the Soviet authorities of cultural and religious facilities for the survivors. This prompted further measures against him. Although he suffered a fifth heart attack in March 1976, he was denied admission to a hospital and succumbed to his sixth and final seizure a month later.

Only after his death was his family allowed to leave for Israel, carrying his remains with them. In keeping with his last wish, the Israel Defense Forces honored his memory with a military burial in Jerusalem. His comrade, Colonel Alshansky, recited *kaddish*. Even in death the Soviet authorities had acted spitefully; they confiscated at the airport the late Colonel's war medals and honors.

22

An International Bank Crisis

Through Senator Hartke I met one of his leading constituents, who not only became one of my closest friends, but who plunged me into the heart of an international banking scandal. Donald Tanselle, President of Merchants National Bank and Trust Company of Indianapolis, came to Washington in early 1974 to see the senior Senator of his state, whom he had helped in various election campaigns. Tanselle told us that he wanted the Senator to pressure the Israeli Government through its Washington Embassy. His bank had $4.5 million involved in the collapse of the Israel-British Bank (I.B.B.) and its London subsidiary. Some 20 banks across the United States were also involved, although the Indiana bank's losses would be the greatest. A number of prominent European and Canadian banks also were caught by the I.B.B. collapse. The American banks alone had suffered a loss of $20 million. The banker, who was to become one of my most intimate and trusted friends, later told me that his initial attitude toward me was one of hostility. That was because, when he asked me to serve as his counsel in the I.B.B. case, I told him bluntly, "If it will be to Israel's detriment, I won't touch it. But if not then I will be pleased to represent you."

274

My major aims were to get justice for clients and to save Israel from losing its credibility among the international banking community—and thus losing its credit standing. When I first was consulted this appeared a plausible projection. Under a proposed bankruptcy arrangement the American banks would get back only about 15 percent of the lost deposits. What I found, to my vast dismay, was a refusal of the Israeli banking and political authorities to accept their responsibilities for what had happened. At first they refused to acknowledge their obligations toward the creditors of the I.B.B. subsidiary in London. Only at a later stage did the Government of Yitzhak Rabin agree to a joint liquidation scheme for I.B.B. in Israel and in England that would enable the creditor banks to recoup a higher proportion of their losses.

I really feared that concern about Israel's credit might spread like wildfire throughout the world banking community and affect Israel's financial pipeline. I proposed in the course of the tortuous negotiations that the Government of Israel enable these banks to recoup part of their losses; in return, the banks would reinvest the recouped money in Israel Bonds, even below the going market interest rates.

As it turned out, Don's bank alone continued to purchase Israel Bonds to the tune of millions of dollars.

I was rather upset at the short-sightedness of the Israeli Embassy in Washington toward the I.B.B. American creditors. It remains unclear to me until this day whether the Embassy's economic personnel grasped in full the financial and political ramifications involved. I also doubt they were totally aware of the ultra-sophisticated lobbying techniques of U.S. banking at the various levels of American Government.

Within a short time I was representing virtually all the American banks involved. Because Don's bank had the largest sum to lose, I decided that I had to take Don to Israel with me, expecting that such a man would become more sympathetic to the country once he experienced it firsthand. First we flew to London to meet with people involved in the liquidation of the London branch. I am afraid I put our English hosts' backs up, especially the Queen's Counsel, whom they had called in. He looked askance at me, no doubt because my casual dress contrasted sharply with his "city gentleman" garb. However, I think I earned his respect after I revealed that he had overlooked knowledge of certain points in English law.

During that London visit I finally won Don's friendship. He told me later that it was not only because of my deft handling of the pompous Q.C., but also because of the fact that I broke off an important meeting with some bankers in the City in order to go to the Marble Arch synagogue to recite *kaddish* in memory of my late father.

That evening I told Don we were flying to Israel the next day. I had bought the two plane tickets and had booked reservations on the morning flight. He was flabbergasted. But actually he rather liked the idea of such a spontaneous move. He fell in love with Israel the moment we landed.

Meeting the Decision-Makers

We met everyone in the Israeli banking world including Bank Leumi's Ernst Japhet and Bank Hapoalim's Ya'acov Levinson. By then we had gotten an inkling of the deep competition between the heads of the two big Israeli banks. They had an intense business rivalry and it also appeared that they were competing for the purchase of the "discredited" I.B.B., with Levinson's people already claiming that the Governor of the Bank of Israel, Moshe Sanbar, was unfairly leaning to Japhet.

When we met the Governor, he was not very helpful. He stated that it was not his responsibility nor that of the state bank to do anything to alleviate the lot of the foreign creditor banks. We decided then and there to go to the top and asked Sanbar if we could meet with the Finance Minister, Yehoshua Rabinovitch. But Sanbar declined to give us an appointment. Then luck stepped in. My friend Noah Klieger, a reporter for the daily newspaper, *Yedioth Aharonot*, interviewed Don and me on the American connection with the I.B.B., and he introduced us to his boss, publisher Dov Yudkovsky. Yudkovsky invited us to his home and listened to our position. Don explained to him that "if Israel is to become a mature nation and be recognized as such by the international community, it must accept its responsibilities. If the I.B.B. issue is not settled satisfactorily it could have long-term repercussions on Israel's position in the world financial market." Yudkovsky—as Don put it—was a truly charming gentleman.

The next morning, Sunday, we were informed that we would get an appointment with the Minister in a day or two. In the interim we met with Chaim Barlev, who was then Commerce and Industry Minister.

Rabinovitch was courteous but evasive and did his best to put off a decision. Finally he set up a committee to consider the joint liquidation idea.

I returned to Washington and was bombarded for assistance and/or ideas from members of Congress who were being lobbied by the banks in their states and localities about the position of the Israeli Government. As it turned out, Rabinovitch came around only some time later. This apparently was after a visit to Washington, when he reportedly was told bluntly by Senator Inouye of Hawaii, Chairman of the all-important Senate Appropriations Committee, that aid to Israel might suffer if the joint liquidation matter was not settled. Indeed, I remember on one occasion hearing Hartke cautioning Israel's Ambassador Simha Dinitz that Israel might encounter mounting difficulties in mobilizing support in Congress because of the banks' lobbying over the I.B.B. case. It was a portent of what I had feared and predicted. All throughout this period, meetings were proceeding with the U.S. and Canadian bank creditors of I.B.B., with the Bank of England, and with Israeli authorities.

The case took years to settle, and in pursuit of settlement I traveled to Israel and London frequently. The amount of pressure brought to bear on the Israeli Government was truly incredible. The Israeli finance, commerce, banking, and industrial heads all were besieged by letters and visits of mini-armies of bank officers and banking authorities. These were not only from the United States. Creditor bankers in other foreign countries were exerting equal influence. I fashioned my role as a kind of shock absorber, because I felt that if another lawyer lacking my sensitivity toward Israel negotiated the case then the ramifications for Israel could have been horrendous and long-lasting.

Don told me of a meeting in Washington in October 1974 of officers of the North Carolina National Bank—including its chairman, Tom Storrs—with State Department officials, led by Deputy Assistant Secretary of Economic Affairs Paul Locker, at which State arranged meetings with Israeli Cabinet Ministers. He said, "Both Shmuel Tamir and his partner Moritz feel that political pressure through the U.S. State Department is the best course of action to pursue at this time...."

On October 29th, the Steering Committee of creditor banks met with Sanbar Zadok (Minister of Justice), and Rabinovitch in Jerusalem. Don reported on their meeting with Sanbar. "...the Bank of Israel did not act in good faith and even now appears to be trying to protect itself. Sanbar flatly refused to consider possible alternative solutions, and was told his attitude reflects adversely on the Bank of Israel, the Israeli Government and can only hurt Israel in the future. It was pointed out to him that, while refusing to discuss alternatives with the United States banks, the Israeli Government, according to press reports, is mounting a rescue operation for the International Credit Bank [I.C.B.], a Swiss entity in which many Israeli citizens and friends have an interest. Prime Minister Rabin is said to be interested in seeing this bank helped." Sanbar denied the I.B.B. story, as did Rabinovitch at their subsequent meeting. Don also reported hearing from I.B.B. London's Special Manager Monte Eckman that "...efforts to find assets of I.B.B. London are actually being impeded by the Bank of Israel.... Eckman feels...regardless of their corporate structure, I.B.B. Tel Aviv and I.B.B. London operated as one bank and the Bank of Israel was, and is, fully aware of this fact."

The London *Sunday Times*, in its issue of November 5, 1974, reported, "Israel is grappling with a $47 million business scandal that could have major repercussions in the City of London.... Investigations [continue] into Israel-British Bank, a medium-sized operation that was on the verge of collapse when the Bank of Israel came to its rescue five weeks ago." The paper reported the indictment of I.B.B. Joint Managing Director Joshua Bension in a Tel Aviv court, which made headlines around the world and shook Israel. He was indicted for offenses involving $100 million, including the theft of $47 million. The London paper also told of deadlocked negotiations on a solution between the Bank of England and the Bank of Israel.

In Israel, the I.B.B. affair blossomed into a full-fledged scandal. The Examiner of Banks, Meir Heth, offered his resignation, and newspapers called for Sanbar to do the same.

Pinhas Sapir, who was Finance Minister at the time, was reported to have advised against taking action, which he finally denied.

The Jerusalem Post reported in February 1975 of an exchange in the Knesset, with current Finance Minister Rabinovitch defending his predecessor, Pinhas Sapir, against attacks from the Likud benches.

By April, *The New York Times* reported from Paris about the difficulties of the International Credit Bank and their ramifications, linking its head, Tibor Rosenbaum, to Pinhas Sapir and other Israeli political figures. It also reported the indictment in a Tel Aviv court of one of Sapir's confidants, Michael Tsur, for "fraud, bribery, and breach of trust" involving $20 million. It noted, "This is the second banking scandal involving Israel," mentioning the I.B.B. affair.

By mid-April I was using the good offices of Amos Eiran, an Israeli political advisor and associate of Prime Minister Rabin. Eiran was hearing from others about the negative effect of the I.B.B. affair on U.S.-Israeli relations. He said he would discuss the affair with Ambassador Simcha Dinitz immediately and report to the Prime Minister in Jerusalem on its ramifications. I later learned that Dinitz also had been approached on the I.B.B. case by Senators Mondale and Bird, apart from Hartke and Bayh.

On the morning of April 16th, I was in contact with Eiran at the Israeli Embassy. He told me that he and Dinitz would recommend strongly to the Prime Minister by phone and/or by cable that from a political viewpoint the situation necessitated an urgent settlement.

On May 1, the newspapers in London and Tel Aviv reported that the I.B.B.'s London branch was being investigated by the City of London Fraud Squad in cooperation with the Israeli police. It appeared that 3.6 million pounds sterling were not recoverable from credit advanced to companies in Switzerland and Liechtenstein.

The scandal—and the pressure—built steadily through May. Finally, in June, *The New York Times* reported from Tel Aviv, "In a sharp policy shift, the Israeli Government this week agreed to pool assets of bankrupt I.B.B. in Israel and Britain for their joint liquidation.... It also offered to renounce 30 million West German marks (approximately $13 million) of claims on the London operation, provided the Bank of England put up $7 million.... A Finance Ministry source has confirmed that the Cabinet asked the Bank of Israel to negotiate with the Bank of England along these lines.... A knowledgeable source reckoned the British operation's assets were worth $20 million and the Israeli's $45 million. Pooling them, the sources estimated, would enable creditors of the British unit to recover 38 percent of their deposits instead of 20 percent as previously reckoned.... The policy shift came after pressure was put on the Israeli Government by American Senators and Representatives with constituents who had large deposits in the London institution...."

In addition to my other cases and interests, I was still representing Don's bank and the other American creditor banks in their efforts to recoup part of their losses. I would try to sound out my connections on the matter whenever I visited Israel, which was often. The I.B.B. Managing Director, Joshua Bension, was convicted and sentenced to 12 years in jail. Thus it was that in 1976 I was drinking coffee and discussing the issue with Ya'acov Levinson and Pinhas Sapir at the Moriah Hotel in Jerusalem. Sapir asked me how the case was proceeding and whether he could be of help. We spoke of meeting in a week's time at his Tel Aviv office. However, that was not to be. Shortly after he left us, Sapir suffered a fatal heart attack. So passed away the architect of Israel's industrial development. Some of his methods were highly controversial, but his vision of an economically viable Israel and his warm personality made up for them.

The Banking Duo

Don and I were again in Israel in late July 1977 watching the upheaval that had overcome the country in the wake of the Likud's ascent to power. With us came the Chairman of Don's bank, Otto Frenzell III, who was made much of in the Israeli newspapers because of his ownership of a hockey team. We were received graciously by Prime Minister Menachem Begin, after a warm welcome by his chief aide, Yehiel Kadishai, and his advisor, Yehuda Avner. The two bankers from Indiana were very taken with the new Israeli leader. As Don told me later, "That man could charm the pants off a snake." Begin was wearing a cardigan and offered us tea, so it was a really homey atmosphere, which impressed the two bankers.

We had had occasion in the past to discuss the I.B.B. affair with Begin when he was Knesset opposition leader. The bankers raised the question of the Government's responsibility for the losses sustained by American banks and others through I.B.B.'s collapse. The case had dragged on for five years. Our meeting took place not long after Begin had pardoned Bension, in one of his first acts as Prime Minister. He asked Don if he had acted wrongly, to which his American visitor replied that it was hardly for him to say, he could not pass judgment. Begin explained, "The man was dying, I had to display mercy toward him."

The Americans explained that the other bankers were not as friendly to Israel as they were and were lobbying their Congressional representatives to exert pressure. It was revealing to hear Prime Minister Begin remark, after we discussed the importance of American aid, that "Israel will never be able to achieve freedom as a sovereign nation by military means only. We will only be properly free if we have economic freedom, and that must involve proper measures even if it means that Israelis have to stop living so well."

Don explained the importance of preserving Israel's banking credibility, and earned Begin's approval by revealing that the Indianapolis bank had recently acquired $1 million worth of Israel Bonds to demonstrate its confidence in the Israeli economy and its faith in Israel. The banker warned the Prime Minister that "investors abroad have lost confidence in Israel's economy, and the best way to rectify that is to restore that trust and thus renew the flow of investments in Israel." Begin promised to do his best.

As we parted from the Prime Minister, I could hardly anticipate to what extent the course of my life would be shaped in the coming three years by decisions and responses to world-shaking events emanating from that room.

23

The Opening of Doors

Through the years I kept in touch with Amos Eiran, who was so helpful in the I.B.B. affair. Simultaneously, he grew closer to Prime Minister Rabin, who was to appoint him his chief advisor and Director General of his Office. During the 1975 "shuttle" of Secretary of State Kissinger between Cairo, Jerusalem, and Washington, when Kissinger was trying to bring about an interim agreement between Egypt and Israel, Eiran contacted me to ask for the legal distinction between the terms *agreement* and *understanding.* I replied, "It's the difference between a woman being pregnant and not pregnant." I wrote out an official memo on the terms and their ramifications and made a special journey to Israel to deliver the explanation to Eiran. My opinion was that the word *agreement* was preferable. I do not know whether my advice was taken, but the document arrived at between the Ford Administration and the Rabin Government was a *Memorandum of Agreement.*

The Door to Peace

During my years working with Senator Hartke I became acquainted with Senator James Abourezk of South Dakota. I considered him to be the most outspoken anti-Israel and pro-Arab member of the Senate. I have always believed in maintaining a dialogue with people with whom I disagree on basic issues. That included Abourezk, with whom I shared ideas and goals in some domestic policy areas, including social justice and the judiciary.

The Senator is of Lebanese-Christian background. Frequently when I visited the Senate I would call on him. He agreed with me that, above all, everything should be done to stop the killing between Israelis and Arabs. I kept telling him that he should use his influence in the Arab world to set up a secret meeting between Arab and Israeli leaders. Israeli contacts of mine close to the Rabin Government had appeared interested in pursuing the matter when I had raised it with them. Abourezk and I resolved that I should go to Jerusalem to try to enlist official support for an attempt at setting up a meeting on neutral ground. We thought London would serve as a good meeting site. Abourezk promised to sound out his Arab friends. We decided to use a code which would be employed by him in a telex message to the Sheraton Hotel in Tel Aviv, where I would be staying. The code would indicate success or failure on his part to get his Arab friends to consent to a meeting with the Israelis.

When I approached Eiran with the idea, he was highly skeptical as to whether Abourezk could indeed deliver, but he told me that the Israeli authorities agreed in principle to go any place, any time, to seek a way of furthering peace. However, the telex message I received from Abourezk substantiated my Israeli friends' skepticism. Originating in Washington, D.C., and dated in Tel Aviv June 16, 1975, it read:

```
NNNN
ZCZC UIB369 CAB0146 2-017096E167
ILTY CO URNX 016
TDMT WASHINGTON DC  16 16 1131A EST VIA RCA


LEON CHARNEY
SHERATON TELAVIV HOTEL
TELAVIV (ISRAEL)


SORRY WE CANNOT SHIP SOUVENEIRS REPEAT CANNOT SHIP
   JIMMY KLOCKER
```

I was most disheartened, but there was compensation in the knowledge that it was neither the first nor the last time that informal efforts at making peace had failed. When I met Abourezk in Washington, he explained that his Arab contacts had doubted that Israel really wanted peace. I felt that the connection with the pro-Arab Senator was worthwhile, notwithstanding the carping from my friends at the American Israeli Policy Committee (the Israeli lobby in Washington, D.C.) who thought it unseemly. I wonder how unseemly they would have thought it if they knew that Senator Abourezk was helpful on occasion in facilitating appeals to the Soviet authorities to let Jews out of Russia?

Taking into account the enmity of the Arab world toward Israel, Anwar Sadat's decision to travel to Jerusalem in November 1977 was truly a momentous step. It must be said that the *interim* agreements signed by the Government of Premier Yitzhak Rabin in 1975, when valuable oil resources were handed back to Egypt, provided the right kind of groundwork that led to the 1979 signing of the peace treaty between the Egyptian President and Prime Minister Begin. The moderation and statesmanship revealed by Rabin in his international dealings should never be ignored.

In April 1977 Yitzhak Rabin demonstrated a high level of *political* morality by acknowledging his accountability as a public figure for his wife's omission in reporting their United States bank account, which was a breach of Israeli currency regulations. He then declared that he was stepping down as leader of the ruling Labor Party and resigning as Prime Minister. This meant his withdrawal from the race for a second term as Prime Minister in the election campaign then under way, which ended in Labor's defeat.

The Door to Gratitude

One of the last acts of Amos Eiran as Director-General of the Prime Minister's office was to write an official letter of congratulations to me at the Yeshiva University dinner that honored me with the school's first Distinguished Alumnus Award. In his letter addressed to the Dinner Chairman, Dr. Benjamin Hirsch, Eiran wrote in part: "In addition to his professional achievements as an attorney, his contributions to other diversified areas, such as the problems of Russian Jewry, or the problems of individuals such as the Jewish refugee from India, Elijah Jhirad,* and numerous others which were not publicized, are laudable...We in Israel have learned to know and appreciate these traits. More than once we have asked for Leon's opinion on different and varied subjects and benefited by his wisdom...."

---

* The author was largely responsible for preventing the extradition of this native of India to his homeland. There were solid grounds for suspecting the reason for extraditing Jhirad was mainly because he was suspected of being a Zionist.

The Door to Service

My experience with resolving the national and international implications of the Israeli-British Bank affair has been an asset in fulfilling my current responsibilities as a member of the Temporary Commission of the State of New York on Banking, Insurance, and Financial Services. New York Governor Mario Cuomo appointed me to the post. It has been fascinating. It has afforded me an opportunity to perceive the space-age financing and the integrated financial services that will be available in 21st century banking. Through this distinguished forum I am gaining a powerful perspective on what makes New York *the* financial capital of the world.

I have also been privileged to become acquainted with some remarkable people—my fellow members of the Commission. Louis Lefkowitz is perhaps the most colorful. At approximately 80 years of age he has the dash and energy of men half his age. As the feisty Attorney General of the State of New York for 22 years he certainly left his mark on Albany, especially as the right-hand man of the late Governor Nelson Rockefeller. I have been privileged to serve on the Commission with such notables as former Governor Malcolm Wilson; New York State Superintendent of Banking Vincent Tece; John Torrell, President of Manufacturers Hanover Trust; John Phelan, Chairman of the New York Stock Exchange; and William Schreyer, President of Merrill-Lynch.

The Door to Political Support

I met the present Governor through my good friend, Rabbi Israel Moshowitz, in March 1982. Cuomo was then Lieutenant Governor of the State and relatively unknown. When Moshowitz urged me to support Cuomo's bid for the Governorship, I told him, "Rabbi, how can I support Cuomo? The entire city is going to Koch, including all my friends in the real estate business. People say Cuomo is a lost cause." Then Moshowitz asked me, "Tell me, Leon, do you like Koch?" I replied: "I don't have any particular love for him, mainly because of the way he treated President Carter. To be honest, when Koch was elected he vowed to remain in City Hall for four years. Now he's eager to break his pledge." Then my friend the rabbi asked me, "And what do you think of Cuomo?" I told him, "I've heard from friends that he has considerable intellectual talents. My political contacts say he has a great future. I think very highly of him." "So," the rabbi retorted, "even though you believe he will lose, if you think highly of him why not go down to defeat with a great man, rather than win with someone you have little respect for." Faced with that argument, I agreed to lunch with Cuomo.

I found him to be an impressive and honest man, and we established immediate rapport, largely because both of us had been engaged actively in the Carter 1980 re-election bid. He had headed Carter's New York State campaign. Cuomo was very frank in assessing his chances, admitting that at that moment he was lagging behind Koch, who had considerably larger financial resources. The candidate outlined his vision for New York State and his aim to maintain its primacy as an international financial and banking center. I promised to give my answer to his request for support after a scheduled visit to Israel.

On my return home, I became a member of New York County's Democratic party and actively joined in Cuomo's drive for the Governorship. In my work for Cuomo's election I met a host of rising figures in the New York political firmament. One I found particularly interesting was Herman (Denny) Farrell, Jr., the elegant leader of the New York County Democratic party. There are some among us who are already betting on his chances of becoming the first black Mayor of New York. And I will chance another risky political forecast: I would venture to predict that Mario Cuomo is destined to continue beyond the Governor's mansion in Albany.

In May 1983, I became Co-chairman of one of the first fundraising receptions in New York for Vice President Walter Mondale's drive for the nomination for the Democratic Presidential candidate. In February I received a letter from Mondale, who wrote:

LC with "Fritz" Mondale, May 1983.

Congratulations at being selected as a temporary member of the Rules Committee of the Convention. The coming months will be both demanding and challenging. Much work remains to be done to ensure a Democratic victory in 1984. We must not lose sight of the fact that we all share the goal of replacing the current Administration and this will require a unified effort. Working together we can elect a Democrat in 1984....

With warmest personal regards,

Fritz

The Door to the Future?

No matter what the outcome of the 1984 Presidential election, it is coincidental that on the day I received Mondale's letter, Ezer Weizman phoned me from Israel to inform me of his plans to re-enter Israeli politics in time for the next general elections, slated for July 1984. Using his pilot's jargon, Ezer asked me to "keep your engines warmed up" on his behalf.

Who knows, perhaps a new back-door channel is about to come into being, one more structured and open than the "peace treaty shuttle" Bob and I traversed while he was in the White House.

Even after Bob formally resigned, we continued to ply the behind-the-scenes byways of diplomacy in trying to resolve matters vital to the United States. Perhaps our attempt to free the American hostages held captive in Iran was the most noteworthy.

24

The Viennese Connection to Iran

It was November 10, 1979 when Bob and I flew to Vienna on a totally secret mission to try to free the Americans being held hostage in Iran. They had been captured November 4th, when thousands of Khomeini militants had overrun the U.S. Embassy in Teheran. The American people were in turmoil, and so was the Administration, from the White House down. Carter in his memoirs disclosed the various "third-party" groups his Administration had contemplated using to approach the Ayatollah, who had little love for America, Americans, or Carter. The list included the Algerians, Syrians, Pakistanis, Libyans, and the PLO. Carter dispatched former Attorney-General Ramsey Clark, known for his espousal of liberal causes, to Teheran in a bid to intercede with the Khomeini regime. Insiders in Washington felt the PLO might try to legitimize itself with the United States by offering to play middleman with the Khomeini people.

My gut reaction was that if the Administration should make
such a policy shift it might well destroy the entire Camp David
peace process. I thought it would be advisable to check out just
what the PLO might be trying to accomplish and what in
actuality it could offer, and the best way to do this would be to
explore the situation through my Viennese connection.

I fished out my telephone book and called the office of the
Chancellor of Austria. It was a bit of a long shot, but I thought
I would try the direct route first. I introduced myself to Krei-
sky's aide, briefly recapped my previous meeting with the
Chancellor, and explained my reason for calling. After a brief
pause, I was delighted to be put right through.

I tried—as best as I could by phone—to sound out the Chancellor on the best approach to tackling the hostage situation.
Kriesky said he would be willing to see me and someone who
could speak for the U.S. Government, even if unofficially.
"Who knows," he said, "your journey here might be productive...."

I called Bob in Atlanta. It was only four days after the
hostages had been imprisoned. I told him of my conversation
with Kreisky and of his willingness to receive "someone" who
could speak for the Administration. Bob immediately conveyed this information to the President, who responded positively to our suggestion of traveling to Vienna to discuss with
Kreisky ways the hostages might be freed. After all, Kreisky
might have valuable information for us. He frequently was a
confidant of Arab and other third world and Eastern countries. Carter advised Bob to contact Secretary Vance. Vance
invited us to work directly with Harold Saunders, whose
duties included heading the American-Iran Task Force.

On Saturday, November 10th, I flew to Washington from
New York and Bob came in from Atlanta. We met with Saunders at his office at the State Department. He briefed us on the
situation in Teheran and the efforts being made to secure the
hostages' release. He did not sound hopeful. Bob then phoned
the American Ambassador in Vienna, Milton Wolf, apprising
him of our impending arrival. We took the Concorde to Paris
that afternoon.

After an overnight stay we proceeded to Vienna. At the airport we were met by Kreisky's top aide and a most cordial Ambassador Wolf. Bob knew Wolf from the election campaign and had met him often at the White House. Wolf, a successful businessman from Cleveland and a leader of its Jewish community, had been a Carter supporter from early on. He had served on Carter's Economic Policy Advisory Committee and was especially close to Senator John Glenn. It was Glenn who had suggested to Carter that he appoint Wolf as an Ambassador to a European country. I think it was good advice. In my opinion Wolf was one of the finest Ambassadors in the Carter administration. Incidentally, Wolf was decorated by the Austrian Government early in 1980. Rudolf Kirchschlager, the President of Austria, personally presented him with the *Great Gold Medal of Honor with Sash*, in behalf of the Republic of Austria, in appreciation for his service. I understand he was the first and only "sitting" Ambassador to be so honored.

It was agreed that our cover would be that of two American lawyers on a business trip. We were all aware of the reputation of Vienna as "the spy capital of Europe." Indeed, in the ride from the airport to the city the Ambassador regaled us with the latest spy story. Every so often the Viennese newspaper, the *Kurier*, printed the number of spies of various powers operating out of and in Vienna.

During our stay in Vienna, Bob insisted on absolute secrecy, and when we were in our hotel rooms, in taxis, or in restaurants, we never discussed our real business. For that, we went to the hotel lobby, and discussed what we had to in the safest manner possible. We were concerned lest the Russians would somehow become aware of our mission.

Viennese Kosher

I found Ambassador Wolf to be congenial, and I discovered that he too came from a traditional Jewish background. Indeed, it was fascinating to see how he and his wife did their best to observe the rules and rituals of their religion, including a kosher kitchen and lighting candles on Sabbath eve, while conducting all the social and diplomatic functions expected of an Ambassador. I imagine theirs must have been the only kosher kitchen in any Embassy in Vienna, apart from that of the Israelis. I was pleased to see that the Wolfs had affixed a *mezuzah* to the doorpost, in keeping with Jewish custom. By coincidence, the Ambassador's residence, which was an imposing palace, had in earlier days been the home of wealthy Viennese Jewish magnates. After the *Anschluss* it had been expropriated by the Nazis, who installed the dreaded S.S. headquarters there. After the war, the U.S. Government purchased it for its Embassy. The building had been used for the historic encounter between President John F. Kennedy and Nikita Khrushchev. In June 1979 the Embassy was the site of a vital round in the SALT Summit talks between President Jimmy Carter and Soviet President Leonid Brezhnev. Ambassador Wolf helped guarantee the smooth flow of the talks by careful behind-the-scenes operational planning. At one point after the meetings, Brezhnev surprised everyone by requesting supper, and Ambassador Wolf suddenly found himself hosting one of the most historic gatherings in modern history. Representing the Russians were Brezhnev, Foreign Secretary Gromyko, Chernenko (who succeeded Brezhnev as leader of the Soviets), and Dmitriy Ustinov, Minister of Defense. Joining them were their American counterparts: President Carter, Cy Vance, Brzezinski, and Harold Brown. Carter mentions in his memoirs that some of the formality dissipated as Brezhnev bottomed up glass after glass of vodka in toasts.

A Kreisky Proposal

On the same Sunday afternoon that we arrived, Chancellor Kreisky received us at his home. He was affable and did most of the talking. He made two preliminary observations. First, in his opinion it had been a mistake to send Ramsey Clark as an official envoy to Teheran. Only a high-ranking official, say Vice President Mondale, *might* have induced Khomeini to see an American emissary at that time, because of the international recognition it would have given him. Secondly, Kreisky added in a tired voice, "Whoever had intervened with Khomeini then, I'm not at all sure that it would have done any good. He's so irrational and irresponsible.... Nevertheless, there's no sense holding back on any further attempt, for the reason that Khomeini is the only game in town." Kreisky proceeded to the main point: if anyone could persuade Khomeini to let the hostages go, it would be Yasir Arafat. Thus the United States must do business with him. Kreisky claimed that the PLO enjoyed clout in Teheran because it had taken the lead in training Khomeini's men in military matters. The PLO and Iranian militants were interchangeable, according to Kreisky. Furthermore, he pointed out, the PLO and Arafat were among the few to have befriended Khomeini while he was in exile.

Kreisky specifically urged that the following course of action be pursued. He could call back to Vienna his Ambassador to Lebanon, Dr. Herbert Amry, whom he trusted completely and who had the best possible relationship with the PLO. Amry would serve as our consultant and as the liaison with the PLO. (Later we learned that Kreisky had already ordered Amry to return to Vienna with this design in view.)

Getting to the heart of his proposals, Kreisky said that Bob and I should meet and talk with the PLO representative in Vienna, Issam Sartawi. Kreisky described Sartawi as a man "who is dedicated to the cause of bringing peace between Israel and the Palestinians at the risk of his own life." The Chancellor urged that Bob overlook the long-standing U.S. commitment to Israel never to deal with the PLO unless and until the PLO first recognized U.N. Resolutions 242 and 338 and Israel's right to exist. It was Kreisky's wish that the U.S. Government take "a demonstrable action openly and directly with the PLO, which should amount to its *de facto* recognition of that organization." However, he went out of his way to assure us that this was not intended as a *quid pro quo* to secure Arafat's active intercession with Khomeini in the matter of the hostages.

Bob did not commit himself on any of the proposals raised

by the Chancellor. He said that he would talk first with Washington. Moreover, he would be only too glad to meet Dr. Amry—but no one else unless so directed by the U.S. Government. That certainly ruled out the PLO.

I then spoke up and said that I was in Vienna as an individual and not as a representative of any Government. However, I said, I thought it might be highly advantageous to clarify the matter with the Israeli Defense Minister. Kreisky agreed, and I placed a call to Ezer in Israel.

We were playing with dynamite. If the PLO had been willing to mediate with the Iranians purely on humanitarian grounds (and for good public relations), the matter might have borne further exploration. But it seemed that they were demanding a *quid pro quo*, "We will do this only if you do that." I was virtually certain Israel would find this unacceptable. This in turn, might color how the U.S. viewed Kreisky's proposal.

I called Ezer from the kitchen of the Austrian Chancellor's home. We spoke mostly in Hebrew. Ezer wanted to be filled in fully and consult with his advisors. "Please come to Israel *immediately*," he asked. I went back to the living room and told Kreisky that Ezer wanted a face-to-face meeting to explore his proposal in depth. Could Kreisky help me get a plane?

Before I left, Bob and I discussed Kreisky's idea. We noted that:

—Kreisky was the leading advocate in Europe of recognizing the PLO.

—Arafat was at that moment in the Kremlin conferring on a new arms deal with the Soviets, with whom Kreisky did his best to maintain good relations.

—Kreisky had overlooked how much the Soviets would gain if the U.S. position in the Persian Gulf eroded.

Moreover, Kreisky had not mentioned how much the Russians would benefit from friction between Teheran and Washington.

Within two hours I was air-borne, the sole passenger in a Lear jet I chartered for $12,000. One more contribution to the cause. I felt as if the world was weighing on my shoulders.

Bizarre James Bond thoughts flickered through my weary brain. One wrong move or word by me could prove explosive, not only between East and West but could destroy the entire peace process. This could have ramifications beyond those I wanted to think about. I must confess that being the only passenger, with such thoughts on this lonely flight, was not exactly my idea of a fun evening. Was I overreacting, I wondered, as my Austrian pilot and co-pilot chatted blithely to each other in German. I slipped on stereo headphones and tried to calm myself by listening over and over again to Frank Sinatra softly crooning, "Strangers in the night, doo-dooby-dooby, Strangers in the night."

As I headed to Tel Aviv, Bob drove to the United States building to use the "secure" phone. He contacted Harold Saunders in Washington and gave him a full report on what had transpired, including my journey. Saunders was most interested to hear from me the moment I got back from Tel Aviv, as he wished to learn of the Israeli reaction. Only then would he be able to flesh out to Bob the reaction of the top people in the Administration to Kreisky's proposals.

From Vienna to Tel Aviv

I was met at the Ben-Gurion Airport by a Defense Ministry car and whisked over to the Ministry and straight into Ezer's office. The tension had made me feel light-headed and feverish.

I briefed Ezer on what Kreisky had said, and sounded him out on whether an Entebbe-type rescue mission might not be mounted. He convened his top military and intelligence advisors, many of whom I had come to know well. They allowed me to sit in on part of their discussions on possible ways to reach the hostages. It was impressive. I think that the Israelis were better informed about the Iranians and on what was going on inside Teheran than most Governments. The CIA, after all, had ignored early alarms from the Israelis about the coming debacle in Iran. At the end of their deliberations, Ezer's advisors concluded that there was no way of launching a successful military rescue operation.

I heard from Ezer that U.S. Ambassador Samuel Lewis had

suddenly decided to leave town and indulge in his favorite
sport, deep-sea diving off the southern Sinai coast. I wondered
whether his abrupt disappearance from the Embassy was not
aimed at demonstrating to outside parties, especially in Iran,
that there was no coordination of information between the
United States and Israel.

When Ezer and I discussed the Kreisky proposal regarding
the PLO, his face grew very stern and he declared, "The United States must appreciate that any *quid pro quo* with the
PLO, even if it is related to the hostage issue, would indicate to
us that the Government of the United States of America is
incapable of fulfilling its commitments to its allies. You
should also convey to your friends in Washington that any
American capitulation in this matter could well deal a terminal blow to the Middle East peace process. How could we trust
the Americans to honor their commitments in the Egyptian-Israeli situation? And I say this with the deepest feelings for
American concern for the safety of 52 American lives in Iran."
We arranged to meet again in the Kirya at 9 a.m. the following
morning. I felt physically terrible, sick to my stomach, flushed
and feverish. I made an appointment with my friend, Dr.
David Sharon, for early in the morning before I was to meet
Ezer. He examined me and told me he could find no clinical
reason for my ill feeling. "You don't seem to have any fever,
but you seem edgy and nervous. Do you have something special on your mind that is upsetting you?" *A good physician*, I
thought, but remained silent, musing to myself, *nothing special, only the world.*

The PLO Beckons

When I returned to Vienna, Bob was waiting at the airport
to brief me on his talk with Saunders (to whom he had suggested that Harold Brown perhaps contact Ezer Weizman). I
disabused him of any notion of an easy way out of the hostage
dilemma. He told me of his previous day's meetings at the
Chancellor's office, first with Kreisky, Dr. Amry, and Ambassador Wolf, and then with only Amry.

Their talk had lasted more than one hour. Amry declared that if Arafat and the PLO played any part in the hostage issue "there would have to be something in it for them." The President, personally or through an authorized representative, should request Arafat and the PLO to help the United States on the hostage issue, he said. The request should be conveyed via Kreisky, he also stipulated. Amry said that thereby the world would see America and the PLO as "partners in solving the Middle East—and the Iranian hostage—problem." He declared, "The PLO wants this to be a clear Presidential request that would be irrefutable, so that the authority of the Presidential envoy could not be denied at a later date." Amry advised Bob that the proposed scenario was the result of two separate discussions. The first was between Kreisky, Amry, and Sartawi, and the second—by phone—was between Sartawi and Arafat.

The Austrian diplomat was honest enough to highlight the opposition of Syria and its President Assad to any PLO intercession on the American hostages' behalf. Not only because Damascus had tried and failed to solve the problem, and did not wish the PLO to succeed where it had not, but also because it did not wish the status of the PLO to be elevated, and that certainly would result from American recognition of the PLO's legitimacy. Amry also advised that, notwithstanding all the current Iranian demands for the Shah's return to stand trial, what the Khomeini people really were interested in was not the former ruler but his money. That prognosis was certainly borne out by later events.

Dr. Amry then made a curious request for rather sensitive information about the hostages—the number of men and women, their ranks of service, the names of any ill persons or family persons with dependents, and so forth. This made Bob begin to wonder what kind of dual role the Austrian might be playing.

After his talk with Amry, Bob returned to the scrambler phone and reported to Saunders, who promised to call back after consultations with Vance.

I had by this time arrived from Israel and briefed Bob and

Ambassador Wolf about my trip. I informed them that the situation in Israel was economically and politically so bad that a miscalculation on America's part could well precipitate an Israeli reaction of an extreme nature. This was a prime reason for being very careful in handling the notion of contact with the PLO.

The three of us returned to the United States security center. It must have been the most heavily guarded and protected place I have ever entered, with almost as much sophisticated, futuristic equipment as in the White House situation room. While we were waiting to be connected with Saunders so we could pass along information about my trip to Israel, I started humming my favorite cantorial tunes to while away the time, with Wolf joining in, much to the amusement of Bob and the curiosity of watching Marine guards.

A Four-Point Strategy

A third meeting, this one with both Kreisky and Amry, was somewhat innocuous and repetitive, because Bob could give no clear reply to Amry's proposals. A further meeting was arranged for the following day. The evening before the meeting our American contingent once again returned to the security center. It was about noon Washington time, and Saunders advised Bob that an hour earlier "the project had been wrapped up." A four-point decision had been adopted, Saunders told him:

1. The Administration would pursue only the private channel of communication with the PLO that had been established some months earlier with Israeli concurrence, and *not* the public channel urged by Kreisky.
2. There would be no public recognition of, nor *quid pro quo* with, the PLO.
3. Bob should explain the decision to the Chancellor, express Washington's appreciation of his advice and helpfulness, and "try to keep the Kreisky connection warm, but not hot."

4. Bob was to inform Ambassador Wolf fully of all developments to date, and also advise Kreisky that, should future communications on this subject be desirable, they would be through the Ambassador.

A fourth and final meeting was held at Kreisky's home with Amry, Bob, and myself present. Bob displayed his best diplomatic talents in explaining the U.S. position. Kreisky said he had known of the private channel and displayed understanding of the American line of "going down only one track at a time." We parted on cordial terms.

While I flew on to Israel, Bob returned to Washington and dined that night with the President at the White House, gave him a full report on the mission, and then caught up on his sleep in the Lincoln bedroom. The next morning Bob briefed Saunders in full at the State Department and submitted a written summary to him and the President.

It was only in March 1981 that Bob released the story of our secret mission to Vienna. It gained immediate worldwide publicity. I was sunbathing in Eilat when I heard of it. Friends I was vacationing with were fascinated to read of my involvement in the case. Curiously, people seemed to be more interested in the private jet flight to Tel Aviv than in other more vital aspects of the mission.

The outcome of that journey to Vienna should certainly put the record straight about Jimmy Carter. After all, there are few politicians who would have declined to tell the story of how they had refused to legitimize the PLO, particularly when the story might have helped the politician in a re-election campaign. But Carter clung to his determination of not doing anything that might jeopardize the lives of the 52 hostages, even at the cost of losing the election in 1980.

25

Controversy at the U.N.

In December 1979 Robert Strauss was succeeded as Middle East envoy by Sol Linowitz, who had previously achieved marked success as U.S. Ambassador to the Organization of American States and as the President's representative in the intricate negotiations concerning the Panama Canal Treaty.

Bob Lipshutz called me to say that Linowitz wished to meet me. I visited him first at his law office in the center of Washington, not far from the White House. (Later I was to meet him in his new quarters in the Old Executive Office Building.) He had a personality which contrasted sharply with that of Strauss, the fast-talking Texan. Linowitz was the archetype of the patrician "East Coast establishment" lawyer, a courtly, soft-spoken gentleman. He was of East European Jewish immigrant stock and had come from a religious Jewish background. He hoped that his upbringing would help him cultivate good relations with the Israeli leaders. He had made his fortune as one of the founders of Xerox Corporation in Rochester, N.Y. during the 1950's. He then became one of the elite Washington lawyers from whose ranks various Administrations recruited their star envoys.

Linowitz was convinced that he could succeed in the Middle East where others had failed. After all, the Canal negotiations had stalled for 14 years before he entered the scene and broke the impasse, so why couldn't he perform the same wizardry in the Middle East? He had a hard task ahead of him, especially since the Americans had lost credibility and prestige with the hostage crisis in Iran and the Soviet invasion of Afghanistan.

The refined lawyer got on extremely well both with Sadat and with Begin; the courtly manners of the trio complemented each other. Linowitz and Ezer took an immediate liking to each other, and the Israeli Defense Minister often referred to him affectionately as "Shloime."

Yet, before Linowitz had served long in his new post, a pall was cast over U.S.-Israeli relations that was to trouble Israel's supporters in America—especially those in the American Jewish community. In Israel, the extremist *Tehiya* Party member Geula Cohen put up for a vote in the Knesset the so-called Jerusalem Law, proclaiming Jerusalem as Israel's eternal capital. It was a purely declarative measure; it affected nothing in Jerusalem's status or development, and other moderate members would have been politically hard-pressed to vote against it. However, it irritated the Administration and caused unnecessary trouble by thrusting the Jerusalem issue onto the world agenda. It even prompted countries that had had their embassies in Jerusalem for many years to move them to Tel Aviv. These included a number of Latin American countries and a friendly European nation, the Netherlands.

The Controversial U.N. Resolution

The Carter Administration from the start opposed Begin's settlement drive, so it did not oppose a Jordanian initiative at the U.N. to set up a Security Council commission to look into the settlement issue. At the same time Israeli Ambassador Evron warned the Administration that its decision not to veto the commission idea would lead to trouble. Then the Israeli Cabinet decided to revive Jewish settlements inside the fundamentalist Islamic city of Hebron. The Carter Administration regarded this as a needless provocation. It happened just as Ambassador Linowitz seemed to be making some progress in the autonomy negotiations. There was a fear that the pro-Arab group at the State Department would be able to maneuver toward punitive action against Israel.

Evron met Vance at this time, and he was reassured that Washington would do all it could to block a U.N. Security Council session on the subject.

Supposedly, instructions were sent to U.S. Ambassador Donald McHenry. But it is not clear how hard McHenry labored to stop the Council from convening, or whether a strenuous effort was made to strike anti-Israel passages from the draft resolution submitted to the meeting. The Israelis were kept in the dark on American intentions. Although the Carter Administration had denounced the settlements as "illegal," the President had promised at Camp David to leave the final determination of the status of Jerusalem to the Egyptian and Israeli negotiators. He had committed the U.S. to either abstaining or vetoing any new U.N. resolutions on Jerusalem's status. The current resolution included references both to the settlements *and* to Jerusalem.

At the President's regular Friday morning breakfast, which focused on foreign affairs, he accepted Secretary Vance's recommendation that the United States abstain on the resolution because of its mention of Jerusalem. Only the next morning was Evron officially informed of the American position, just hours before the vote was taken. Evron pointed out that references to Jerusalem were especially abhorrent to Israel because of such phrases as "occupied Palestinian territory." Vance assured Evron that all references to Jerusalem had been deleted. In Carter's memoirs he recorded that Vance phoned him that day at his Camp David weekend retreat and assured him that all references to Jerusalem had been deleted. Accordingly, Carter authorized him to instruct McHenry to vote for the anti-settlement resolution. However, Evron met Vance that day and pointed to *seven* references to Jerusalem in the draft. Vance blurted out, "I didn't realize it." The Secretary then called McHenry, who protested that it was too late to go back on the U.S. position, that he had committed himself to vote for the resolution. Vance apparently feared that McHenry might resign, and did not relish another scandal over a prominent black official quitting the Administration—so soon after Andrew Young had resigned.(This had resulted largely from the disclosure that Young had met secretly with a PLO representative.)

As was to be expected, the Israelis and their supporters throughout the United States were incensed. The reverberations were heard within the White House. Mondale and Jordan advised the President of the furor caused by the U.N. vote and showed him the resolution. Carter expressed his surprise at the mention of Jerusalem in it. When he phoned Vance and Vance's deputy, Warren Christopher, to check out the matter, they too expressed surprise. A meeting was held with Evron, and the Administration issued a statement saying that the vote at the U.N. "was cast in error through a breakdown of communications with the U.N. delegation."

The incident certainly damaged the Administration's image and raised questions over the President's ability to command and the Secretary of State's ability to see those commands carried out. It also harmed the effectiveness of the Linowitz mission, especially after Prime Minister Begin publicly scolded the Carter Administration over its stance. Carter, who was deeply engaged at the time in primary election struggles with Senator Edward Kennedy, even invited a group of Jewish leaders to the White House to be reassured by him and Vice President Mondale of the Administration's support of Israel. However, many in the Jewish community reasoned that if Carter would upset Israel's friends only six months before the elections, what would he do afterward?

Linowitz subsequently told me of his personal efforts to try to block the U.N. resolution. He had talked to the Foreign Ministers of France, West Germany, and other West European countries on the matter, and he had committed himself to work against the resolution. If it had been left to him, he said, he could have forestalled what happened. The Ambassador said, "When we were in The Hague for the autonomy talks, I told Dr. Burg that it would happen...the inclusion of the words 'dismantling of settlements' was really clumsy language...I told Ezer Weizman straight out that Carter was under pressure."

Linowitz went on to say that he had clout and he would use it. In his opinion the Israelis were hanging on to the fact that 1980 was an election year, believing that Carter would not move and risk being defeated. "But," he added, "Carter will move in any case." An autonomy scheme was to be agreed upon by a May 26 deadline, and Linowitz discussed the kind of concessions Israel might make as the deadline came nearer, so as to show that some progress was being made. But as time passed, the deadline evaporated. He had begun to entertain doubts about the Israelis' good will in the negotiations.

Carter and Linowitz concurred on the need to canvass support among a wide range of Israeli leaders so as to try to coerce Begin into joining the U.S. initiative. But, as I warned Linowitz time and again in our phone conversations and at our meetings, this was not the way to deal with the Israeli Prime Minister. In fact, some of my friends in Israel charged that the U.S. stand at the Security Council had only bolstered Begin's increasingly extremist position. Disagreement within Israel with the Prime Minister's views could be represented by Begin and his supporters as siding with external forces hostile to Israel.

The Back Door to the U.N.

Bob and I still actively used our back-door channels. Usually we worked via Atlanta, with Bob conveying my input back to the White House in Washington. Thus, on March 20, 1980, Bob recorded the following:

Leon going to the White House on Sunday.... Good conversation with Sol L., who's frustrated on a number of points. He doesn't want J.C. to walk into problems.

Sol does not understand the weakness of the Government. Its demise may be imminent?

Again on March 26, 1980:

Credibility is *the* big problem...as U.S. has not expunged our vote.... Reagan making concerted effort.

Then from Israel on April 7th my notes contain the following message to Bob:

The hostage situation affecting Israel's attitude.... Sol has lost some credibility...because of sense of self-righteousness. You may be satisfied with your position but you have to remember you are dealing with people who have spilled a lot of blood....

From RJL to Phil Wise [Carter's Appointments Secretary] April 11, 1980

—I plan to come to Washington Sunday afternoon and stay at least until Monday evening.

—Leon Charney has been in Israel for more than a week and will remain there several more days...probably until after Begin leaves Washington.

—Leon has talked with me almost daily and will speak with me on a secure line Monday morning, Washington time.

—I will then complete my report to the President, and would

like to see him Monday between noon and evening...or, if necessary, Monday night.

From Leon Charney in Tel Aviv—U.S. Embassy secure line—April 14, 1980

9:30 a.m.   Refer back to Article 6 "concept"...*in writing*. Need a new preamble...which will be a reconfirmation of the Camp David agreements...sole guide...IMPORTANT! About 70-80% of the military arrangements...transfer of power from Israeli military government, to civilian Palestinian authority. Not pinned down but can be done (See Sol L.) (Refer C.D. Sect. 3/24.) Enough to "start an autonomy" if we can get an election...use "Gaza first" approach.

Shoot for completing *this* by May 26...momentum, progress. Then O.K. to continue committee meetings in Washington...to work. Set a date for the elections.... Set a date for resolving unresolved 20% to 30% of items(?).

From Leon Charney, April 15, 1980

Kissinger quoted: "Autonomy not a valid concept."
E.W.'s trip. Arrives Wed. April 23.
        3 days, N.Y.
        2 days, Minnesota.
        4 days, Washington.

On April 17, Bob wrote to the President suggesting he meet

privately with Ezer during his upcoming trip to Washington. (Carter had expressed the desire for a face-to-face meeting with Ezer when I'd greeted him at a recent White House reception.)

Ezer and the President met on Tuesday, April 29th at 1:00 p.m. They talked alone for about 35 minutes.

On April 30th, I was able to convey the gist of their conversation, which Bob duly recorded:

J.C.—"Our grapevine works very well!"*

They went into specific ideas about autonomy...U.N. vote, Jewish vote discussed. Asked Ezer to consult with J.C. "thru channels." Peres made a good impression.... Leon placed call today to Fritz.

Meanwhile the furor over the U.N. vote had not abated, and as an actively involved worker in New York for the re-election of Carter and Mondale, I was perturbed at the backlash effect on the campaign, especially the primary battle against Kennedy. So I wrote the following letter to Bob:

New York,
May 8, 1980

Robert J. Lipshutz, Esq.
Haas, Holland, Levison & Gilbert
2300 Harris Tower—Peachtree Center
233 Peachtree Street, N.E.
Atlanta, Georgia 30303

Dear Bob:

I am sure you recall that I was in Israel when the United

---

* Pres. Carter referring to the back-door channel of Lipshutz and Charney.

States did not veto the U.N. Security Council Resolution 465. It is public record that there was an unbelievable and vociferous outcry from and amongst the "Jewish vote" in the United States. At that time, the then Secretary of State Cyrus Vance announced to the world that it was his error in communicating with the President that caused Ambassador McHenry to allow the U.N. Resolution to pass.

Subsequently, the President announced that he disavowed the vote in the U.N. Upon disavowing the vote, the President was instantly subject to immense criticism. Many people claim that the only reason the President disavowed the vote was because he was involved in the New York State primary against Senator Kennedy, and that there was an excellent possibility that the so-called Jewish vote would go against him and ruin his chances in New York State.

I and my friends in Israel had no problem believing the President's version about the error in communication, and that had all the facts been related to him correctly, he would have vetoed the Resolution.

There remains, however, the following question:

"If the President in the first instance would not have voted for the Resolution, then why has he only disavowed the Resolution and not expunged the same from the record?"

Without having the President expunge the same from the record, an inference arises, that the only reason this disavowal took place was because of political considerations in the United States, and that the only purpose for the disavowal was a political one. I do not believe this, nor do my friends, for in reality, the President caused more political problems for himself by calling for a disavowal than if he had done nothing.

It is my belief that the average person concerned with the President's credibility takes the position that a person who makes a mistake, corrects his mistake. If this was an honest error and there was no intention that the United States be part of this Resolution, why not expunge the entire record and Resolution from the record? If the record is not expunged, then there remains the nagging doubt in the minds of many that the President was not telling the truth and that it was merely a political move to placate the "Jewish vote," that in reality the President wished to have the Resolution go forward.

Conclusion
1. Therefore, it is my opinion that the U.N. vote must be expunged first and foremost to keep the President's credibility untarnished.
2. Attached are political reasons why the President, in my opinion, must expunge the U.N. vote.

If I can be of further assistance, please do not hesitate to call. Warmest regards.

Sincerely,
Leon H. Charney

P.S. In Vietnam when Johnson screwed things up, if he had told the truth, he would have won [the election].

I kept in touch with Linowitz. On one particular occasion we met in his sumptuous rooms in the Old Executive Office Building. We had a long and serious discussion about the status of the peace process. Suggestions were even raised that Prime Minister Begin might perhaps be persuaded to change his position if he were to see how the American public was viewing him.

Knowing Begin, I was convinced that this type of tactic would make him dig in only more. I perceived that Linowitz had a strong, personal affection for the Israeli leader, and I believe the affection was mutual. I told him that we had to keep in mind that we were *American* Jews, and that our sons, grandsons, and relatives would not be in the firing line as would be the relatives of Israeli citizens. I felt it was not the role of American Jews to offer judgment as to how Israel should proceed; rather we should try to illuminate the Israeli position to the American public. I often wondered whether some of the official leaders of organized American Jewish groups had not begun to feel that they had a right to tell the elected Government of Israel what to do and how its sons and daughters should spill their blood—while they and their kin remained safe 5,000 miles away.

Sol Linowitz, in my opinion, is both a good Jew and a loyal American, who perceived his limitations and was deeply concerned for Israeli security and peace in the Middle East. He genuinely thought that the moment of history was at hand when peace could be achieved after so much bloodshed. He did not want to lose the moment. He worked patiently and arduously toward this goal.

An Appraisal

When I next visited Israel, Abrasha filled me in on developments. Ezer had pulled out of the autonomy negotiations, leaving Abrasha behind as an advisor. Abrasha had persuaded the Egyptians to stay on by assuring them that Ezer would be back. Any progress that had been made was due to the work of the three groups of expert advisors. The Israeli Ministers tended to "speechify" and competed for media attention. The most publicity-minded was Shmuel Tamir, who ran to reporters all the time.

In Abrasha's view, Carter had picked two such prominent Jewish Democrats (Strauss and Linowitz) as his envoys because he wished to prevent Begin from ever charging him with anti-Semitism if and when the talks ran into crises. Abrasha thought both envoys were way out of their depth in Middle East negotiations. Strauss thought the Middle East was Texas but with more sand dunes. Linowitz thought he was going to work the way he did in Panama. Abrasha thought Linowitz was a gentleman but a rather naive one, and much more Jewish in feeling than Strauss. Both lacked experience in the region's problems and they were not professional diplomats—unlike Philip Habib, whom Abrasha described as a classic negotiator. In Abrasha's view, both Linowitz and Strauss had reached the conclusion that Israel was being too independent of America and had reacted negatively. Moreover, as novices lacking experience, they allowed themselves to be totally guided by the professional experts and did not provide leadership. As Jews they had to prove to the Administration and to Egypt their even-handedness toward Israel, so they leaned over backward in the other direction, not taking into account the considerable concessions made by Israel. As for the other American negotiators, Abrasha thought Alfred Atherton more professional than Robert MacFarlane, while Richard Fairbanks was a really nice guy.

26

One Year Later

There were clouds hanging over the Carter Administration —the biggest one being Iran—when I arrived in Washington one day late in March 1980 for the special celebration arranged by the President and Mrs. Carter to mark the first anniversary of the signing of the Israel-Egypt peace treaty. The East Room at the White House was beautifully decorated, and some prominent leaders of the American Jewish community were present. We all enjoyed the Hebrew melodies played by a smartly turned-out Marine ensemble, melodies which included such favorites as "Jerusalem of Gold." Don Tanselle had flown in from Indianapolis for the occasion, and I introduced him to President and Mrs. Carter, who were standing in the reception line greeting each guest.

At one point, Don and I were standing in a corner having a drink and chatting with Defense Secretary Harold Brown and

Robert Strauss. Brown spoke affectionately of Ezer and mentioned the party they had held the week before to mark the new
defense agreement with Israel. Bob Strauss reminisced about
his short term as Carter's Middle East envoy, during which
Bob Lipshutz and I had been asked to brief him from time to
time. Bob Strauss was already being spoken of as the President's choice to run his re-election campaign, and he began
discussing the mood of the Midwest electorate with Don.

Just then two Marines in dress uniform with white gloves
approached me and announced, "Mr. Charney, the President
would like to see you." Don gave me a startled look, and I
followed the Marines to a smiling President at the other side of
the hall. He put his arm around my shoulder as a demonstration of affection. I did likewise to him. We strolled together to a
quiet corner of the stately room in this informal manner, 500
pairs of curious eyes following us. A golden hush had descended all around us: what were the President and Leon
discussing so intently for fifteen minutes? One must understand that every gesture, nuance, or movement of a President
is scrutinized by the press and the other on-lookers anxious to
find hidden meanings. In any case, to be called by the President in such a manner before such a visible audience is a
tremendous ego message.

The President told me that he wished to emphasize his
regard for me and his gratitude for what I, a private citizen,
had performed for his Administration. He then said he was
troubled. Shortly before coming to the reception he had been
notified of a report from Jerusalem that the Israeli Cabinet
had voted by a narrow margin to establish a new Jewish
settlement in Hebron, a hotbed of Islamic fundamentalism.
This would be another obstacle on the road to peace. I, in turn,
informed him that Ezer Weizman had been absent from the
meeting to show his dissent.

The President said he was deeply anxious about getting the
peace process moving again. He spoke warmly of Bob Lipshutz and told me of Bob's recent visit to Washington from
Atlanta. He said that he hoped this connection between us
would continue, and then hugged me and flashed his famous

grin as we parted. As I walked back to where Don was standing, I felt many curious glances from those who had seen the symbolic way in which the President had singled me out for recognition and esteem. Especially curious was Israel's Ambassador, Eppy Evron.

A Year Remembered

It hardly semed a year had passed since the signing of the peace treaty. I had logged record mileage on the Ben-Gurion-JFK air route and kept the back-door channel humming. Bob's resignation from the White House in September had not diminished the activity or value of our efforts. If Bob was not available, I would communicate with the President directly, as instructed.

In Israel, after the treaty had been signed, Begin came more under the influence of party extremists and seemed intent on isolating Dayan and Ezer, the two Ministers who had been most instrumental in bringing about the peace agreement. Soon Dayan quit the Cabinet; he had become mortally ill. The peace momentum slowed down completely, and the target date of late May 1980 for the completion of Palestinian autonomy negotiations looked like a mirage beckoning in a Middle Eastern desert. I had had intimations since March from Ezer that he could take it no longer and had resolved to resign. I had promised him that the moment he made such a move I would be with him 24 hours later to help plan his re-entry into private life. As the decision boiled over inside him, he kept calling me from Tel Aviv—sometimes twice a day.

Ezer Resigns

The day he informed me of his resignation decision I was in the midst of a real estate deal involving $3.5 million. I asked the other party to postpone the closing for at least a week, but my request was refused. I had previously advised Bob in Atlanta that Ezer was on the verge of resigning and assumed he had brought the matter to the President's attention. When I informed Bob of Ezer's concrete decision, he urged me to fly to Washington and meet with the President. As it turned out, I met not with Carter but with his National Security Advisor, Zbigniew Brzezinski, to whom I had been introduced by Bob. He wanted to know why Ezer was resigning and what I thought the consequences of this action might be. I explained the crisis over the defense budget and Ezer's impatience with the sluggishness of the peace process. I told him that, as far as I could understand Israeli politics, Sharon would eventually take over Defense. However, I could not respond to his question about how Ezer's departure might affect the peace process and relations with the Egyptians—especially Sadat—who had such faith in Ezer.

Just then the phone rang. It was a call my office had forwarded from my banking partners in Zurich. I promised to call back as soon as possible, which I did after emerging from Brzezinski's room. My partners in Switzerland were most understanding when I explained to them the reasons for my delay in closing the real estate deal. They both concurred with my decision, and revealed once more their largeness of heart and the depth of their Jewish commitment by being prepared even to forfeit the deal, if it was for the sake of Israel. (Later we had to resort to litigation over that transaction, although the court "found" for us.)

I took the first flight to New York and the first connection to Ben-Gurion via Athens. A neighbor on the journey was Senator Daniel Patrick Moynihan, who aired the widespread American disquiet about an Israeli Government without Ezer Weizman. It was a long flight, lasting 20 hours. I broke my own record for jet lag. At the airport to meet me were Ilan and his wife, Rachel, who was in tears over Ezer's resignation. Both Ilan and, later, Abrasha hoped that I could utilize the grace period granted to Israeli Ministers to prompt Ezer to withdraw the resignation letter. On the plane I had written a series of questions to put to Ezer, the aim being to present him with the pros and cons of such a far-reaching decision. I never advised him to resign or not to resign. I thought such a fateful decision had to be his own solitary judgment. However, as soon as we met, I perceived that he was firm about resignation and would not be budged. He was intractable.

The next morning was Sunday, a working day in Israel. They say you get your Monday morning feeling on Sunday there. I sat discussing the resignation matter in Abrasha's office. He had always been friendly with Ariel Sharon, and told me that even Sharon did not want Ezer to go.

It was like sitting *shiva*—the week-long ritual mourning period. I was the sounding board and the protective shield, sitting at his side as he cleared out his desk. I was among the bystanders at the farewell ceremony put on by the Israel Defense Forces in his honor. There were many wet eyes among people there.

Calls came in from all over the world expressing regret. I told Ezer that President Carter would like to speak to him, so he asked me to put through a call to Washington. The White House switchboard replied that they would put me through to Camp David. The familiar and famous voice came on the phone, and I said, "Mr. President, here's Ezer." Carter wished him well, trusting he was doing what was best for himself, his country, and the cause of peace. As Ezer was conversing with Carter, the other phone rang. It was Harold Brown on the line from the Pentagon. I had to put the Secretary of Defense on hold, explaining that General Weizman was on the phone to the President.

The next morning Ezer had to appear at the Knesset and formally submit a letter of resignation. That night his friends gathered to discuss the form the letter would take. I was unhappy with Ezer's appearance on Israel TV; in explaining his resignation, he shot off a blast at Begin. Some of his friends at the time advised him badly, both on the resignation itself and on the suggestion that he go public about the reasons. My American background showed. I considered it a matter of fair play, and thought it unwise to pursue an abrasive course. Perhaps I just did not grasp the nature of jugular-vein politics prevailing in Israel. I may have been wrong, but I think I was right.

When Ezer got locked in on anything, that was that. I recall questioning him on whether his presence was not necessary in the Cabinet to avoid the possibility of another war. He told me that he was resigning not only over the budget, but because peace was being whittled away, and he did not want to be a party to this. I tried to advise him that he could wield influence much better from within than without, but he said no. It was my impression that his advisors had persuaded him that once he quit, the Government would fall, because other liberal Ministers would follow him—neither of which happened.

He was also ill-advised on the contents of his letter of resignation to Begin. I counseled him that it should be an historic document that spelled out his reasons for resignation in a dispassionate manner. However, he took contrary advice from other friends. Finally, Ilan, with a heavy heart, took the letter to the Prime Minister's office.

Public Person, Private Life

We started discussing how to handle his projected memoirs, *The Battle for Peace.* Initially, I talked over the matter with some of his friends and their lawyers. But I found their general approach reprehensible and resolved not to work for them. I doubt if anyone wants to be treated like an assistant clerk. So I sent a message to Ezer through Ilan that I was opting out of the deal and declined to work with such people. Ezer called me soon after and we settled that I would start immediately arranging his publication rights as part of my task of putting together his entry into private life.

I left for home the next day and put the machinery in motion. All was ready when he arrived in Manhattan ten days later. Ezer Weizman was very much in the headlines still, and Walter Cronkite's interview was a masterpiece of its genre. We met with a dozen publishers before we secured the deal, which must have been a record advance payment for a former Israeli Cabinet Minister. In fact, I was assured by people in the publishing business that only a few very established American writers could get such a generous royalty advance. We even wrapped up an advance agreement with the Book-of-the-

Month Club with a party at the St. Regis Hotel. All in all, it was quite an experience in the book trade. In Israel, I managed to arrange a mutually profitable contract with the mass circulation *Yedioth Aharonot* through its publisher, Dov Yudkovsky, one of the most honorable men I have met anywhere in business. Then Ezer went back to Israel to put his book together.

Not only did the Israeli Government not fall as Ezer's advisors had predicted, but Begin fulfilled one of his most cherished dreams of emulating his late and great political adversary, David Ben-Gurion, in serving as both Prime Minister and Defense Minister. (In 1981, after the elections, he was compelled to hand over the Defense portfolio to Ariel Sharon.) In the United States the Carter Administration remarked that "it is the worst of all possible worlds," a Begin Government minus Ezer Weizman.

27

A Campaign and an Olive Branch

Our back-door channel continued to work after a fashion until late 1980. Thus Bob recorded the following for the end of August 1980:

From Leon Charney, August 26, 1980

—Ezer going to Egypt *this* Saturday. Any ideas from J.C.?
—Leon wants to continue dealing thru RJL!
—Leon mentioned that E.W. will be in in N.Y. October 21; but we agreed he would have to come earlier for our purposes, which he is willing to do (but all the arrangements must be handled thru the usual channels).

The Presidential campaign was getting up steam. I recall phoning Bob when he was staying with the Carters at Camp

David at the end of August. I passed on the message that Ezer had been invited to Egypt by Sadat for a five-day visit at the end of the month. "Does the President have any message to convey to President Sadat?" I asked. Bob passed the message on:

To Phil Wise, August 27, 1980, 2:45 p.m.

Re: E.W. trip to visit Egypt on Saturday-Sunday, August 30-31, 1980. (Direct, RJL w/President (?) or via Sol L.?)
—Visit ostensibly to visit with Egyptian Defense Minister Ali, but he also is invited to a one-on-one meeting with President Sadat.
—Does the President have anything which he wants Ezer to convey to Sadat or recommend to him? (Keeping in mind that Sadat probably has more confidence in and friendship for E.W. than any other Israeli...and, probably, next to President Carter, more than *any* other non-Egyptian.)
—Urge that all U.S. communications be "secure." Only message to E.W. will come from L.C. and be carefully transmitted.
—Re: E.W. coming to U.S. in October and "speaking out," he is receptive, but prefers to handle the basic arrangement through our previously established channel of communication: Charney/Lipshutz.
NOTE: Either Leon C. himself or a reliable courier with letter from L.C. to E.W. can leave N.Y. Thursday p.m. (August 28) and get to Israel before E.W. leaves.

From Phil Wise, August 27, 1980, 5:10 p.m.

—Response from the President:
"No. I believe Ezer understands situation well. His views are compatible with mine."
—Five days in Egypt.

> *From Leon Charney, August 30, 1980*
>
> Leon called after lengthy talk with E.W.
> Sam Lewis had come to see E.W., and among other things,
> asked him if he was going to run for P.M. E.W. told him that as
> of now it was 70-30 negative.

Then, in late October of 1980, Ezer found himself at the fulcrum of a political tempest that swept the United States and Israel, with candidate Ronald Reagan and the Israeli Cabinet issuing protests.

When I talked to Bob in Atlanta that fall, I mentioned that Ezer was back in the U.S. to be a guest speaker at the Weizmann Institute of Science, named after his famous uncle. This was an exception to his rule of never addressing Israeli charity events. Bob said that the President would surely love to meet once more the Israeli he liked best. An invitation to the White House or to Camp David would soon be forthcoming, Bob assured me. However, the President's schedule was in the hands of his campaign organizers and neither plan worked out. It was therefore suggested by White House officials that Ezer, Re'uma, and I join Air Force One in Washington and share the one-and-a-half-hour flight to Cleveland with the Carters. (There would be a short campaign stopover in West Virginia.)

Sparks on the Campaign Trail

When I told Ezer about the invitation, I cautioned him about the pros and cons of joining the President on the campaign trail. On the one hand, people might accuse him of endorsing Carter. On the other hand, Air Force One was the traveling White House; it could be argued that the Weizmans were making a courtesy call on the Carters. As to the West Virginia campaign stop, I advised Ezer to maintain a low profile so that people would not charge him with getting involved in American elections. Ezer's response was, "I'll make the decision when I'm on the plane."

We were picked up at National Airport by a White House limousine and driven to Andrews Air Force Base to join the Presidential party on Air Force One. We were quite impressed by its luxurious interior design. The red, white, and blue decor was not only patriotic, it was in good taste. Ezer, Re'uma, and I sat in the V.I.P. lounge with the other guests: Senator Jennings Randolph of West Virginia, Kentucky Governor John Y. Brown, West Virginia Governor Rockefeller, and a group of White House staffers. There was piped-in music, and I think it was playing *They're Playing Our Song*. Robert Strauss, now Chairman of the Re-Election Committee, was also in the lounge. I, of course, knew him from when he was the President's special Middle East envoy. We discussed the election campaign, and Strauss thought Carter and Reagan had fairly equal prospects, with the outcome hinging on the upcoming

On the plane. Left to right: LC, Mrs. Weizman, Jimmy Carter, Ezer Weizman.

TV debate and on what happened with the U.S. hostages in Teheran.

From the moment we got on that plane, it was crystal-clear that the Carter staff wanted Ezer to endorse their man. When we stopped at the Tri-State Airport in Wayne County, West Virginia, Ezer said to me: "Look, Leon, I'm not a hypocrite. I love that man. I want to give him back a bit of what he gave to us. I don't care what the press has to say." "Ezer, you're a big boy," I replied. "Do as you deem fit." At the time, I could not judge whether he was doing himself good or harm, but I admired the man for having the courage to stand by his convictions. This is one of Ezer's great attractions: he is governed by a sense of political integrity coupled with a warm and loyal heart.

To understand the background of the political bomb that Ezer set off, one must recall the still-echoing rumpus from 1972 when the then Israeli Ambassador Yitzhak Rabin virtually endorsed Richard Nixon over McGovern. Perhaps with that ruckus in mind, Prime Minister Begin had been discreet in talking of Carter. Ezer, however, had publicly called for Carter's re-election on three previous occasions. "I am not the Ambassador nor a civil servant, I'm an elected politician. I have the right to speak my mind. I hope to see Mr. Carter in the White House for another four years," he had said.

Well, Ezer went out onto the tarmac and was immediately tackled by a reporter.

Q. Do you endorse Mr. Carter for re-election?
A. Of course I do.
Q. Why?
A. Look, it's very simple and straightforward. I took part in one of the greatest achievements for the State of Israel— Mr. Begin, Mr. Dayan, and myself in Camp David with President Carter. I think what I watched there and what he contributed to my country is a thing deserving of praise, and that's why he invited me and that's why I'm here to thank him.

Photo by United Press International Inc.

On the campaign trail: President Jimmy Carter seated in foreground; Ezer Weiz-man and LC walking behind platform; Air Force One in background.

Q. You don't think it's interfering in our political process?
A. No, I'm just enjoying it.
Q. How long do you plan to campaign here?
A. I'm not campaigning. I'm just attending. I'm leaving in Cleveland, going back to New York, then to Washington. I'm watching for the first time in my life an American election.
Q. But are you endorsing him?
A. Look, the man has done a lot for my country. Do I have to thank him or not for that?
Q. Well, Reagan has gone all-out for Israel.
A. I don't know Mr. Reagan.

We left Air Force One in Cleveland. My friend Milton Wolf (who had been U.S. Ambassador to Austria) arranged for a limousine to take us to a reception he had organized at his home. Three hours later we were en route back to New York aboard Wolf's private plane. In the privacy of the Lear jet, Ezer and I discussed the ramifications of Ezer's activities that day, particularly his press conference at the airport. (This became a very controversial issue in Israel.) Ezer reiterated his feelings, that the State of Israel was deeply indebted to President Carter, and that as a private citizen he had the right to speak out the truth as he saw it.

I spent the next day fending off phone calls from the heads of official Jewish organizations, blaming *me* for Ezer's support of Jimmy Carter. I recall one particularly irritating exchange with one of these guardians of the community's interests, just when an Israeli reporter happened to be present. As the reporter wrote later that week, "Charney says: 'Can anyone tell Ezer what to do?' " I think that put it in a nutshell.

An Olive Branch Offered

The back-door channel became part of history, but my friendship with Ezer remained steadfast. Indeed in 1981, shortly after the second Begin Government was sworn in, I was involved in a behind-the-scenes effort to bring about a rapprochement between Ezer and Begin. A third party urged me to approach one of the few surviving confidants of Begin—Ya'acov Meridor, before he became Economic Coordinating Minister in the second Likud Cabinet. We met in his office at the El Al building in Tel Aviv. I had already informed Ezer of my initiative. We spent an hour discussing Ezer, and I told Meridor that, while I could hardly commit myself on Ezer's behalf, I was sure he would make up with the Prime Minister if only to save the nation from war. I urged Meridor, "You are one of the few men who are on such friendly terms with Menachem Begin. Maybe a meeting could be arranged on neutral ground?" Meridor was a long-time admirer of Ezer and had been instrumental in bringing him into the Golda Meir Government as a Likud Minister in 1968. He was very much in favor of bringing about a reconciliation that would pave the way for Ezer's return to a Cabinet post. However, Meridor's advocacy notwithstanding, Begin rejected the idea. Someone explained to me later that Begin could not forgive Ezer for the tone of his resignation letter. Someone else said that perhaps Begin did not wish to have Ezer around to save the country from war. This I do not believe. However, it is my opinion that history will show that Begin's not reconciling with Weizman at this juncture was one of his worst political decisions and the beginning of his personal downfall. Indeed, a year later Begin allowed Ariel Sharon to let loose the dogs of war on Lebanon. It was to prove the undoing of both men.

"By My Spirit"

I think a favorite memory of my association with Ezer Weizman in those years was when he agreed to make one of his rare exceptions and address a Jewish National Fund memorial dinner in Minneapolis. It was in commemoration of the late Senator Hubert Humphrey, in the presence of the Humphrey family. Ezer was in sparkling form, and when the White House liaison with the Jewish community, Al Moses—who had substituted for Vice President Mondale—came up to

us I was introduced whimsically as, "My man in Havana."
Moses said, "Really. And how's the weather in Cuba? Which
section of Havana do you live in?" I hope he appreciated the
joke.

In his address, Ezer excelled himself, encapsulating his
vision of peace and what he wished for Israel and the Jewish
people in a phrase from the Book of the Prophet Zechariah—
part of his Bar-Mitzvah confirmation—"Not by might, not by
power, but by My spirit, saith the Lord."

28

An "Unsung Hero"

It was a sultry Friday late in May 1983. The weather had come as a relief after an over-long rainy spell that had strained New Yorkers' collective reserves of equanimity. Hurrying through the bustle of LaGuardia Airport, I soon found the V.I.P. lounge. A pretty stewardess met me. "Mr. Charney? This way, please." She led me into a corridor and from there I was conveyed up an escalator and around another corner by a succession of very polite, poker-faced Secret Service men. I was escorted through two doors, encountering a departing group of men and women wearing the kind of self-important faces that so often characterize New York's local politicians. Then I was ushered into a small room where I found former President Jimmy Carter.

He had come up North for a speaking engagement and was leaving for a fishing trip. The former President was wearing a navy-blue blazer and radiated a glow of perfect health and good humor. His bright blue eyes, which could show an almost Arctic coldness when he sought to register displeasure, were gleaming with a welcoming warmth. My first, instinctive response was to reflect, "Here is a man who has found the secret of inner peace. In a world where the pressure to 'make it'

330

never stops, he's reached the very top. After all, what can there be beyond being the President of the United States?"

The atmosphere in the small room was cordial and relaxed. The President personally served his guests coffee and Coke, quipping from behind his famous grin, "We dare not drink anything else in Atlanta"—a reference to the well-known headquarters of the Coca-Cola empire. He inquired after my health and recalled his enjoyment at having talked with me by phone a month earlier when I'd telephoned Ezer Weizman's home in Caesaria. Carter and his wife had been spending that Friday evening as dinner guests at the Weizman house during their first visit to the Middle East since he had left the White House. Carter came on the line after Ezer and I had exchanged Sabbath Eve greetings.

An Interview

An interviewer who was with me early in my meeting with the President that day expressed surprise that there had been no United States response to the President's offer to mediate between Nicaragua and El Salvador through his Emory University International Crisis Center. Carter answered with a smile, "I have not yet mentioned that proposal in this country." He had enunciated that novel idea while in Israel on his previous Middle East trip, during an address to the Tel Aviv University convocation that was conferring an honorary degree on him.

The interviewer then remarked, "Unlike Ronald Reagan, you did not give the green light to Begin to go into Lebanon, did you?" Carter nodded his agreement with the utmost vigor. He vehemently concurred with the view uttered recently by his former Vice President, "Fritz" Mondale, that, unlike the Reagan White House with its carrot-and-stick methods, the Carter Administration had never threatened to suspend arms supplies to Israel. He also supported Mondale's stand that his previous Administration, unlike the Republicans, "had preferred to air our differences between ourselves."

It was a curious, almost abstract experience hearing the President discuss my role.

Q. *"Shortly after the signing ceremony at the White House, you kindly wrote a very warm letter to Leon Charney, thanking him for personally having been most helpful to you and your Administration in your efforts to achieve peace. Could you perhaps elaborate?"*

A. *"From the very first time I met Leon—late in 1977, I think it was—I found him to be a source, if a somewhat mysterious source, of advice. Admittedly, at first it was a source I regarded with some trepidation, for I did not know him well. Since then I got to know him better through Bob Lipshutz. I found him knowledgeable of the situation in Israel in matters that didn't come to me from the State Department and other official sources, offering me inside advice, Ezer's advice, and his own advice. After the treaty was signed, I recapitulated to myself the people who had been helpful."*

Q. *"There were not many?"*

A. *"There were very few people who had been so exceptionally helpful. I can tell you that there were few people to whom I'd like to write that. [He smiled a broad smile.] It was indeed rare for me as President to send notes like that. I wrote the letter on my own. No one asked me to do it."*

Q. *"While Counsel to the President, Bob Lipshutz chose a public occasion to pay tribute on your behalf to Leon Charney as 'one of the unsung heroes of the peace process.' Perhaps you could recall the circumstances warranting that description?"*

A. *"I don't want to exaggerate what Bob Lipshutz has said, but there were so very few people who played such a significant role and were unsung. There were, on the other hand, so many sung heroes. [He had a slightly sardonic twist of the mouth.] I agree wholly with Bob."*

Q. *"Do you remember that in your White House, Bob and Leon were often referred to as The Odd Couple?"*

A. [He grinned broadly.] *"I like that."*

Q. *"Your role in securing the release of thousands of Soviet Jews is not widely known. Why is that?"*

A. *"I don't know why that should be. After all, during my Administration we secured the emigration of over 50,000 Jews from the Soviet Union in one year alone! Now, compare that to the 2,400 Soviet Jews who have managed to get out during one year of Ronald Reagan's Administration."*

Q. *"It's also not widely known that you did your best to help secure the release of Anatoly Shcharansky, wrongfully condemned to prison on imaginary treason charges."*

A. *"That is so. I did what I could for that unfortunate man. I even sanctioned Leon's initiative to fly to Vienna to obtain the good offices of Chancellor Kreisky in seeking to influence the Kremlin to release Shcharansky."*

Q. *"How do you explain the attitude of so many American Jews toward you?"*

A. *"I am afraid that I did discern the not-all-that-supportive position of the American Jewish community after Camp David. I think it was caused by our having to address some controversial issues, like withdrawal and Palestinian rights...otherwise we could not have achieved the peace treaty...I hope and pray the results will bear up. We did what was right and what was compatible with Israel's interests.... We don't want it undone."*

After the interviewer departed, the President recalled to me some of the difficulties encountered during the negotiations. When I recalled in particular the problems involved in framing Article Six of the treaty (as to whether the agreement did or did not supercede Egypt's military commitment to other Arab lands), I remarked, "That was a bleak Friday night." Carter rejoined with a grin, "Yes, that was a tough one." He then proceeded with familiar complaints about his dealings with Begin. Seeking a more cheerful subject, I drew his attention to the manifest success of the peace treaty he had engineered, reminding him how it had held up during the war in

Lebanon. Above all, not one soldier had died in Sinai since the treaty. He could not but concur.

We spoke about the time in mid-1980 when I had been approached regarding working a "Back Door Channel" for the Republicans. I reminded the President that when I had asked for his reaction he told me, "Do anything for peace." He stressed that peace was the overall objective, partisan politics should play no role. The plan had been to put me in touch with high ranking foreign policy leaders in the administration. The idea fell through. I never received a confirming call from the two administration envoys with whom I had lengthy discussions. I told them that the plan could only work if it were based on the same concept as the role I had played in the Carter Administration; I insisted on having direct access to the President, as I had had before. Carter reflected, "Yes, that's perfectly correct. You most certainly did have direct access to me. And I always knew you were loyal."

We both felt it was unfortunate that the momentum of the Camp David Peace Process was not continued in the new administration. It is possible that the entire Lebanese crisis might have been averted had the Reagan Administration given a higher priority to the Middle East and the Camp David Peace Process. In my opinion history will show that this was one of the critical errors of the foreign policy of the Reagan Administration.

As we parted, Carter advised me in his most avuncular manner to watch my weight, declaring with a smile, "A blessing on your head and success in your endeavors." On past occasions he had shown a liking for this phrase from a song in *Fiddler on the Roof*. Finally, he promised to send me a copy of his memoirs.

My relationship with Jimmy Carter's White House had developed from one of Presidential trepidation to that of utmost trust, from being referred to in confidential memoranda as "an American citizen and a New York attorney" to "the American attorney and friend of Ezer Weizman" to "our friend Leon."

I suppose I was in the fortunate circumstance of being my own boss, of having a well-run law office, and of possessing sufficient means that allowed me independence of action. At the same time I was not subject to family obligations. Above all, I had freedom of movement.

Though the President asked me to call him directly whenever I deemed the matter sufficiently urgent, on the whole I kept to our regular channel of communication, through Bob Lipshutz. Bob and I enjoyed the overwhelming advantage of immediate access to the President without having to resort to the tortuous corridors of the Governmental bureaucratic apparatus. Hence the efficiency and immediacy of the flow of our information and counseling. Bob liked to say, "Cy Vance has at his disposal the entire State Department staff to produce reports for the President; Zbig has the collective work of his National Security Council personnel; while my input comes from you."

Window on the World

A retrospective discussion with Bob brought home the diversity of that input. A private trip to Paris in November 1978, for example, produced insights on President Carter's greater popularity with influential European business circles as a result of his economic measures. This was at variance with media reports current at the time. I was also able to report from my own connections in the international banking community that a half-billion dollars had been transferred from Iran to numbered bank accounts in Switzerland during the previous two weeks. The particular significance of this report—which was made evident during my next visit to Washington—came from the rising agitation against the Shah in Iran and the recent arrival in France of his powerful opponent, the Ayatollah Khomeini.

I also conveyed advance knowledge of the impending departure for Canada from Israel of Israel's two top negotiators— Foreign Minister Moshe Dayan and Defense Minister Ezer

Weizman—to confer with Prime Minister Begin, who was there at the time.

I was able to offer the President an extra window on the world. Thus it was that early in February 1979 I conveyed to Bob from Jerusalem the insight of a member of Begin's inner circle that "the whole thing will be signed by March." That was over a month before the signing ceremony on the White House South Lawn, when many questions still hovered over the success of the peace process. In fact, reflecting on the somewhat skeptical climate at the time, I had mentioned in my report "my many doubts about my source's accurate comprehension...."

Reflections

When Bob resigned as White House Counsel and sought to put down on paper his perspective or our relationship, he wrote:

> *"Our partnership developed, or rather, it evolved, together with our trust and friendship. There was no specific turning point in the connection. It grew organically. The President was cognizant of who Leon was and where his sympathies lay. The information provided by Leon, weighed up against that derived from our sources, afforded the President some most valuable insights. He was enabled to ascertain what was of real weight in the Israeli positions, what was rhetorical, and what was substantive."*

For my part, I did my utmost to convey to the President how far he could go with the Israelis, and what they could find acceptable.

Bob went on to recall:

> *"In the discussion on the interpretation of Article Six of*

*the peace treaty, we managed to convey to the President
the absolutely vital importance to Israel of this mechan-
ism for peace...I am also sure we did a sterling job in
conveying to the President the urgency of raising the aid
level for the redeployment scheme, to mention one issue
alone. At first I volunteered material; in due time the
President frequently asked for our input."*

I was always curious about how far I had been subject to
security surveillance, because of my special access both to the
White House and to the Israeli Defense Ministry. At a later
stage Bob admitted to me wryly that he had asked "to have me
checked out from the appropriate quarters." As for the Israelis, I can only assume that I was subject to thorough scrutiny. I
remember the security men around Ezer admitting me to his
presence and saying to one another in Hebrew, *"Charney
beseder, haver shel Ezer* (Charney is OK, he's a pal of Ezer's)."
At the White House there was a standing order at the Secret
Service desk to let me through. Yet walking the tightrope so
gingerly did cause me some spiritual stress. It was natural
that I felt hurt at the animosity that "the mysterious Mr.
Charney," as Ezer liked to refer to me, generated at both ends
of the tightrope.

I entered the back-door channel fairly well equipped from a
professional viewpoint. I had been involved in international
law since 1972. During the time I served as special counsel to
Senator Hartke I was advisor to him on subjects of his concern, such as immigration and international trade, and my
law practice brought me to engage in legal affairs with the
Netherlands Antilles. Nor should I omit the considerable
grounding I obtained in international financing and banking
laws through my active involvement in the Israel-British
Bank scandal, which encompassed three continents. In addition, I had been asked by an aide of Prime Minister Yitzhak
Rabin to give my counsel on the interim agreement discussions between Israel and Egypt.

Evaluations

In a rare admission, Ezer also has gone on record with a positive evaluation of the unofficial channel. He said, "I think every Government leader should have one. It might have been good and useful for Prime Minister Begin to have had a similar conduit.... The best example of how it worked was the military-aid issue. Through the existence of this back-door channel, we were able to sound out the other side informally, before official channels had managed to start discussing the problem. The main thing in bilateral relations of this kind is to prevent lasting and damaging mistakes. When the two sides meet formally, everything must be put down in writing, and then it is very difficult to reverse one's position. Because by then it has become a commitment binding on one's Government." Here he added significantly, "Moreover, an unofficial channel does not commit one's Government in any way, and should the informal and preliminary contacts not work out, then one's personal prestige is not affected for the worse either."

I found no conflict in myself between my sentiments toward America and Israel. As a Jew I believe that peace is the central factor of my credo. I abhor the way some of my fellow Jews brandish the Bible in order to justify making war. That is neither my kind of Bible nor my kind of religion. I felt I could perhaps benefit best as an illuminator, but I was most careful never to take up positions.

I have never feared to tell the truth whenever I felt it was required. When I discerned that the President was going too far in pressuring Israel, I would see to it that the appropriate view reached him. Considering all the requirements piling up on a President daily, it is not all that easy to get his ear. Bob and I did so, however, as frequently as was needed. A review of the years of the Carter Administration points out that Carter devoted more time to seeking to bring peace to the Middle East than to any other single issue at home or abroad.

I think that one of the quiet achievements of our channel was to persuade the President to accept the approach of a *selective gradualism.* Through this approach one carefully establishes the attitude that problems can be resolved. This is done by dealing in the beginning with those aspects and issues which have an available solution, and leaving the most difficult problems for the end. It is a confidence-winning and face-saving method. Both of these qualities are supremely important in this area. My attitude in negotiation is motivated by a philosophy of never seeking perfection. That way lies failure. Or as my late father would sagely say, "If you look for perfection, you're going to get migraine."

Negotiations mean compromise. Whenever I embark on them I follow the rule enunciated by Leon Trotsky, taking one step backward for every two steps forward. The partnership between Bob and me worked because we were both moderate in outlook. We came from two different worlds—he eats grits and I eat kosher food. He is from Atlanta and I am from Bayonne. He was—and remains—an idealistic person, a courtly gentleman, a very honest man, and a first-class lawyer. He played a most important role in advising the 39th President of the United States. His frankness was of indisputable value, but he was too low-key for the intrigues of Washington, which in the end caused him to leave the White House and return home.

I would be equally frank with Ezer, and I pride myself on being one of the few friends he has who is not afraid to tell him the truth to his face. He might blow up at me, but in the end he would quiet down, because he needs someone to talk to, someone he can trust. I would come to his office and he would ask me to discuss matters with Abrasha. (Now *that* man is a computer. He is one of the brightest men I have ever met, and at this point he must be an international expert in the techniques of conducting negotiations. After all, he has taken part in 23 negotiations with the Arabs and the Americans on Israel's behalf, either as the leader of the delegation, its deputy chief, or as number-three delegate.)

We would sit in Abrasha's office up the corridor from that of Ezer and talk for hours at a time, tossing ideas in the air. I knew those that would be acceptable to the United States,

while Abrasha knew the Egyptian mentality, not to mention
the Israeli position—which it was his job to formulate, in
many cases. His kind of flexible mind was often beyond the
dogmatically closed mental processes of ideologically motivated politicians. He used to explain to me that the Egyptians
were motivated by the desire to avoid becoming a Soviet surrogate, and that they had finally come round to the conclusion
that their problems would not be solved through war. He
described himself as "an optimist by nature and a pessimist
by arrangement." He kept telling me that there should be no
doubt at all about it—Egypt needed peace out of self-interest,
not out of any sudden love of Israel. For him, the Camp David
agreement was less a peace process and more an instrument to
avoid war. Its prime achievement, as he put it, was to save the
lives of thousands of Israeli boys who might otherwise perish
in the sands of Sinai. I recall having been told by an Egyptian
scholar I met in Washington through Bob that the Egyptians
were fed up with the general Arab attitude of being ready to
fight to the last Egyptian soldier.

Abrasha's technique in written agreements was to leave
things open for the various sides' interpretations. As this
veteran military diplomat put it, "An agreement between
nations is like the *Ketuba* [the marriage contract]. Just as
couples don't study the small print each day, so nations must
learn to live with the document as the basic premise for a new
life together."

It was Abrasha who used to tell me that Ezer may have had
many advisors, but I was among the few to whom he always
listened. He would say to me, "If we didn't have you, we'd have
to invent you, because you have Ezer's ear and you can reach
the ear of the American President."

Keeping the Faith

As usual, the President kept his word. One day I arrived at
my office to find a package waiting for me. Inside was a copy
of President Carter's memoirs. I opened the fly-leaf and read
the autographed inscription:

"To Leon Charney, my fellow Middle East Negotiator.
Jimmy Carter"

I trembled as the realization hit me. Here was the former President of the United States elevating me to the position of his fellow negotiator in one of the great diplomatic triumphs of the 20th century—the conclusion of a peace treaty between an Arab nation and a Jewish state.

I felt fulfilled. It had been well worth the loneliness and frustration. My years of work were rewarded: I had received my "diploma" as Special Counsel.

August 22, 1979

MEMO TO: ROBERT J. LIPSHUTZ, THE WHITE HOUSE
FROM: LEON H. CHARNEY

WEST BANK AND GAZA AUTONOMY PROPOSAL

Herewith is an outline of a proposed method of resolving the current autonomy questions relating to Gaza and the West Bank based upon my most recent insights and observations.

POINT I

It is imperative that any and all proposals with respect to the above emanate from and stay within the FRAMEWORK OF THE CAMP DAVID AGREEMENT. Any variation or

343

deviation from this could cause a breakdown of the entire negotiating process.

POINT II

The history of the region has shown us that to try to resolve all the issues concerning the above areas in a very expeditious manner will in all likelihood result in failure. This memorandum is, therefore, dedicated to proposing conceptually a way whereby the negotiating process will progress and at the same time allow sufficient space and time for the principal parties to digest the fact that they are now living in peace. Given such time and space, it can be assumed that the principal parties themselves will look forward to insuring the fact that a future peace amongst all the parties should come into being. It can reasonably be expected that the population of the principal countries will develop trust and confidence between and amongst themselves and thus this trust will give rise to a spirit and aura which will allow for certain issues that cannot be settled as of this day to be solved after the passage of time as will be enumerated below.

POINT III

It is proposed that the autonomy talks be broken down into two areas:

A. Issues which are capable of resolution immediately by the present parties.
B. Issues which are not capable of resolution today and should be postponed to the future.

By postponing many of these issues, we are able to defer tackling the Palestinian participation, which is a very serious and complex issue. Notwithstanding this fact, there is no need to break down or slow down the negotiations but rather continue the process under the terms and conditions that I will set forth below.

POINT IV

By letter agreement between the President, Egypt and Israel, it is understood that in the event Jordan does not join the autonomy talks, then Israel, Egypt and the United States shall proceed with the same under the Framework of the Camp David Agreement. Thus, without entering into the Palestinian problem, the above parties are fully capable of arriving at an agreement as to which issues can be resolved as of this date and which issues should be postponed to the future.

POINT V

Article A1(a) of the Camp David Framework calls for a transitional arrangement for the West Bank and Gaza for a period not exceeding five years.

Article A1(c) states that "As soon as possible but not later than the third year after the beginning of the transitional period, negotiations will take place to determine the final status of the West Bank and Gaza and its relationship with its neighbors and to conclude a peace treaty between Israel and Jordan by the end of the transitional period."

Thus the Camp David Framework is a source which allows us to break up the transitional autonomy periods into two time frames, three years and two years.

The three year period which I shall refer to as the "temporary transitional autonomy" will [be used to] resolve issues capable of resolution immediately.

The two year period following the temporary transitional autonomy will be used to negotiate issues that require arduous negotiations and are not capable of resolution at this time.

By following this process, we will allow for a digestive period as outlined above in Point II so that the principal parties can acclimate themselves to the evident situations that have come about because of the peace treaty and the transitional autonomy. This concept is totally workable since only the consent of the United States, Egypt and Israel is necessary.

POINT VI

It is proposed that political efforts during these three years will allow for changes in attitudes and understandings between principal parties and further will allow for a check and balance system to develop so that the principal parties will become less fearful of cohabitation with their neighbors and will feel more comfortable, in that the security arrangements that will be in existence will prove to be sufficient and capable. It is hoped that with the accomplishment of the above, future autonomy propositions which are stubborn as of today will become amenable to solutions. Furthermore, this time period will allow sundry elements to influence the status of Jordan and it is very much hoped that they will then become a party to the process.

POINT VII

It is an established fact that the Egyptians have some solid influence in Gaza. Thus it is proposed that the first temporary transitional autonomy be implemented in Gaza. It is believed that because of the Egyptian influence in Gaza, there will be sufficient inhabitants of the area to partake in an election and it is naturally very vital to the autonomy process.

POINT VIII

This memorandum supports the proposition that the present autonomy talks should definitely not press for a final solution at this time. It is submitted that the following issues be deferred and *not* discussed or negotiated until the end of the three year "temporary transitional autonomy period." The areas which will be subject for negotiation during the latter two year period will be the following:

A. The status of Jerusalem (but see Point X B below).
B. The resettlement of refugees (but see Point X D below).
C. Definition of borders.
D. Permanent economic relationships.

POINT IX

It is a basic assumption of this memorandum that the final autonomy proposal will become sufficiently attractive so as to entice the inhabitants of the area to accept autonomy...[to achieve] a comprehensive peace in the area.

POINT X

The following are areas or issues which are subject to specific arrangements during the three year temporary transitional autonomy:

A. *Source of Authority in the Region*—It is believed that once the security needs of Israel are accomplished basically through Israeli military control, civil matters which do not affect the security of Israel would be susceptible to control by the autonomy council. I do not believe that Israel will yield on its position with respect to a military governor for the entire three year period. It is possible that further study by me of the region may produce a more relaxed solution; however, at this writing it is not likely. It would be a compromise on the part of Israel to accept any civil authority in this region at this time. There is also the question of the Israeli veto over the autonomy committee which would consist of four parties. I do not believe that Israel will yield on this position also. A possible solution to the problem would be to have some excellent and strong staff work which clearly could define the areas of authority and the solutions that could be achieved in the event a problem arose. You would thus have a problem-by-problem solution process. There is also the possibility of revolving time

periods wherein the military government would rotate
for several periods of time with the autonomy council as
to the final and supreme authority of the land. A combined factor can be created whereby the inhabitants of
the region will achieve a localized citizenship and at the
same time the security of Israel will not be compromised.

B. *Jerusalem Vote*—It is proposed that during the three
year temporary transitional autonomy period that the
subject of Jerusalem be in no way discussed, nor should
Jerusalem by any implication become a party to the
autonomy process during these three years. What can be
accomplished is the setting up of some kind of election
district in Jerusalem which in no way recognizes that
Jerusalem is part of the autonomy process. It is proposed
that the Arab citizens presently residing in Jerusalem
formally declare their citizenship to Jordan and be
granted a dual election right. This means that they will
be capable of voting in the municipal elections of Jerusalem and they will be capable of voting in the autonomy
process as citizens of Jordan on the West Bank. I believe
this can be accomplished; however, it must be very clear
to all parties that Jerusalem itself is not a part or a party
of the autonomy.

C. *Settlements*—An agreement should be made between
the parties that existing settlements will remain and will
be legally capable of thickening. Parties would then
establish by stipulation an agreement as to a small
number of settlements that can be established within the
next five years. Therefore, Israeli citizens would have
the right to purchase land from Arabs on the West Bank
providing the Arabs want to sell and the citizens of the
West Bank and Gaza would be given the ability of purchasing land in Israel providing the Israelis were willing
to sell.

D. *Sovereignty Over Land*—It is proposed the land on the
West Bank and Gaza be divided into five categories:

a. Land whose sovereignty is the autonomy council

b. Lands closed for security reasons
c. Lands owned by Jewish settlements
d. Lands for settling refugees
e. Lands reserved for strategic purposes

This last category would not be subject to negotiation during the three year period but would be reserved for negotiations and talk in the latter two year period.

E. *Internal Security*—Since this issue is most vital to the security of Israel, it is proposed that, for the three year temporary transitional autonomy period, all internal security control be under Israeli defense forces with the distinct understanding that after three years there will be a re-examination of this concept providing that terrorist activities and the state of war ceases.

F. *Water Rights*—It is believed that this problem can be solved by establishing a common Israeli/Arab Water Authority.

G. *Conflicts of Law*—It is felt that different juridical systems under sundry governmental systems such as trusteeships or autonomy plans be studied and emulated so that a system be developed whereby due process and equality be established for the benefit of the inhabitants of the area. It is believed that a solution in this area is not very difficult.

Bimah	Reader's stand in synagogue.
B'rith	Religious circumcision of a male infant.
Diaspora	Referring to Jews in voluntary or forced "exile" from the Holy Land.
Hanukah	Eight-day festival commemorating defeat of Syrian Greeks by Maccabees, 165 B.C.E., and rededication of desecrated Temple in Jerusalem.
Irgun	An "underground" Jewish group that used what many considered radical methods to push the British out of Palestine and establish a Jewish state.
High Holy Days	Major Jewish holy days, particularly Yom Kippur and Rosh Hashona.
Herut	Israeli party calling for the territorial integrity of Eretz Israel within its historic boundaries on both sides of the Jordan.
Heder	Elementary Hebrew school.
Kaddish	Prayer recited in memory of the dead.

351

Kashrut	Kosher. Observing dietary laws.
Kedushah	Proclamation of the holiness and kingship of God by the congregation during the service.
Ketuba	Traditional marriage contract.
Kfir fighters	Israeli-produced fighter aircraft.
Kibbutz	Communal agricultural settlement in Israel.
Kirya	Israeli compound housing the Government Administration.
Kosher	Food prepared in accord with traditional Jewish law.
Knesset	Israeli Parliament or Congress.
Labor	See: Mapai.
Likud	Non-socialist Israeli political alignment consisting mainly of the Herut and Liberal parties.
Mapai	Israel's Socialist Labor Party, generally considered liberal.
Meshugga	Crazy.
Mezuzah	Container for parchment containing Bible quotations, attached to the right post of gates and doors in a Jewish household.
Midrash	Homiletic commentary on the Biblical canon, divided into legal and ritual (Halakkah) and legendary, moralizing, folkloristic, and anecdotal (Haggadah) parts.
Minyan	The minimum of ten Jewish adult males required for communal prayers.

Moshav	A Zionist small holders' agricultural settlement in Israel.
Mozel tov	Good luck.
Mussaf	Additional prayer service for Sabbaths and festivals immediately following morning prayer.
Nu	A long, drawn-out "well."
Pogrom	A riot or murderous assault against a Jewish community, especially in Russia and Eastern Europe.
Purim	Social and convivial Jewish festival celebrating the rescuing of Jews from destruction at the hands of Haman, premier of Persia. It is marked by masquerades and plays.
Rabbi, Rebbe	Literally "my master" or "teacher." Originally applied to Talmudic scholars, later to religious judges. Today rabbis function very much like clergymen of other faiths, providing pastoral guidance and supervision of religious ceremonies.
Rosh Hashana	First day of the month of Tishri. (New Year.) The shofar is sounded at the service. It is the beginning of the Ten Days of Penitence.
Sabra	A native-born Israeli.
Shabbos	Sabbath. Seventh day of the week, last day of creation in Genesis, day of rest and reminder of divine justice on earth.
Shacharit	Morning prayer.
Shiva	Seven-day period of mourning after the burial of a close relative.

Shofar	The unadorned ram's horn sounded on Rosh Hashona and at the conclusion of Yom Kippur.
Shtetl	Yiddish word for "small town."
Siddur	Prayer book.
Succot	Fall harvest festival lasting seven days.
Talmud	Lengthy works of Biblical interpretation formulated from the 3rd to the 6th centuries in order to present a new set of laws which would reinterpret the ancient Mosaic concepts to the sons of Israel living in a pagan world.
Tehiya	Right wing political party in Israel.
Tel Hai fund	A fund originally established to aid injured members of the Irgun and their families. It has evolved into a political and charitable fund.
Torah	The Jewish scriptures.
Yad Vashem	Memorial in Jerusalem to the victims of the Holocaust.
Yarmulke	Skullcap.
Yeshiva	Talmudic school of higher education.
Yiddish	Language widely spoken and written by Jews, derived from Middle High German, incorporating some Hebrew words and Slavic elements and using Hebrew print and script.
"Yiddishkeit"	Jewishness.
Yom Kippur	Day of Atonement, the holiest day in the Jewish year.

355